THE RIGHT TO PUNISH

What gives international courts the authority to punish individuals for international crimes? Through the lens of political philosophy, Luise Müller provides an original perspective on the justification of the authority of international criminal courts and tribunals. She argues that institutions of international criminal justice are permitted to pierce the sovereignty of states in order to punish high-profile politicians for genocide, crimes against humanity, war crimes, and other mass human rights violations. Their right to punish is justified by virtue of their function to deter mass violations of fundamental human rights. However, to legitimately exercise that right, international criminal justice institutions must fulfil two conditions: first, they must conduct criminal trials with the highest level of fairness; second, they must treat those who are subject to their authority as equals. This last condition can be satisfied by international criminal justice institutions by including procedures of democratic decision-making and democratic accountability.

LUISE MÜLLER is a postdoctoral research associate at Freie Universität Berlin. Before joining the Institute of Philosophy at Freie Universität, she held research and teaching positions at the Humboldt University of Berlin, the University of Hamburg, and the Technical University Dresden and was a visiting scholar at King's College London and Columbia University.

STUDIES ON INTERNATIONAL COURTS AND TRIBUNALS

General Editors
Andreas Føllesdal, University of Oslo
Geir Ulfstein, University of Oslo

Studies on International Courts and Tribunals contains theoretical and interdisciplinary scholarship on legal aspects as well as the legitimacy and effectiveness of international courts and tribunals.

Other books in the series:

Mads Andenas and Eirik Bjorge (eds.) *A Farewell to Fragmentation: Reassertion and Convergence in International Law*

Cecilia M. Bailliet and Nobuo Hayashi (eds.) *The Legitimacy of International Criminal Tribunals*

Amrei Müller with Hege Elisabeth Kjos (eds.) *Judicial Dialogue and Human Rights*

Nienke Grossman, Harlan Grant Cohen, Andreas Føllesdal and Geir Ulfstein (eds.) *Legitimacy and International Courts*

Theresa Squatrito, Oran R. Young, Andreas Føllesdal, Geir Ulfstein (eds.) *The Performance of International Courts and Tribunals*

Robert Howse, Hélène Ruiz-Fabri, Geir Ulfstein and Michelle Q. Zang (eds.) *The Legitimacy of International Trade Courts and Tribunals*

Marlene Wind (ed.) *International Courts and Domestic Politics*

Christina Voigt (ed.) *International Judicial Practice on the Environment: Questions of Legitimacy*

Martin Scheinin (ed.) *Human Rights Norms in 'Other' International Courts*

Freya Baetens (ed.) *Legitimacy of Unseen Actors in International Adjudication*

Shai Dothan *International Judicial Review: When Should International Courts Intervene?*

Silje Langvatn, Mattias Kumm, Wojciech Sadurski (eds.) *Public Reason and Courts*

Daniel Behn, Szilárd Gáspár-Szilágyi, Malcolm Langford (eds.) *Adjudicating Trade and Investment Disputes: Convergence or Divergence?*

Sondre Torp Helmersen *The Application of Teachings by the International Court of Justice*

Daniel Behn, Ole Kristian Fauchald, Malcolm Langford (eds.) *The Legitimacy of Investment Arbitration: Empirical Perspectives*

Eric De Brabandere *International Procedure in Interstate Litigation and Arbitration: A Comparative Approach*

Chiara Giorgetti and Mark Pollack (eds.) *Beyond Fragmentation: Cross-Fertilization, Cooperation and Competition among International Courts and Tribunals*

Stavros Brekoulakis and Georgios Dimitropoulos (eds.) *International Commercial Courts: The Future of Transnational Adjudication*

Mark Gillett *Prosecuting Environmental Harm before the International Criminal Court*

Sassan Gholiagha *The Humanization of Global Politics: International Criminal Law, the Responsibility to Protect, and Drones*

Ezgi Yildiz *The European Court of Human Rights and the Norm Against Torture: Between Forbearance and Audacity*

Christina Voigt and Caroline Foster (eds.) *International Courts versus Non-Compliance Mechanisms: Comparative Advantages in Strengthening Treaty Implementation*

THE RIGHT TO PUNISH

Political Authority and International Criminal Justice

LUISE MÜLLER

Freie Universität Berlin

CAMBRIDGE
UNIVERSITY PRESS

CAMBRIDGE UNIVERSITY PRESS

Shaftesbury Road, Cambridge CB2 8EA, United Kingdom

One Liberty Plaza, 20th Floor, New York, NY 10006, USA

477 Williamstown Road, Port Melbourne, VIC 3207, Australia

314–321, 3rd Floor, Plot 3, Splendor Forum, Jasola District Centre, New Delhi – 110025, India

103 Penang Road, #05-06/07, Visioncrest Commercial, Singapore 238467

Cambridge University Press is part of Cambridge University Press & Assessment, a department of the University of Cambridge.

We share the University's mission to contribute to society through the pursuit of education, learning and research at the highest international levels of excellence.

www.cambridge.org
Information on this title: www.cambridge.org/9781009378130

DOI: 10.1017/9781009378109

First published 2024

A catalogue record for this publication is available from the British Library

Library of Congress Cataloging-in-Publication Data
Names: Müller, Luise, author.
Title: The right to punish : political authority and international criminal justice / Luise Müller, Freie Universität Berlin.
Description: Cambridge, United Kingdom ; New York, NY : Cambridge University Press, 2024. | Series: Studies on international courts and tribunals | Includes bibliographical references and index.
Identifiers: LCCN 2023050342 (print) | LCCN 2023050343 (ebook) | ISBN 9781009378130 (hardback) | ISBN 9781009378093 (paperback) | ISBN 9781009378109 (epub)
Subjects: LCSH: Punishment. | Criminal procedure (International law) | International crimes–Law and legislation. | Criminal justice, Administration of. | Fairness. | Equity (International law)
Classification: LCC K5101 .M85 2024 (print) | LCC K5101 (ebook) | DDC 345/.0773–dc23/eng/20231031
LC record available at https://lccn.loc.gov/2023050342
LC ebook record available at https://lccn.loc.gov/2023050343

ISBN 978-1-009-37813-0 Hardback

CONTENTS

ACKNOWLEDGEMENTS

Since this book started as a dissertation many years ago, I would like to begin by thanking my former doctoral advisors Bernd Ladwig and Stefan Gosepath. Their careful and detailed feedback has been enormously helpful in improving the argument of the book, and I am deeply grateful for their continued support. Probably the best unforeseen side effect of pursuing a career in academia is that I have not only gained colleagues, but also friends, and thus I want to thank Jan Brezger, Andreas Cassee, Sara Gebh, Jakob Huber, Tamara Jugov, Andreas Oldenbourg, Cord Schmelzle, and Daniel Voelsen. I am grateful to Sophie Eisentraut, Patrick Gilroy, Christian Kreuder-Sonnen, Mathis Lohaus, Maurits Meijers, Gil Murciano, Sören Stapel, Zoe Williams, and Wiebke Wemheuer-Vogelaar for discussing or commenting on parts of the book. Tom Christiano, Andreas Føllesdal, Turkuler Isiksel, Larry May, Peter Niesen, Jim Nickel, Kit Wellman, and Michael Zürn all took the time to answer my questions or discuss parts of the argument with me, and these conversations have improved the book enormously.

Parts of this book were presented at the political theory colloquium at Freie Universität Berlin, the practical philosophy colloquium at Freie Universität Berlin, the Work-In-Progress Sessions at Columbia, quite a few Berlin Graduate School for Transnational Studies workshops, a Justitia Amplificata Workshop in Bad Homburg, and the Hamburg-Berlin Workshop. I am grateful for the helpful discussions and comments. I also thank the Fritz Thyssen Stiftung and the Berlin Consortium for German Studies for generous financial support. During the final stages of writing the manuscript, Christian Neuhäuser and his colloquium invited me to Dortmund, where I was able to discuss a major change I was contemplating to one of the chapters. Around the same time, a conversation with Catherine Lu allowed me to see more clearly the argument I needed to make. I am grateful to both for their time and support. The editorial team at Cambridge University Press – first Tom Randall and then Marianne Nield and Biju Singh – were professional and patient. I am also grateful to the two anonymous reviewers for their excellent advice, and to Andreas Føllesdal and Geir Ulfstein for helpful comments and for including the book in their excellent series.

A special thanks goes out to my best friend Mirjana, the most kind and generous friend I can imagine. Finally, I am enormously grateful to my husband Fabian, who always manages to make everything easier for me, and this includes parenting and writing books. I dedicate this book to my parents. Having their support in every single important thing that I do has enabled me to follow my interests wherever they lead me – even to strange places like philosophy departments.

ABBREVIATIONS

E, followed by book, chapter, and section number	John Locke, *An Essay Concerning Human Understanding*
ELN, followed by page number	John Locke, *Essays on the Law of Nature*
L, followed by paragraph number	Thomas Hobbes, *Leviathan*
MM, followed by page number	Immanuel Kant, *Metaphysics of Morals*
I or II, followed by paragraph number	John Locke, *Two Treatises of Government*

1

Introduction

1.1 The Radical Project of International Criminal Justice

On 17 March 2023, just over a year since Russia began waging an aggressive war against its neighbouring country Ukraine, the Pre-Trial Chamber II of the International Criminal Court (ICC) in The Hague issued two warrants of arrest. The ICC's Prosecutor, Karim Khan, had opened an investigation into the situation in Ukraine and the commission of potential war crimes less than a week after Russia invaded Ukraine in 2022. He immediately sent staff to collect evidence on the ground. Based on that evidence, the judges argue that they have reasonable grounds to believe that at least hundreds, if not thousands, of Ukrainian children were illegally transported to Russia and given up for adoption. One of the warrants is for the arrest of Maria Lvova-Belova, Commissioner for Children's Rights in the Office of the President of the Russian Federation. The other arrest warrant is for the President of the Russian Federation himself – Vladimir Putin. The ICC alleges that Lvova-Belova and Putin are criminally responsible for the war crime of unlawful deportation of population[1] and of unlawful transfer of population from occupied areas[2] of Ukraine to the Russian Federation.

The ICC's decision to seek an arrest for Putin is radical: it is a highly controversial step of the ICC to indict a sitting head of state, let alone a president of a state with a permanent seat on the United Nations Security Council. Putin is now a suspect at large, and under article 59 of the Rome Statute, any one of the 124 ICC member states is now obligated to arrest Putin if he enters their territory and deliver him into the custody of the

[1] Prohibited under article 8(2)(a)(vii) of the Rome Statute. UN General Assembly, *Rome Statute of the International Criminal Court (last amended 2010)*, 17 July 1998, ISBN No. 92-9227-227-6, available at: www.icc-cpi.int/sites/default/files/NR/rdonlyres/ADD16852-AEE9-4757-ABE7-9CDC7CF02886/283503/RomeStatutEng1.pdf

[2] Prohibited under article 8(2)(b)(viii) of the Rome Statute.

ICC in The Hague for trial. The Kremlin swiftly dismissed the arrest warrants as 'outrageous' and 'unacceptable', denying that the ICC has jurisdiction over Russian officials.[3] Indeed, neither Russia nor Ukraine is a member of the ICC. So why did the Prosecutor decide to open an investigation? According to the Rome Statute – the treaty establishing the court – the ICC can initiate investigations under a number of principles. First, a member state can refer itself to the ICC and give it permission to open an investigation.[4] The other principle under which an investigation into a situation in a member state (or involving a citizen of a member state) can be initiated is by decision of the Chief Prosecutor. This principle finds application when member states fail to investigate a situation on their own territory because they are either unwilling or unable to do so.[5] The third principle under which an investigation can be initiated is by United Nations Security Council resolution. A referral to the ICC by the Security Council in principle allows the ICC to investigate situations in non-member states, although any permanent member of the Security Council may veto the referral.[6]

The Ukraine situation is special: although Ukraine is *not* a member of the ICC, it has permitted the ICC to exercise jurisdiction over international crimes committed on its territory.[7] Despite this, it is unlikely that Putin will appear before the ICC – certainly not in the near future, and probably not at all.[8] The court has no enforcement tools of its own

[3] www.reuters.com/world/europe/icc-judges-issue-arrest-warrant-against-putin-over-alleged-war-crimes-2023-03-17/.

[4] Examples of such a self-referral include Uganda, Mali, Gabon, and the Democratic Republic of the Congo.

[5] Kenya, Côte d'Ivoire, and Afghanistan, for example, have been the focus of such a *proprio motu* investigation.

[6] In 2005, the Security Council referred the situation in Darfur, Sudan, and in 2011, it referred the situation in Libya. A planned referral of the situation in Syria failed in 2014 because Russia and China vetoed it.

[7] Under article 12 (3) of the Rome Statute.

[8] The *formal* influence that powerful states have on the court is very limited; the only exception is the Security Council's power to defer an investigation for reasons of maintaining peace and security. Under article 16 of the Rome Statute, the Security Council can defer an investigation or prosecution for one year. The formally limited role of powerful states is unusual for international institutions. Bosco argues that it probably resulted from the participation of civil society groups in the process that led up to the drafting of the statute. Civil society groups were able to 'shape and amplify' the message of smaller, less powerful states, while the larger powers did not manage to dominate the proceedings as a coherent group negotiator (Bosco 2015, 7). The limited formal influence is mirrored in several institutional features: for example, the 'one-state-one-vote' majority voting

and relies on the state parties for financial, diplomatic, intelligence, military,[9] and police support. Cooperation from the state parties is vital for accessing witnesses and evidence, the delivery of arrest warrants, and the search and arrest of suspects. Without the help and provision of the resources of states, the ICC cannot perform any of its essential functions. In that sense, the ICC relies fundamentally on the political goodwill and support of states – and while legal considerations matter, states will always also consider the political implications of their actions, especially during an active war.

One might therefore be puzzled why – in light of the slim chance of actually seeing Putin in the defendants' dock – the ICC decided to go ahead and publicly issue the warrants for arrest. Piotr Hofmański, the ICC's president judge, explains the intention of making the warrants of arrest public: 'the judges of the chamber … decided to make the existence of the warrants public in the interest of justice and to prevent the commission of future crimes'.[10] In their press release, the ICC reiterates the claim that the arrest warrants, having been made public, may 'contribute to the prevention of the further commission of crimes'.[11] To my mind, this reasoning – that the ICC's actions prevent further crimes – gives us a first, rough answer to the following questions: Is the ICC morally justified to prosecute and punish alleged perpetrators of international crimes, even if their states have not consented to the ICC's jurisdiction? And if it is, on what grounds?

procedure for the election of judges and prosecutors, or the rule that no two judges may be citizens from the same state (Bosco 2015, 8).

9 Seventy-three per cent of global armed forces are non-members of the ICC while only 27 per cent are members (Bosco 2015, 7).

10 www.icc-cpi.int/news/situation-ukraine-icc-judges-issue-arrest-warrants-against-vladimir-vladimirovich-putin-and

11 This is in line with article 58 (1) (b) (iii) of the Rome Statute. On the decision to make the arrest warrants public, the press release states:

> The Chamber considered that the warrants are secret in order to protect victims and witnesses and also to safeguard the investigation. Nevertheless, mindful that the conduct addressed in the present situation is allegedly ongoing, and that the public awareness of the warrants may contribute to the prevention of the further commission of crimes, the Chamber considered that it is in the interests of justice to authorise the Registry to publicly disclose the existence of the warrants, the name of the suspects, the crimes for which the warrants are issued, and the modes of liability as established by the Chamber. (www.icc-cpi.int/news/situation-ukraine-icc-judges-issue-arrest-warrants-against-vladimir-vladimirovich-putin-and)

This book is the result of approaching these questions from a political philosophy perspective. The history of and the contemporary rhetoric surrounding international criminal justice (ICJ) and its institutions suggest that beyond their nature as international contracts between states, or even military impositions of victorious states, there is a further *moral* claim that supersedes such conceptualizations. Statements like as the ones we find in the Preamble of the Rome Statute about 'atrocities that deeply shock the conscience of humanity' which are 'the most serious crimes of concern to the international community as a whole' reveal that behind the mere technical legality of ICJ lies a normative promise of universal scope. My aim is to understand under what circumstances this universal normative promise can be rightfully redeemed. Assuming that the content of the moral rules that frame international criminal law – the prohibition of genocide, the prohibition of slavery, crimes against humanity, war crimes, and aggressive war – is not in dispute, the real challenge for political philosophers lies with justifying the scope and nature of *institutions* that prosecute and punish such crimes in the absence of unanimous state consent. Do international institutions such as the ICC have justified political authority to prosecute and punish alleged perpetrators of mass human rights violations, even if their states have not consented to their prosecution? Judge Hofmański's argument – that arresting and putting Putin on trial might help prevent further crimes – illustrates the core of the argument I advance in this book, which is that ICJ institutions are justified by virtue of their function to deter mass violations of human rights, which everyone has a natural duty to secure and protect. But that authority comes with conditions: ICJ institutions must operate with the highest level of fairness, and they must treat those who are subject to them as equals. This last condition, treating subjects as equals, yields the – perhaps surprising – result that the source of the ICJ institutions' authority must be democratic decision-making procedures. In a sense, then, I undertake an attempt to address a concern that was voiced by Madeline Morris in 2002: namely, that an undemocratic ICC with global jurisdiction presents normative problems for its legitimacy (Morris 2002).

1.2 From Nuremberg to The Hague

The Rome Statute that established the ICC came into force in 2002. But the historical precedent for prosecuting state agents under criminal charges was set in the German city of Nuremberg over fifty years earlier, right after the Allied forces' victory over Nazi Germany. The choice of a criminal trial as a means to deal with the atrocities committed by Germany was not obvious at all during the war. In his memoirs about the Second World War, Winston Churchill recounts a telling incident at a vodka-infused banquet that was hosted by Joseph Stalin during the Tehran Conference on 29 November 1943. The evening's atmosphere involved 'a good deal of gaiety', many toasts, and some teasing by Marshal Stalin, which Churchill said he did not resent, until

> the Marshal entered in a genial manner upon a serious and even deadly aspect of the punishment to be inflicted upon the Germans. The German General Staff, he said, must be liquidated. The whole force of Hitler's mighty armies depended upon about fifty-thousand officers and technicians. If these were rounded up and shot at the end of the war, German military strength would be extirpated. (Churchill 2005, 330)

Churchill writes that he categorically rejected Stalin's proposal, saying that the Soviets must be under no delusion that he would ever allow it. But Stalin was insistent:

> 'Fifty thousand,' he said, 'must be shot.' I was deeply angered. 'I would rather,' I said, 'be taken out into the garden here and now and be shot myself than sully my own and my country's honour by such infamy.' At this point the President [Franklin D. Roosevelt, L.M.] intervened. He had a compromise to propose. Not fifty thousand should be shot, but only forty-nine thousand. By this he hoped, no doubt, to reduce the whole matter to ridicule. Eden also made signs and gestures intended to reassure me that it was all a joke. (Churchill 2005, 330)

Churchill left the banquet full of indignation after Roosevelt's son, Elliott, stood up and said how cordially he agreed with the Marshal's proposal. Stalin and Molotov followed Churchill, eager to reassure him that they were only joking. But Churchill was actually not so sure:

> Stalin has a very captivating manner when he chooses to use it, and I never saw him do so to such an extent as at this moment. Although I was not then, and am not now, fully convinced that all was chaff and there was no serious intent lurking behind, I consented to return, and the rest of the evening passed pleasantly. (Churchill 2005, V:330)

Was Stalin's proposal – to shoot fifty thousand Nazis as a means of bringing justice after the Second World War – really a joke? It would certainly not have been out of character for a man responsible for the 1950s purges in the Soviet Union, or the massacre of twenty-two thousand Polish officers and Polish prisoners in the Katyn forest and other sites.[12] Perhaps, if Churchill had reacted differently, Stalin's proposal would have gained momentum towards the end of the war. What else to do with the scores of German officials who had planned and carried out crimes so massive that they were beyond comprehension? Leaving the prosecution and punishment to the Germans themselves was not an option. The German judiciary was deeply involved in the crimes. Even from a purely practical perspective, it would not have been possible: in 1945, there was effectively no German state – its institutions were dissolved. In fact, the German criminal justice system did not start prosecuting Nazi crimes until more than ten years later.[13]

The Allied powers chose a different path: in August 1945, they established the International Military Tribunal (IMT). Twenty-two Nazi leaders[14] were tried before it. The trial took place between November 1945 and October 1946 in the German city of Nuremberg. The judges presiding over the trial were citizens of the four victorius powers: the United States, France, Great Britain, and the Soviet Union. The US Supreme Court Justice Robert Jackson was elected prosecutor and opened the trial on 21 November 1945, a mere ten months after the liberation of Auschwitz and seven months after Hitler's suicide. Jackson opened the court proceedings by acknowledging that the decision to prosecute the defendants under criminal charges expressed the 'victory of reason over vengeance': 'That four great nations, flushed with victory and stung with injury stay the hand of vengeance and voluntarily submit their captive enemies to the judgement of the law is one of the most significant tributes that Power has ever paid to Reason.'[15]

[12] These massacres were themselves war crimes and crimes against humanity but were left unprosecuted – thus begins the long story of selective prosecution in international criminal law.

[13] Since 1958, about 18,500 prosecutions were investigated by German authorities for their involvement in international crimes, according to the Central Office of the Land Judicial Authorities for the Investigation of National Socialist Crimes in Germany.

[14] Number 23, Robert Ley, committed suicide three days after receiving the indictment. Dr Gilbert, the psychologist on duty at the prison where the prospective defendants were held, reports that Ley, when he received his indictment, was furious:

> He said he could not prepare a defence, that he knew nothing about any of the crimes alleged. He stood against the wall, arms raised as if in crucifixion, and asked why the victors did not shoot their prisoners if they had wanted more sacrifices. 'But why should I be brought before a Tribunal like a c . . . c . . . c. . .', Gilbert supplied the word 'criminal'. (Tusa and Tusa 2010, 133)

[15] Justice Robert Jackson's Opening Address to the International Military Tribunal at Nuremberg, Germany, 10 November 1945, quoted in Tusa and Tusa (2010, 8).

The idea to prosecute major Nazi leaders in the form of an international tribunal was not the first attempt at punishing officials under international criminal law.[16] It had a historical precedent: the Treaty of Versailles included an article that provided for the criminal prosecution of Kaiser William II of Hohenzollern 'for a supreme offence against international morality and the sanctity of treaties' before a special tribunal.[17] However, neither the crime of 'offence against international morality' nor the crime of 'offence against the sanctity of treaties' legally existed in international law, and in the end, the Allied powers decided that the article could not be enforced (Bassiouni 2014, 1052). Furthermore, the Kaiser was in Dutch exile, and the Dutch refused to hand him over, regarding pressure as an illegitimate infringement on their sovereign right to choose their own 'guests' (Tusa and Tusa 2010, 18). An Allied Powers Commission also urged for the prosecution and punishment of the perpetrators of the 1915 genocide of the Armenians in Turkey. Talaat Pasha, the architect of the genocide, had fled to Germany after the surrender of the Ottoman Empire in 1918. Besides the protection Talaat Pasha was afforded by the German authorities, the Allied powers were unwilling to put any serious political effort into punishing those responsible for the genocide of the Armenians.[18]

[16] For two accounts of very early international criminal law punishment and the first international criminal tribunal, in 1474, see Bassiouni (2014, 1047ff).

[17] Peace Treaty of Versailles, article 227. The Peace Treaty of Versailles was drafted during the Paris Peace Conference in 1919, after the end of the First World War.

[18] It appears that Adolf Hitler referred to the Armenian genocide and the subsequent impunity in the context of the invasion of Poland in 1939. According to the document L-3, which was introduced as Exhibit Nr. USA 28 in the trial of Hermann Goering during the Nuremberg Trials, Hitler pointed out that nobody cared about the Armenian genocide:

> Ich habe den Befehl gegeben, und ich lasse jeden füsilieren, der auch nur ein Wort der Kritik äussert, dass das Kriegsziel nicht im Erreichen von bestimmten Linien, sondern in der physischen Vernichtung des Gegners besteht. So habe ich, einstweilen nur im Osten, meine Totenkopfverbände bereitgestellt, mit dem Befehl, unbarmherzig und mitleidslos Mann, Weib und Kind polnischer Abstammung und Sprache in den Tod zu schicken. Nur so gewinnen wir den Lebensraum, den wir brauchen. Wer redet heute noch von der Vernichtung der Armenier?

> I have given the order, and I will have anyone who utters just a single word of criticism shot, that the final goal of the war does not consist in reaching specific lines, but in the physical extermination of the enemy. And so I have allocated my skull and crossbones formations (*Totenkopfverbände*) to the East, with the order to send men, women, and children of Polish descent

The Nuremberg Trials marked a sea change in a long history of impunity. When Nazi General Alfred Jodl signed the document of unconditional surrender in May 1945, passing Germany's sovereignty to the Allied forces, he said that he hoped that the Allied forces would treat the German people with generosity (Tusa and Tusa 2010, 13). After having freed the concentration camps, having seen the piles of dead bodies, and having heard the chilling testimonies of the half-dead survivors, it seems almost lunatic to hope for generosity towards those responsible for these crimes. Indeed, US Treasury Secretary Henry Morgenthau advocated a post-war plan that included summary punishment for a few dozen Nazi leaders. Against this, the US Secretary of War Henry Stimson brought up the idea of legally prosecuting and punishing Nazi criminals. For a brief while, it looked as if Morgenthau's plan would prevail, but Roosevelt was ultimately swayed onto the Stimson plan (Tusa and Tusa 2010, 60f). Stalin wanted to put the Nazi leaders to death, but not without a previous trial. Only the British were adamant that 'political justice by joint executive action' of the Allied forces was the only way to deal with the major war criminals: 'for the principal Nazi leaders a full trial under judicial procedure was out of the question'.[19] However, Roosevelt's successor, Harry Truman, was a wholehearted supporter of a criminal trial and wanted to implement his plan as soon as possible. The United States had given the impulse for a legal prosecution of those responsible for the war and the massive atrocities committed. With the support of the Soviets and the French, the British were finally persuaded.

Since the end of the trials in Nuremberg, there have been a few more instances of international criminal trials. The International Military Tribunal for the Far East (IMTFE) was established in January 1946. With its seat in Tokyo, it prosecuted twenty-eight Japanese military officials, excluding, among others, the Japanese Emperor Hirohito. Both the IMT and the IMTFE only prosecuted the crimes committed by the losers of the war, not the ones committed by those who had won. Another problem was that there was no explicit international law on the basis of which the IMT and the IMTFE could operate. Technically, both tribunals prosecuted and punished retroactively and therefore in

and language to their death without mercy or pity. This is the only way to get the living space we need. Who still talks about the extermination of the Armenians these days?

[19] From the minutes of War Cabinet Meeting, 12 April, quoted in Tusa and Tusa (2010, 65).

breach of one of the most fundamental principles of criminal law: *nullum crimen, nulla poena sine lege.*[20]

During the Cold War period, the idea of ICJ lay dormant, and the momentum that was gained after the end of Second World War dissipated. Neither the crimes committed by the United States in Latin America or Vietnam, nor the crimes committed by France in Algeria, nor the crimes committed by the Soviet Union in Afghanistan and on their own territory were ever prosecuted.[21] After this long hiatus, in 1992 the Security Council established a Commission of Experts to investigate violations of international humanitarian law in the former Yugoslavia between 1991 and 1994 (Bassiouni 2014, 1057f). In May 1993, the International Criminal Tribunal for the former Yugoslavia (ICTY) was established by the United Nations. It was the first international criminal tribunal since the Nuremberg Trials and the IMTFE in Tokyo. A year after the establishment of the ICTY, in November 1994, the Security Council established the International Criminal Tribunal for Rwanda (ICTR), which was operative for almost twenty years until it formally closed its doors in December 2015. In Rwanda, the international effort to prosecute those responsible for the mass atrocities was supplemented by national courts as well as about 12,000 *gacaca* courts, traditional community courts that heard over 1.2 million cases during their operative time between 2005 and 2012.

The first permanent, treaty-based international criminal court, located in The Hague, was established in 2002.[22] The Rome Statute had been adopted four years earlier, long after Trinidad and Tobago had asked the United Nations (UN) General Assembly to reopen the negotiations for a permanent international criminal court in 1989. After the momentum

[20] For a discussion on the ex post facto and *nullum crimen sine lege* problem, see Altman and Wellman (2009, 82ff). It can be argued that the IMT and IMTFE prosecutions of at least some war crimes/some serious violations of the laws and customs of war that had been regarded as crimes under customary international law were not in breach of these two principles. Case law from the International Criminal Tribunal for the former Yugoslavia [JCE Decision – 21 May 2003] asserts that criminal liability must be 'sufficiently foreseeable' and that the law providing such liability must be 'sufficiently accessible' to warrant a criminal conviction and sentencing; and it can be argued that this had applied to at least some crimes. I am grateful to an anonymous reader for Cambridge University Press for pressing me to consider this.

[21] The only exception was the investigation and prosecution of two US soldiers, William Calley and Ernest Medina, for their involvement in the My Lai massacre.

[22] A few months earlier, in January 2002, the UN and Sierra Leone agreed to establish the Special Court for Sierra Leone, another international criminal tribunal. I thank an anonymous reader for Cambridge University Press for spotting and pointing out an earlier imprecision regarding the timeline.

gained with the two ad hoc tribunals in The Hague (ICTY) and Arusha (ICTR), and a lucky combination of government changes in some of the global powers – the election and then re-election of the Democrat Bill Clinton to the White House, the shift from a Tory to the Blair-led Labour government in the UK, and a socialist majority in France, leading to Lionel Jospin being the socialist prime minister cohabiting with President Jacques Chirac – the path was cleared to enter real negotiations for a permanent court (Bosco 2015, 44).

The conference to establish and adopt a statute for such a court was held in Rome in June and July 1998. According to a German delegate, the outcome of the final vote was completely unpredictable. The long nights, the parallel working groups, and the subsequent lack of communication between the delegates and the home governments – the delegates were often simply too tired to report back to their governments and receive instructions for further negotiation – were probably conducive to the politically ambitious draft that eventually emerged from the Rome sessions. Due to the looser communication channels to their national capitals, the delegates took many decisions on their own, without checking their governments' position first (Bosco 2015, 48). Another factor that likely contributed to the eventual high number of yes votes was the fact that the organizing committee of the Rome Conference (known as 'the Bureau') strategically held off on any voting as long as possible with the result that delegates were mostly in the dark about the other delegations' positions.

With the deadline approaching, the Bureau decided against suspending and postponing the conference and prepared a draft statute. India and the United States, actively trying to bully the supporting states to draft in exceptions and special competences for the major global powers, proposed last-minute amendments in an attempt to suspend the final vote, but they were blocked by a number of small states, among them Norway, Malawi, and Chile (Bosco 2015, 50). Immediately, an open vote on the draft statute was held. According to the German delegate, at that moment, the outcome of the voting procedure was completely up in the air: the delegates had no time to properly check back with their governments and basically had to make a decision on the spot. Smaller undecided states looked nervously to the regional powers who nervously looked to the other regional powers. Somehow a cascade of yes votes had started, and the dynamic gripped the whole room.[23] Once it was clear

[23] According to the personal recollection of a delegate, told in personal communication.

that the draft statute would be adopted, celebratory cheers broke out. Observers recounted that they had never seen such an outbreak of emotion in a diplomatic conference before (Bosco 2015, 50).

The vote count to establish the court was at 120. Seven states voted against establishing the court, definitely including the United States, China, and Israel, and possibly including Syria, Iraq, Libya, Qatar, Cuba, or Yemen.[24] After the statute had received the critical number of sixty ratifications in April 2002, it formally entered into force in July 2002. Then-UN Secretary-General Kofi Annan summarizes what must have been an immense sense of achievement for those who had devoted their time to the establishment of the court over the years: '(t)he establishment of the Court is a gift of hope to future generations, and a giant step forward in the march towards universal human rights and the rule of law'.[25] Two distinctive features of the ICC are its permanent nature and its connection to the Security Council. The IMTs in Nuremberg and Tokyo as well as the ICTR and the ICTY were tribunals connected exclusively to the crimes they were established in response to. The ICC, on the other hand, is a permanent court. Just like the earlier tribunals, the prosecutions are focused on senior military, political, and security officials, but the ICC can also prosecute heads of states – an unprecedented competence that is rarely used. Besides the arrest warrant for Putin, the only two other cases in which the court issued an arrest warrant for a head of state were for Omar al-Bashir in 2009 and 2010 and for Muammar Gaddafi in 2011.

1.3 Justifying the Political Authority of ICJ

The argument I develop and defend in this book is that an institution like the ICC indeed possesses the authority to prosecute and punish individuals (regardless of their diplomatic status) when it helps us discharge universal moral duties that we have independent of consent. But its authority depends on two conditions: first, whether institutions of ICJ operate in accordance with minimal procedural fairness; and second, whether those

24 There is some dispute over the identity of the states that voted against the treaty because the vote was officially unrecorded. The United States, China, and Israel have made their vote public, and the other four are most commonly identified as belonging to the group that voted against the establishment of the ICC. Bosco writes that the opposing states (apart from the three secure ones) were Syria, Iraq, Cuba, and Yemen (Bosco 2015, 50).

25 Kofi Annan on 20 July 1998, UN Press Release L/2890, www.un.org/press/en/1998/19980720.l2890.html.

subject to such institutions are treated as equals. When these conditions are fulfilled, institutions have the right to prosecute and punish perpetrators of mass human rights violations. That is the main claim of this book.

To indicate the ambition and limits of this study, let me clarify my methodological assumptions. I am writing in a tradition – often broadly called analytical political philosophy – in which we are often primarily concerned with justification.[26] The concept of justification is seldom explicated when it is invoked, so before I begin to elaborate the main argument of the book, I am going to define the conditions under which a justification is successful. Justification, as A. John Simmons argues, is largely a 'defensive' concept:

> Justifying an act, a strategy, a practice, an arrangement, or an institution typically involves showing it to be prudentially rational, morally acceptable, or both (depending on the kind of justification at issue). And showing this, in the standard cases, centrally involves rebutting certain kinds of possible objections to it: either comparative objections – that other acts or institutions are preferable to the one in question – or non-comparative objections – that the act in question is unacceptable or wrong or that the institution practices or sanctions wrongdoing or vice. (Simmons 1999, 740)

The justification of ICJ that I present in this book involves showing that, under the right circumstances, punishment beyond the state is morally permissible. I show that it is morally permissible by considering two non-comparative objections, namely (a) the (abolitionist) objection that the practice of punishment itself is *impermissible*, and (b) the sovereigntist objection that foreign states or international institutions are not permitted to pierce a state's sovereignty and punish its constituents. This is no small task, because although many of us consider it a given, punishment is coercive and a drastic intrusion into the moral autonomy of persons. John Rawls rightly notes that

> [t]he subject of punishment, in the sense of attaching legal penalties to the violation of legal rules, has always been a troubling moral question. The trouble about it has not been that people disagree as to whether or not punishment is justifiable. Most people have held that, freed from certain abuses, it is an acceptable institution. Only a few have rejected punishment entirely, which is rather surprising when one considers all that can be said against it. (Rawls 1955, 4)

[26] For an excellent, more general perspective on the ICC, see Leila Sadat's book (Sadat 2021).

A moral theory that centres on permissibility is one that requires merely that institutions (or acts) do not breach applicable moral rules, even if, in some respects, other institutions (or acts) are preferable. Compare this 'permissibility justification' approach with another approach Simmons calls 'optimality justification' (Simmons 1994, 63ff, 1999, 741). A moral theory that centres on optimality is one that requires institutions (or acts) to be *the best possible* institutions in order to be justified. In contrast, I consider my argument successful if it shows that international punishment is merely *permissible*.

When studying something of utmost moral urgency – such as the protection of fundamental human rights – it seems natural to suppose that permissibility justifications are not sufficient and we have reason to focus on optimality.[27] After all, it is not merely *permissible* to protect human rights; rather, it is morally obligatory. And while that is correct, this book is not concerned with human rights protection in general, but whether we are permitted to establish a system of institutional punishment with the aim of enforcing fundamental human rights. My intention in this book is not to explain whether we are morally obligated to protect human rights, but that prosecuting and punishing human rights crimes is a permissible way to enforce – and therefore protect – fundamental human rights. In that sense, I provide a permissibility justification that applies to the *mode* of human rights enforcement.

Defending an optimality justification is not a viable strategy for this study. Part of the reason is that we ultimately lack the necessary empirical knowledge that would allow us to describe an optimal institution without unduly speculating about the essential features of such an institution. Protecting human rights globally is a complex task that likely requires experimentation and several interlocking strategies. I therefore argue that ICJ is *but one* way in a multidimensional approach to the protection of human rights. What political philosophy can contribute is to specify our political goals and analyse what mechanisms are morally permissible and likely effective to reach those goals.

My focus on a permissibility justification on these grounds also reveals the limits of my argument. Because the aim is merely to demonstrate permissibility, I do not discuss comparative objections. Comparative objections are objections advocating an alternative mechanism or system

[27] I am grateful to Cord Schmelzle for bringing up this point and to him and Bernd Ladwig for pressing me to clarify the reasons for focussing on permissibility rather than optimality.

that is purported to be morally superior or more effective. There are two sets of circumstances under which it makes sense to discuss comparative objections. The first is when the relevant alternative is incommensurable with a system of ICJ; that is, when supporting the relevant alternative would damage the project of ICJ and vice versa. The second set of circumstances is when the two options are commensurable, but resources are so scarce that they suffice for only one of the alternatives. The morally right decision under both sets of circumstances is in support of the most effective option, all things being equal. For our purposes, the issue of incommensurability is not especially virulent. A system of criminal justice is commensurable with a variety of other actions or arrangements that protect fundamental human rights. Think of state punishment: not only is it commensurable with other policies designed to promote basic rights (welfare, education, policing, etc.), but the integration of different strategies that support each other can amplify its general effectiveness.

The problem of scarce resources is, however, more worrying. Maintaining a permanent system of ICJ is financially burdensome: trials are slow in delivering results (they often take years), and the court must be staffed by a large number of highly specialized professionals. There are also high costs for imprisoning people in humane conditions, sometimes for the rest of their lives. But making a reasonable assessment of optimal resource allocation presupposes that we have data that allow us to assess the relative effectiveness of the available alternatives. That is neither the case now, nor will it likely be in the future. To a large extent, there is uncertainty about what alternatives would be more effective: we simply do not know the likely effect of devoting more resources to alternative instruments for human rights protection. For example, would the effectiveness of foreign aid or human rights campaigning substantially increase if we invested more resources? Or would such resource pooling on just one mechanism be detrimental, perhaps because it amplifies unforeseen side effects? For the moment, as a matter of practical concern, the best way forward is to experiment with combinations of morally permissible and likely effective actions and arrangements, and hope that activists, public servants, and political scientists build more robust practical knowledge from those experiments.

Such an approach is germane to the type of non-ideal theorizing that I am interested in. While ideal theory works under the premise of strict compliance, '[n]onideal theory asks how this long-term goal [of building ideal theory institutions, L.M.] might be achieved, or worked toward, usually in gradual steps. It looks for courses of action that are morally permissible and politically possible as well as likely to be effective' (Rawls 2003, 89) – under the condition that agents are partly non-compliant. Note how Rawls's view is similar to Simmons's description of permissibility justifications when he says that the courses of actions are justified when they are permissible, possible, and likely to be effective. These different kinds of judgements require distinct kinds of arguments: while judgements of moral permissibility lie squarely within the field of moral and political philosophy, judgements of likelihood of effectiveness require theoretical as well as empirical foundations of the kind that social scientists offer.[28]

Is the criminal law itself part of ideal or non-ideal theory? Rawls argues that it mainly belongs to non-ideal theory, except for that part that covers the assurance problem (Rawls 1999, 277).[29] The assurance problem is a type of generalized prisoner's dilemma: because persons in a well-ordered system of social cooperation lack full confidence in one another, they 'may suspect that some are not doing their part, and so they may be tempted not to do theirs' (Rawls 1999, 211). Some constraining arrangements, including penal sanctions, are necessary to ensure compliance – and therefore the fundamental stability of the cooperative scheme – even in ideal theory, but, as Rawls remarks, 'their main purpose is to underwrite citizens' trust in one another. These mechanisms will seldom be invoked and will comprise but a minor part of the social scheme' (Rawls 1999, 505). With the focus on the moral permissibility of ICJ, two types of non-compliance must be considered: the non-compliance of individuals and the non-compliance of states. Table 1.1[30] organizing the different types of partial compliance in non-ideal theory is helpful for understanding how the two dimensions of non-compliance overlap:

For an analysis of the permissibility of ICJ, I focus on both individuals (2) and international relations (3). In fact, what makes ICJ an interesting subject of political philosophy is that in it, these two dimensions overlap: in this book, I will analyse both deliberate individual non-compliance (2a) and deliberate or unfortunate non-compliance of nations (3a, 3b). The overall goal is two-dimensional: to show that individuals committing crimes may permissibly be punished[31] and that states that fail to comply

[28] For a similar point, see Simmons (Simmons 2010, 19). I survey some empirical work measuring the effectiveness of international criminal prosecutions in the concluding chapter.

[29] I am grateful to Bernd Ladwig for this reference.

[30] The table is an adaptation of Simmons (2010, 17).

[31] In chapter two of his book, Simmons (2016) notes that while in the *Theory of Justice*, Rawls argues for such a tripartite scheme, by the time we get to the *Law of Peoples*, Rawls

Table 1.1 *Different types of partial compliance in non-ideal theory.*

	Non-ideal theory	Permissible action
1. Basic structure within the state	a. Deliberate non-compliance: institutional injustice, for example racial discrimination in basic rights	Civil disobedience, conscientious refusal, non-civil resistance of citizens
	b. Unfortunate non-compliance: lack of political culture, poverty	Temporary adjustments guided by the general conception of justice, aimed at full compliance
2. Individuals	a. Deliberate non-compliance: wrongs and crimes	Intervention in personal autonomy in the form of punishment and/or payment of reparation
	b. Unfortunate non-compliance: immaturity and insanity	Paternalism
3. International relations	a. Deliberate non-compliance: outlaw states violate their constituents' fundamental human rights or are outwardly aggressive	Intervention in a nation's sovereignty in the form of military intervention or just war, maybe payment of reparations
	b. Unfortunate non-compliance: burdened societies lack the political culture or are too poor	International assistance

with their function of protecting human rights (which is what justifies their claim to sovereignty in the first place) may have their sovereignty pierced by a particular type of institution: an international court that operates fairly and democratically.

1.4 Overview of Chapters

I begin my substantive argument in Chapter 2, where I examine whether punishment is morally permissible. This question is important because

seems to have dropped the individual dimension of partial compliance and now speaks of ideal theory having only two parts, the basic structure and peoples (Rawls 2003, 4).

prosecution and punishment are generally regarded as the main functions of ICJ. It lies at the heart of what institutions of ICJ – like the ICC, or the special tribunals – do. To begin, I reconstruct John Locke's argument for the permissibility of punishment. Locke argues that we have a moral duty to 'preserve humanity' and we can discharge that duty by exercising our 'natural executive right' – that is, a right to punish in the state of nature. The Lockean argument is consequentialist in nature: punishments are effective in enforcing rights because they deter crimes. Therefore, the moral justifiability of punishment depends on the correctness of the claim that punishment deters crimes. I then discuss several objections against the consequentialist structure of Locke's argument. To counter these objections, I argue for a mixed theory that distinguishes between justifying the *practice* of punishment and justifying the *distribution* of punishment within that practice. To explain the latter, we must take into account considerations of normative individualism, egalitarianism, and pragmatism. Taken together, these arguments imply that coercive punishment is permissible for natural rights enforcement.

In Chapter 3, I examine why and under what circumstances the sovereignty of states can be pierced. To begin, I presuppose that persons have some fundamental rights independently of their membership in any political community. These rights are routinely called basic human rights. With Christopher Wellman, I argue that a state's legitimate power over its people and territory depends (among other things) on its performance in protecting those rights. If individual states fail at this task, those states have no right to complain about other parties stepping in and ensuring the enforcement of human rights. I then turn to the question of how third parties *acquire* the right to intervene. I distinguish between two approaches: the international harm principle and the duty view. According to the international harm principle, the international community has the authority to punish criminals when it has been harmed by their crimes. I argue that the view is implausible and introduce an alternative approach – that I call 'the duty view' – which instead argues that the international community acquires the right to punish because all persons have a moral duty to preserve humanity by helping to enforce their fundamental human rights. Normally, we discharge this duty through a system of just states in a moral division of labour. But when states fail to protect the fundamental human rights of their citizens, not only is outside interference permissible, but the duty to preserve humankind falls back to everyone. In fact, we are in a state of nature vis-à-vis that state, and in that situation, we all have an equal right to punish perpetrators of human rights crimes. Finally, I come back to Locke to argue that since we are all equals in the state of nature, our natural executive right must be exercised competitively. This leads to problems because people are biased and have competing interpretations when they exercise this right. Because such competitive punishment is incompatible with our equal status as moral authorities, we have reason to leave the state of nature and submit to an impartial institution that exercises the right on our behalf.

In Chapter 4, I then approach the question of in what sense, and to what extent, such an institution has political authority. I take institutions with legitimate authority to be justified in wielding political power, where this political power is backed by the threat of coercion. Against the position that international institutions are in principle not coercive, I claim that applying an adequate conception of coercion – which takes the concept of enforcement as paradigmatic for coercion, rather than the concept of pressure – enables us to understand some international institutions as coercive. It also lays open the assumption that a single conception of authority applied to all international institutions misconceives the diversity in aims and purposes of international institutions. Instead, different institutions require different standards of legitimate authority. In light of these two arguments, I distinguish between institutions that coordinate morally mandatory aims, and institutions that coordinate mutually advantageous aims. Both of them can be plausibly understood as coercive, even though their authority differs in scope and in the standards they must satisfy. Finally, I discuss whether the standard of state consent is an appropriate standard for international institutions. I conclude that while it is plausible for institutions that coordinate mutual advantage, it is implausible as a standard of legitimacy for institutions that coordinate morally mandatory aims – like ICJ institutions.

In Chapter 5, I argue that international institutions that pursue morally mandatory aims must satisfy two criteria to justify their claim to legitimate authority. First, they need to operate on a set of rules that ensure fair trials. But while fairness is a necessary condition for the legitimate authority of the international exercise of criminal justice, it is not a sufficient condition. To show what is missing I discuss three theories that all share a common instrumental understanding of ICJ institutions. None of them, I argue, is capable of answering the 'subordination complaint'. When some rule, others are subordinated to their rule – and the point of legitimate institutions is to address how this fact can be reconciled with the equal status of persons. Pointing out that some institutions are particularly fair and particularly effective in enforcing rights by meting out punishment is not a satisfactory answer to the subordination complaint. An adequate way to respond to the subordination complaint is to vest institutions with democratic procedures that ensure all subjected to the coercive rule of an institution have an equal opportunity to influence the rules that govern them. For ICJ institutions to gain political authority, I argue that they must provide institutional procedures that make democratic decision-making possible. The democratic requirement is *not* justified because democratic decision-making necessarily leads to better or more just outcomes. Rather, the democratic requirement is justified by the idea that authority can only be legitimate if its subjects have equal control over the institution that rules them. In the final part of Chapter 5, I highlight two strategies that enable states and individuals to exercise equal control over the court. The first strategy involves a legislative assembly that deliberates and decides on questions of criminal justice and institutional design. The second strategy seeks to make judicial law-making, where it is inevitable, more accountable to the public.

In the Conclusion, I offer some remarks about the relation between the argument I developed over the course of the book, and whether applying it to our structurally unjust real world leaves the argument vulnerable to a number of criticisms. I discuss two issues in more detail: first, whether the unequal distribution of international crime prosecutions taints the legitimacy of the ICC, and second, whether the ICC does in fact deter crimes. Both issues are serious, but ultimately, I conclude that they do not weaken my argument. I end the book by highlighting just how radically the project of ICJ departs from earlier strategies of dealing with war and human rights violations.

2

The Permissibility of Punishment

2.1 Punishment and International Criminal Justice

Why have international criminal justice (ICJ)? What is its purpose? The literature attributes several aims to the project of ICJ: it contributes to the processing of the past and helps with reconciliation (Bogdandy and Venzke 2014, 67); it expresses humanitarian or universal values (Luban 2010); it ends impunity and brings justice to the victims (Bachrach 2000); and it engages in a communicative enterprise with the defendants, calling them to account (Duff 2010). There is no reason to assume that ICJ exclusively serves one single purpose; it potentially serves all of these at the same time (May and Fyfe 2017). But while all of these aims are important, each of them is often *better* served by other mechanisms than ICJ: the expression of collective values is certainly better served with other means than with expensive, lengthy, and highly complex law cases. The same is true for its capacity to communicate with and call to account the defendant: a better institutional alternative might be a truth commission or a community trial. There is a similar problem with the aim of reconciliation: although international criminal trials sometimes help process what happened in the aftermath of political violence, reconciliation cannot justify the practice of international criminal law, because it is not at all clear that reconciliation is best served with a trial – much less with a trial that takes place far away from the place where the crimes were committed, as is often the case in ICJ proceedings. At best, it seems overly optimistic to say that international criminal trials are vital in helping a society scarred by unspeakable violence. In some cases, criminal prosecution might in fact do the opposite, and reconciliation is better served by generous amnesty laws.

In that sense, it is not clear that any of these aims can be the foundation for an argument about the permissibility of ICJ. That is why we need a stronger basis to show that ICJ is permissible. The reason is that ICJ primarily operates through the criminal prosecution and punishment of individuals. Any argument in favour of ICJ must be able to stand the considerable pressure coming from the deeply invasive nature of punishment. The practice of punishment is particularly difficult to justify because it often infringes basic rights: it limits a person's right to own property, to freedom of movement, or to freely choose their employment. If we take seriously the natural liberty of persons, we need a sturdier explanation as to why an institution is permitted to inflict evil on a person for the sake of punishing them. We need a story that explains why criminal acts make such rights infringements permissible.

It is not clear that the aims cited in the literature on international criminal law are by themselves sufficient to make that story plausible: just because some aim would be desirable does not necessarily imply that we can use the practice of punishment to reach it. To justify the practice of punishment, the aim must be extraordinarily important, and punishment must contribute significantly to the realization of this aim. None of the aims I described above entirely qualify in this sense: for example, the expression of humanistic values seems in fact important, but neither does it seem so important as to justify the criminals' deprivation of liberty, nor is punishment the best way to express those values. The same goes, I suggest, for the aims of reconciliation or calling defendants to account. Instead, I argue that our main focus should be on the role that ICJ plays in the protection and enforcement of fundamental human rights. In fact, I argue that this is the main purpose – the purpose that contributes most significantly to its justification – of a system of ICJ. As we will see, this involves an argument that emphasizes the deterrent function of punishment, but is, at its core, a 'mixed theory' that draws a conceptual connection between the importance of some rights and their punishability.[1]

I argue that punishment is justified because it is instrumentally valuable in reaching an aim that is independent of the nature of punishment, namely the enforcement and protection of important rights. However, this does not mean that the choice of punishment to serve this aim is arbitrary. One major reason that speaks in favour of a system of punishment is that a modern and liberal system of punishment takes seriously

[1] I do not discuss retributivism – the idea that the morally guilty deserve to suffer – as a rationale for punishment. Part of my reason is that to me, it seems like 'a mysterious piece of moral alchemy, in which the two evils of moral wickedness and suffering are transmuted into good' (Hart 1968, 234f). While retributivists have developed complex and subtle arguments in support of it (see the overview in Walen 2021), I will not be able to discuss and refute them in this study. For the purpose of my argument, I hope that it suffices to make the positive argument for deterrence.

the separateness of persons and is compatible with the view that under normal circumstances, persons are, and can be held, responsible for their actions. Viewing ourselves as autonomous, equal, and responsible individual agents precludes a variety of other systems of rights protection, such as extreme levels of surveillance or pre-emptive imprisonment for potential criminals. A system that is grounded in individual liability to punishment and that imposes sanctions in a foreseeable manner is a more acceptable and realistic alternative than other forms of law enforcement, given that it operates under circumstances that ensure the quality of the law (Fuller 1958). The idea that we are separate, autonomous, and responsible individuals is deeply anchored in our conception of ourselves and is too important to be potentially overridden by other considerations, such as high effectiveness. A narrow cost–benefit analysis that treats goods and threats as weighable against each other misjudges the complexity and importance of the values that are at stake in designing institutions of justice. Even a far more effective system of rights protection may not be legitimate if it would mean sacrificing innocents or curtailing everyone's personal autonomy and privacy to an intolerable degree.

To begin, I discuss the concept of punishment, and how it is distinct from other measures of rule enforcement. I then offer a systematic interpretation of John Locke's argument for a natural right to enforce fundamental rights. Locke's intuitive idea is that rights imply their own enforcement. While there are several ways to enforce rights, punishment is an effective enforcement mechanism because it tends to deter rights violations. In short, the argument is that a system of punishment is permissible because rights require enforcement, and a practice of punishment is one way of ensuring the enforcement of rights.

Before I begin with the substantive argument, allow me to comment on the scope of the argument: my argument for punishment is limited to ICJ. This entails that it refers to a specific kind of criminal action, namely those crimes that are most serious and are usually referred to as international crimes: among them are aggressive war, genocide, crimes against humanity, and war crimes.[2] Whether punishment is an appropriate means of social regulation for less serious crimes and actions is beyond the scope of this book. I tend to think that it is permissible only for a much narrower range of crimes than is usually the case in most states, but such an argument requires a different justification, and one that I am

[2] For a full list, see the Rome Statute, articles 5–8.

unable to provide here. I also want to be clear that a system of punishment is compatible with a larger and coordinated effort to enforce human rights with the help of tackling the socio-economic and cultural circumstances that generate a hostile climate for human rights. It is also compatible with efforts for reconciliation and other non-legal and non-punitive ways of rehabilitation, such as truth commissions and community service. Because punishment is only one permissible way of ensuring the protection of fundamental human rights, a pluralist effort to prevent human rights violations will be most successful overall.[3] I merely argue that an ICJ system is a permissible and effective mechanism to enforce some human rights. Both conditions – permissibility and effectiveness – are treated in non-comparative, sufficiency terms. The permissibility condition can be satisfied with a theoretical argument that shows that punishment is morally permissible, given that criminals forfeit some of their own rights by committing a crime. Whether punishment is also effective – in the sense that it deters future crime – is an empirical question. In the concluding chapter, in which I discuss how far my argument applies to the real world, we will see that there is reason for cautious optimism about the effectiveness of international criminal law in deterring future rights violations.

What is the nature of punishment? To begin, consider the following definition made by early modern philosopher Thomas Hobbes, who argues that punishment is: 'an evil inflicted by public authority on him that hath done or omitted that which is judged by the same authority to be a transgression of the law, to the end that the will of men may thereby the better be disposed to obedience' (Hobbes L, §18).

Hobbes defines punishment as an infliction of an evil, which makes a person worse off than before. But what exactly constitutes an evil is itself contentious: it might be thought of as a harm, or as a setback of interest, of a deprivation, or as a deprivation of rights. Hart argues that punishment must involve pain or other consequences normally considered unpleasant (Hart 1968, 4). But what distinguishes punishment from other forms of unpleasant treatment that result from a transgression of the law? Take the examples of compensation and penalties: compensations normally involve the deprivation of money or assets; penalties are impositions of fines. Both these treatments are, technically speaking, evils that are inflicted by public authority[4] as a result of a legal

[3] See also Drumbl (2007), who argues for a multidimensional effort to prevent atrocities.

[4] Punishment has a public nature which distinguishes punishment from mere vengeance. The real-world phenomena are certainly difficult to distinguish, but analytically,

transgression. But punishment and compensation are conceptually distinct: compensation is an approximation or a restoration of the *status quo ante*, that is, to the state before the crime was committed. To compensate is to return what one has unjustifiably taken from another. Therefore, compensation is usually considered a distinct measure of justice, and offenders often receive both punishment and a compensation order for the same crime.

To distinguish between penalty and punishment, Feinberg (1965) argues that punishment is distinguished from a mere penalty by its 'condemnatory character'. While penalties can be understood as admission-cost regulation – 'price tags' – on a certain kind of behaviour, punishments are meant to express moral condemnation of the criminal behaviour. Parking fines are an example of the former, while punishments are an example of the latter. Consider the example Philip Pettit gives on the intuitive distinction between punishment and penalty:

> The idea that criminalization is nothing more than admission-cost regulation is hardly any more fetching . . .. Imagine appearing as an offender in a criminal court and explaining to the judge that you are perfectly happy to accept the standard penalty, since you understand that you were only entitled to do what you did, provided you were willing to pay the associated costs. Imagine representing yourself, in other words, as entirely free of remorse or regret. You suggest that the assault or burglary or fraud, like the parking in our earlier example, was worth it: if not worth the actual cost to be imposed, at least worth the expected cost involved. Were you to deliberate and represent yourself in such a manner, it would be clear to all involved that for whatever reason, whether of stupidity or cynicism, you just did not understand what criminalization entails. (Pettit 2014, 135)

Similarly, Rawls argues that punishments 'are not simply a scheme of taxes and burdens designed to put a price on certain forms of conduct and in this way to guide men's conduct for mutual advantage. It would be far better if the acts proscribed by penal statutes were never done' (Rawls 1999, 276f). Feinberg, Pettit, and Rawls argue that the nature of punishment involves moral censure and the understanding that the crime should not have been committed in the first place.

Hobbes's definition also concerns the content of the criminal law: what type of behaviour may be punished? How do we determine what belongs to the criminal law and what belongs outside it? Hobbes defines

vengeance is 'angry', motivated by 'lust for blood' and 'schadenfreude' (Feinberg 1970, 103). Punishment is 'righteous' and justifiable.

punishment as the consequence of a transgression of the law. This mirrors the principle of *nullum crimen sine lege:* that is, punishment requires a law that specifies what constitutes a crime. But what acts should and can be criminalized depends on the political community: a conservative position might refer to the socially internalized moral rules that a society happens to have (Devlin 1965), while a liberal position paradigmatically refers to the principle of harm for answering this question (Dworkin 1966; Hart 1967; Feinberg 1987). There are also limits to feasibility when we consider what acts ought to be criminalized. Crimes should not be impossible to prosecute, and their eschewal should not be over-demanding: for an example, think of how the criminalization of lying would be close to impossible to police.

Hobbes's definition of punishment as a consequence of a legal transgression also rules out pre-emptive sanctions: punishment is always a *consequence* of a criminal act. However, not every transgression of the law automatically results in punishment. That something qualifies for punishment requires two general rules: a criminal act (*actus reus*) and a guilty mind (*mens rea*). Although a person might have transgressed the law, the punishment can be precluded in cases where, for example, they did not intend the crime, or did not know it was a crime, or did not have the choice not to commit the crime. These exemptions are described by the absence of the *mens rea* requirement for punishment.

The definition also speaks to the purpose or aim: what justifies the general practice or the system of punishment? Punishment is a notoriously difficult problem in moral philosophy, and the debate on its justification is nowhere near a consensus. Theories that seek to justify punishment are either backward-looking, forward-looking, a mix of backward- and forward-looking, or abolitionist. Backward-looking theories mostly circle around the concept of retribution, the core idea being that a crime has destabilized a moral equilibrium and thus requires rebalancing by harming the criminal, who has deserved the harm by their action. Forward-looking theories are about deterrence, that is, that the threat of sanctions helps deter future crimes.[5] Mixed theories argue

[5] Hobbes seems to view punishment as goal-oriented and justified by its general deterrent function: ('to the end that the will of men may thereby the better be disposed to obedience'). A distinction is usually drawn between general deterrence and special deterrence: whether a system of punishment deters potential future crimes by any person, or whether it deters potential future crimes of that particular person receiving the punishment. I say more on this later in the chapter.

that both deterrence and retribution have a role to play in the justification of punishment. They might also introduce further aims of punishment, like reconciliation, releasing social pressure, or expressing social values and calling offenders to account. Abolitionist positions reject both backward- and forward-looking theories: they argue that punishment cannot be justified without reaching for reasons that rely on implausible grounds. All four positions are mainly concerned with the aims of punishment.

Finally, when we consider the problem of punishment in a political context, there is another dimension that is especially important: the dimension of authority. Who has the right (or duty) to punish? Is the right to punish an individual right, or a collective right, or both? Under what circumstances and with what standing may institutions or individuals punish? What is it that gives one person or collective coercive power over another? Punishment is conceptually tied to the idea of standing in a relationship of authority, although not necessarily a public or institutional authority. This leads to the further question of which authority may permissibly punish. Persons may be liable to punishment from one agent, but not from another – and *vice versa*, agents may have the standing to punish some, but not others.

Both the aim of punishment and the question of authority are central to my argument. The main question of this book is whether, and why, international institutions have the right to punish individuals that are normally subject to their own governments. To answer that question, we need to first ask what gives *any* institution – including the state – the authority to punish in the first place. Note that the authority states de facto claim is extensive: states do not only claim the right to define and determine who gets which kind of punishment for what action, but also normally claim the right to *exclude* other agents from punishing their citizens. How do we explain such an extensive claim to authority?[6]

Before I discuss how *institutions* acquire the right to punish, I will argue that the practice of punishment is permissible in the first place. To do so, I offer an interpretation of an argument made by John Locke. The reason I focus on Locke for a theory of permissible punishment in

[6] The relative dearth of discussion concerning this question might be due to the fact that matters of punishment are largely discussed in the field of moral philosophy, where relations of political authority are not central. Christopher Wellman argues that another reason why the issue of authority in discussions of punishment has attracted relatively little attention is that political philosophers tend to be 'unreflective statists' (Wellman 2009, 420) who uncritically assume the sole authority of the state.

the context of ICJ is twofold. First, Locke offers a compelling view that takes seriously the idea that persons are equal to one another. Indeed, as Jeremy Waldron argues, the Lockean theory might very well be 'as well-worked out a theory of basic equality as there is in the canon of political philosophy' (Waldron 2002, 6). The premise of basic equality is the most important ground for my argument against subordination and therefore in favour of a *democratic* authority of ICJ institutions that I develop in the later chapters of this book.

Second, the Lockean justification of punishment is conceptually independent of the state.[7] Locke's core argument is that political institutions acquire the right to punish by the voluntary transfer of the right to punish from individuals. Individuals, Locke argues, have a natural right to punish (what he calls a 'natural executive right') in the state of nature: they are permitted – under certain circumstances – to punish individuals for transgressions of the (natural) law. Locke introduces the idea of a natural right to punish as a 'strange doctrine' (Locke II, §9 and §13), and it remains a controversial view. One of the reasons for its controversiality is perhaps that an individually held natural right to punish immediately evokes ugly connotations of vigilantism, 'mob justice', and brutal punishment driven by base motives. But despite its initial counter-intuitiveness, it is helpful in the context of ICJ because it does not presuppose an already constituted political community like the state. Or so I will argue.

2.2 The Natural Right to Punish

Locke offers a view that allows room for a particularly pertinent worry about international crimes: namely that the failure to punish can itself be an injustice – especially when the institutions normally responsible for punishing instead enable the crimes. It is in this sense that Robert Nozick

[7] Contrary to Locke's view, Hobbes argues that just as there can be no real rights in the state of nature, there can be no real punishment in the state of nature. Persons are allowed any means to preserve themselves in the state of nature, and therefore there can be no 'private punishment': only when it comes from authority can the infliction of an evil be properly called punishment. Consequently, the origin of the state's right to punish is not an individual natural right to punish, but the individual's natural right to do whatever is necessary to preserve oneself; by laying down that right, as Hobbes argues, the sovereign is justified to use the necessary means (within the limits of the natural law) to preserve everyone (Hobbes 1651, 214). I thank Timo Pongrac for pressing me to clarify my reasons for concentrating on Locke.

asks whether Locke's general right to punish is really so counterintuitive: 'If some great wrong were committed in another country which refuses to punish it (perhaps the government is in league with, or itself, the wrongdoer), would not it be all right for you to punish the wrongdoer, to inflict some harm on him?' (Nozick 1974, 137).

The story of the Argentinian movie *El secreto de sus ojos* from 2009 provides a powerful illustration of the intuitive plausibility of Locke's argument. The story is mainly set in the times of the Argentinian military dictatorship and Dirty War (1974–1983) and revolves around Benjamin Esposito, a federal justice agent, who in 1974, together with his colleague Irene Menendez Hastings, is assigned to a case of a young woman who was raped and murdered. The widower of the victim is devastated, and Esposito promises him that the killer will face justice. Esposito and Hastings eventually catch the killer, Isidoro Gomez – the victim's childhood friend whose obsessive romantic advances were rejected by the victim. He confesses that he killed her out of his wounded male pride, and is put on trial, found guilty, and sentenced to prison.

About a year later, the widower sees how Gomez appears on television as a part of a security detail for the Argentinian president. It turns out that Gomez was hired right out of prison by the Argentinian intelligence service to do the 'dirty work' in a death squad for the dictatorial government, hunting down and killing perceived enemies of the military junta. Seeking revenge for his imprisonment, Gomez threatens Esposito and Hastings and kills their common friend in an attack originally planned on Esposito's life. Esposito flees to a remote corner of Argentina where he is safe. Decades later, Esposito writes a book about the affair and sets out to find out what happened to everyone. He finds his former colleague Hastings, but he cannot find Gomez. When Esposito seeks out the victim's widower – to whom he had promised that the killer will face justice – to find out what happened to Gomez, the widower confesses to have taken revenge for his wife's murder by having kidnapped and shot Gomez in 1975. After the widower's confession, Esposito leaves, but with an awkward feeling that he has not yet discovered the whole truth. Going back to the widower's house, Esposito watches the – by now elderly – widower take an orange into a small shed adjacent to the main house. When he follows him, he discovers an old man – Gomez – in a makeshift prison cell. Instead of having killed him in 1975, the widower has imprisoned Gomez for thirty years next to his private home.

The plot is a compelling illustration of the plausibility of a natural right to punish, especially because the widower did not simply seek revenge – he could have killed Gomez as a retribution for having murdered his fiancée – but, instead, imprisoned him in an attempt to imitate what he thought *should have been* the state's just punishment. In a situation of state terror, in which judicial and government institutions have perverted their original function – that is, to serve justice and to protect the innocent – do we really think that the widower acted wrongly? The government's brutal decision to not only release the legally convicted murderer from prison, but vesting him with deadly power is overwhelmingly unjust.

An illegitimate state imposing unjust laws comes close to what Locke considered the 'state of nature' (Simmons 1989).[8] Those familiar with Locke's general theory of political obligation will be familiar with the idea that a state's right to punish can only be explained in reference to prior individual rights. No public institution has any power unless it is granted to it by its subjects. Locke argues that individuals possess an equal right to punish lawbreakers in the state of nature. For Locke, the state of nature is a state of fundamental and absolute moral equality:

> A *State* also of *Equality*, wherein all the Power and Jurisdiction is reciprocal, no one having more than another: there being nothing more evident, than that Creatures of the same species and rank promiscuously born to all the same advantages of Nature, and the use of the same faculties, should also be equal one amongst another without subordination or subjection. (Locke II, §4)[9]

It is a state in which all persons share the same faculties and a common nature: 'all that share in the same common nature, faculties and powers, are in nature equal, and ought to partake in the same common rights and privileges' (Locke I, §67).

Because every person in the state of nature is 'furnished with like faculties, sharing all in one Community of Nature, there cannot be supposed any such *Subordination* among is that may Authorize us to destroy another, as if we were made for another's uses, as the inferior

[8] The state of nature is a description of the moral relations between persons rather than a description of a historical or territorial state (Simmons 1989, 460).

[9] Locke's emphasis on the equality in the state of nature is an important part of his reply to Robert Filmer's 'Patriarcha, or the Natural Power of Kings'. In it, Filmer argues that political authority of some over others is natural by virtue of a natural inequality of persons. Locke's treatises are written as a rebuttal of Filmer's work (Waldron 2002, 16).

ranks of Creatures are for ours' (Locke II, §6).[10] All persons have the same desire for self-preservation and the rational capacity to pursue projects in life, and all persons must have the same rights to do so (Simmons 1992, 81ff). An unequal distribution of rights was justified only if persons were unequal regarding these two fundamental desires. But Locke assumes that everyone has the same desire for self-preservation and pursuing a plan of life. Of course, not all persons are equal in every sense. Clearly, some are stronger or more intelligent, but neither strength nor intelligence bears on the two fundamental desires. Differences in age or virtue are consistent with equality of authority, Locke insists (Waldron 2002, 31). Rights that protect the two fundamental desires then must be distributed equally. In Simmons's words, 'no person is any better than another at *being a person*' (Simmons 1992, 82), and therefore, nobody is justified in subordinating another. The fundamental equality of persons in the state of nature is, in modern terms, an equality of status.[11] Equality is the default, and those who argue for unequal status and unequal distribution of rights must give reasons why they depart from this presumption (Simmons 1992, 81). Unless

[10] Locke seems to think that animals ('inferior creatures') are made for human use. This somehow sits uncomfortably with his more general approach of rights, especially when looked at it from the religious perspective. One of the reasons why he thinks humans ought to respect one another and not harm one another is because they are the 'workmanship' of God, sent into the world by Him and therefore his property (Locke II, §6). And it is absolutely forbidden to destroy God's property without reason. This, however, should also be true of the animals; although they might not have the same faculties as humans in terms of rationality, they do have the same desires of self-preservation and happiness.

[11] I follow and emphasize Simmons's reading of Locke, which defines the ground of natural equality in a more or less secular way. There is another side in Locke that grounds our rights and duties in the obedience to God. Simmons argues that both readings are equally supported by the text; Locke was writing in the seventeenth century, a time of transition between a time when the thinking about duties was centred around the picture of God and a time when moral thinking started to take other persons as genuine sources of moral duties (Simmons 1992, 99). I find that this secular approach is of more systematic use for my project. Locke's own view is, as Simmons argues, therefore not inconsistent, but merely overdetermined. For a reading of Locke that argues against the possibility of bracketing out the religious underpinnings in Locke's defence of basic equality, see the important work of Waldron (2002, 2017). In it, there is also an enlightening discussion of Locke's somewhat awkward insistence that there is a natural difference between men and women, which gives rise to a difference in authority. Waldron shows how this argument is inconsistent with Locke's general direction in his political theory, namely to deny 'that natural differences among humans give rise to basic differences of authority' (Waldron 2002, 35). For a feminist interpretation of Locke's egalitarian commitments, see the work of Butler (1978).

individuals are given exceptional rights by others (or God), there is no reason to think that natural rights are distributed unequally.

So: what natural rights are there? Simmons argues that there are three types of rights in Locke: general rights, consensual special rights, and non-consensual special rights (Simmons 1992, 87). The general rights are the right(s) of self-government: our 'equal right to freedom from harm and interference by others, provided only that our actions stay within the bounds of natural law' (Simmons 1992, 85). Consensual special rights arise from our voluntary actions and include our political rights: Locke's justification for the state famously involves the voluntary consent of the governed. They also include other rights, for example conjugal rights. The third category of non-consensual special rights are rights that 'derive from relationships not based in promises or consent' (Simmons 1992, 87). Nonconsensual special rights arise from special moral relationships that are involuntary and as such include, for example, parental and filial rights. This category also includes the natural executive right,[12] which permits that

> all men may be restrained from invading other's rights, and from doing hurt to one another, and the law of nature be observed, which willeth the peace and preservation of all mankind, the execution of the law of nature is in that state (of nature, L.M.), put into every man's hands, whereby everyone has a right to punish the transgressors of that law to such a degree, as may hinder its violation. (Locke II, §7)

As Locke argues here, the law of nature 'wills' the peace and preservation of all mankind. Just as we have a duty to 'preserve ourselves' (and not to 'quit' our station 'wilfully', that is, not to commit suicide), we also have a duty '*to preserve the rest of Mankind*' (Locke II, §7). Simmons argues that Locke's conception of the moral law has a rule-consequentialist superstructure, with the 'preservation of mankind' as its ultimate goal (Simmons 1992, 50). The purpose of the natural executive right is thus to give everyone permission to enforce this law of nature, which commands everyone to preserve everyone else. The argument that gets Locke from a *duty* to preserve mankind to a *right* to enforce the law is the following: first, the concept of moral duties and moral rights entails the existence of natural law. For why else would we have moral duties if it was not because there is a law of which duties and rights are part? But if we can accept the idea that there is natural law,

[12] For an interpretation of the right to punish as a special right, see Müller (2019b).

then, Locke implies, we must accept that there are sanctions for non-compliance with the law:[13]

> What duty is, cannot be understood without a law; nor a law be known or supposed without a lawmaker, or reward and punishment ... Since it would be utterly in vain to suppose a rule set to the free actions of men, without annexing to it some enforcement of good and evil to determine his will, we must, wherever we suppose a law, suppose also some reward or punishment annexed to that law. (Locke E, 2.28.6)

The law of nature would be 'in vain' if persons were not allowed to enforce the obligation to act according to the law. Why? Because our internal motivation, such as our moral conscience, is often insufficient for obeying the law. If it was sufficient, there would be no need to enforce law externally. But because it is not, the law would lose its point if it could not determine the will of those who are under its obligation.[14] But then why do some individuals break the law and are disobedient? Perhaps one might argue that the cause of disobedience is not insufficient internal motivation, but simply epistemic uncertainty about what the law is. As we are in the state of nature and have no positive (moral) law, we might simply not know what the law is, even though we would possess enough internal motivation to obey it – if only we knew what it was. The ambiguous term Locke uses in the passage quoted above is 'to determine

[13] Elsewhere, he argues: 'for the *law of nature* would, as all others laws that concern men in this world, be in vain, if there were nobody that in the state of nature had a *power to execute* that law, and thereby preserve the innocent and restrain offenders, and if any one in the state of nature may punish another, for any evil he has done, every one may do so. For in that *state of perfect equality*, where naturally there is no superiority or jurisdiction of one, over another, what any may do in prosecution of that law, every one must needs have a right to do.' (Locke II, §7)

[14] This argument is not to be confused with the Austinian argument that enforcement is the *source* of the obligation to obey: John Austin argues that the law simply is an aggregation of commands, and that the potential sanctions behind these commands are the cause of an individual's obligation to comply with them. As Hart has argued, this 'gunman-writ-large conception' (because in Austin's picture, there is no distinction between a gunman who commands you to φ 'or else ...', and legal rules, thereby saying that the law is nothing but a gunman writ large (Hart 2012)) of law blurs the necessary distinction between being compelled by force vs. being obligated for normative reasons. Locke understands the relation between sanctions, obligations, and law differently from Austin: the obligations to comply with the law originate with the normative validity of the laws itself, and the sanctions are merely a mechanism to make sure the law is being followed. Locke does not think that the obligation stems from the sanctions that are attached to the law (Simmons 1992, 27), but that sanctions are justified because the natural law obligates.

the will': if we do not attach good and evil to determine a person's will, rules will be in vain.

But further textual evidence suggests that the problem of disobedience is *not* caused by problems of knowing what the law is. To see why, let us have a closer look at Locke's idea of natural law. The moral law is given by God and God is perfectly wise, and so the moral law that He gives us is the most ideal set of laws to advance the goal of preserving mankind (Simmons 1992, 51). Rational persons should be perfectly able to resolve any conflicting claims by appealing to the natural law – in fact, the natural law is almost easier to understand than the positive law (the law of the commonwealth):

> yet it is certain there is such a law, and that too as intelligible and plain to a rational creature and a studier of that law as the positive laws of commonwealths, nay, possibly plainer; as much as reason is easier to be understood than the fancies and intricate contrivances of men, following contrary and hidden interests put into words; for truly so are a great part of the municipal laws of countries, which are only so far right as they are founded on the law of Nature, by which they are to be regulated and interpreted. (Locke II, §12)

Our *specific* moral duties follow from knowing the law of nature and applying it to the empirical conditions of human life, where those conditions are revealed by our senses (Locke E, 4.12.11; Simmons 1992, 23). For example, the duty to preserve humanity applied to the empirical condition of human life implies a duty not to kill my neighbour. But if we can indeed know our specific moral duties, then the reason for not acting according to them must be the weakness of our internal motivation, not that we cannot know what the law is.

Locke also explains that when a person transgresses the law, that person declares themselves as living by other rules than those of reason and common equity (Locke II, §8). In other words, criminals wilfully put themselves above the law. This argument is also reinforced by what Locke takes to be the aim of punishment, which is to make the criminal repent, and deter the criminal and others from 'doing mischief' (Locke II, §8). Deterrence obviously only works when criminals have a *choice* to commit or not commit the crime – which they did not have, were they simply confused about what the law is.

To make persons comply with the law and mitigate the problem of disobedience, we need to introduce an external enforcement mechanism: the right to execute the law. Locke claims that there are no better means of enforcement available in the state of nature than punishment. Notice that the concepts of enforcement and punishment are not identical in Locke's picture: punishment is *one way* of enforcing the law. But Locke argues that in the absence of public institutions, punishment is the only available external enforcement mechanism of the law besides thwarting attacks.[15] How plausible is this claim? To understand it, let us first turn to the concept of enforcement. Enforcement is the organized or unorganized effort to secure compliance with a rule or body of rules. This can be done by a variety of actions. For example, self-defence – warding off attacks to protect oneself – is probably the most immediate form of enforcement: it immediately terminates the encroachment on the person. Similarly, punishment is a form of enforcement, as it prevents rights violations prospectively.

To show how enforcement and punishment are related, Locke makes a consequentialist argument that progresses in two steps. First, he points out that persons are free in the state of nature, but they are not free to do whatever they please. The law of nature prohibits persons to commit suicide or kill others; indeed, they must 'preserve' themselves and others:

> Every one as he is bound to preserve himself, and not to quit his Station wilfully; so by the like reason when his own Preservation comes not in competition, ought he, as much as he can, to preserve the rest of Mankind, and may not unless it be to do Justice on an Offender, take away, or impair the life, or what tends to the Preservation of the Life, the Liberty, Health, Limb or Goods of another. (Locke II, §7)

Because we have a duty to preserve humanity, transgressions of the law must be prevented. The only way this can be done is by either restraining or punishing the offender. This will deter them from offending again, and it will set an example to other potential offenders, so that they are put off from violating rights:

> In transgressing the Law of Nature, the Offender declares himself to live by another Rule, than that of reason and common Equity, which is that measure God has set to the actions of Men, for their mutual security: and

[15] Rocio Ferrecio Lorca argues that Locke is mistaken here. It makes perfect sense, she claims, that enforcement only entails the right to defend and the right to protect, but not the right to punish because right enforcement is not strictly dependent on punishment (Lorca 2016). That is certainly correct, but I read Locke as saying the punishment is an *effective* mechanism of deterrence, not a necessary mechanism. In that sense, Locke's argument depends on the empirical claim that punishment does indeed effectively deter rights violations and that it is permissible. I claim that both of these conditions are fulfilled.

> so he becomes dangerous to Mankind, the tye, which is to secure them from injury and violence, being slighted and broken by him. Which being a trespass against the whole Species, and the Peace and Safety of it, provided for by the Law of Nature, every man upon this score, by the Right he hath to preserve Mankind in general, may restrain, or where it is necessary, destroy things noxious to them, and so may bring such evil on any one, who hath transgressed that Law, as may make him repent the doing of it, and thereby deter him, and by his Example others, from doing the like mischief. (Locke II, §8)

When a person transgresses the law of nature, they declare themselves as living by other rules than the law of nature (which is the law of reason and equality) and therefore become dangerous to others. It is under these circumstances that punishment – doing justice to an offender – is permissible because it creates a climate of deterrence that ultimately helps to hinder rights violations. One might object that this argument actually justifies much more than only the right to punish: if what matters is our moral duty to preserve our fellow humans against offenders, then we might also be justified, for example, to pre-emptively use force in order to restrain a potentially dangerous offender (Simmons 1992, 136). I believe the objection is correct, but unproblematic: punishment is only one mechanism that protects fundamental rights and can exist among other mechanisms. In that sense, Locke is a pluralist about fundamental rights protection. In fact, this explains why Locke supposes a natural *right* to punish, instead of a *duty* to punish – even though the right is derived from the duty to preserve humanity. Punishment is just one of many ways to create a deterrent climate conducive to the protection of the fundamental rights of others. In that sense, it is not a natural right justified by its capacity to protect a supposed interest in punishment, but by its capacity to enable the protection of others' rights.[16] Hence, the right to punish is instrumentally valuable for fulfilling the duty to preserve humanity, but it is not a conceptual necessity *simpliciter*.

Locke gives another argument for why there must be a natural right to punish, but this one is less convincing. Locke argues that only the natural executive right can explain why it is permissible to punish foreigners on the state territory. Here is his argument: foreigners are subject only to the

[16] Thwarting attacks on others, supporting just institutions, and giving to charity may be structurally similar.

authority of their own states because, according to his theory of obligation, they have consented to their own state and not to the state they are visiting. Locke seems to be assuming that foreigners thus remain in a state of nature with respect to the host government so that the host government has no right to punish them unless there was a right to punish in the state of nature (Simmons 1992, 133). Therefore, it is inexplicable how they can be punished if not for the reason that there is a natural executive right to punish that is possessed by all:

> Those who have the Supream Power of making Laws in England, France or Holland, are to an Indian, but like the rest of the World, Men without Authority: And therefore if by the Law of Nature, every Man hath not a Power to punish Offences against it, as he soberly judges the Case to require, I see not how the Magistrates of any Community, can punish an Alien of another Country, since in reference to him, they can have no more Power, than what every Man naturally may have over another. (Locke II, §9)

This argument is systematically much weaker, and three problems with his argument stand out. First of all, Locke deduces his conclusion from the stipulation that governments must be allowed to punish foreigners on their territories. But it may well show that the stipulation is wrong: maybe the magistrates are indeed not justified in punishing aliens of another country. It is entirely conceivable that, instead, they must leave them alone or extradite them to their native country. Otherwise, the argument is circular: Locke basically asserts that governments have the right to punish, deduces that persons must have had the right to punish in the state of nature, only to then use the natural right to punish as a justification for showing that governments have the right to punish.

Second, this argument does not show what Locke wants it to show: if the foreigner is in fact in the state of nature with the government and therefore may be punished by it, by extension the foreigner finds himself also in the state of nature with all other citizens of the state. This would mean that the government has no exclusive right to punish. And third, Simmons shows how this argument can be refuted with Locke's own reasoning about tacit consent. Given that the alien is on the foreign territory by choice, the government can assume that the alien has tacitly consented to observe the laws by moving their body on the territory. The consequence of this reasoning is that the state has the right to punish not because previously there was a private executive right, but because the alien has consented to the laws of the state and therefore has consented to the state's authority to punish him. Simmons thus rejects Locke's claim that an alien is in the state of nature with respect to the host government.

The fact that individuals have a natural executive right itself does not play any role in the justification of punishment here.[17]

In light of these weaknesses, I find the first, more systematic account of the natural executive right much more plausible. To summarize the argument: the idea of moral rights and duties only makes sense if there exists law, and that the existence of law implies it is enforceable. The only enforcement mechanism in the state of nature consists in either averting or punishing breaches. Thus, having the duty to preserve humanity, we must resort to punishment to hinder the breaches of law. And since nobody is above anybody else in the state of nature, the right to punish is distributed equally among all rational adults.

2.3 Punishment's Aim

We have seen that right to punish is explained by everyone's duty to protect other members of the human community. For this argument to work, Locke relies on the idea that transgressions of the law can be deterred by punishing the transgressor. In that sense, Locke defends a forward-looking theory that identifies deterrence as the aim of the practice of punishment. Both special deterrence and general deterrence play a role in the justification of punishment for Locke: for example, he says that 'Each transgression may be punished to that degree, and with so much severity, as will suffice to make it an ill bargain to the offender, give him cause to repent, and terrify others from doing the like' (Locke II, §12). So, punishment deters both the actual offender ('make it an ill bargain to the offender' and 'give him cause to repent' = special deterrence) and potential offenders ('terrify others from doing the like' = general deterrence).

But that claim opens the door to several objections that have been made against deterrence theories of punishment. First, how can Locke explain that every transgression of the law may permissibly be punished, and not only those acts whose punishment will be directly useful for the climate of deterrence? Obviously, not every act of punishment will directly contribute to deterrence,[18] and not every failure to punish a criminal will damage the climate of deterrence. If we take the consequentialist core of the deterrence argument seriously, we are forced to conclude that the only justifiable punishment is that which directly

[17] For a similar rejection of Locke's 'foreigner' argument, see the discussion in Lorca (2016).

[18] I am grateful to Michael Zürn for pressing this point. I reply to it further below.

contributes to the climate of deterrence. But this renders the idea of punishment absurd: to punish *means* to sanction transgressions of the law – and fairness demands that equal cases are to be treated equally.

Second, how can Locke justify a prohibition of the punishment of innocents? It might be the case that punishing one innocent person every now and then will be conducive to deterring future crime. Third, deterrence-based arguments lend themselves to justify disproportional punishment: smaller, but recurring crimes are, according to the deterrence logic, to be met with strong punishment, whereas big, but seldomly occurring crimes are to be met with weak punishment. There seems to be something wrong with that, and although Locke says that punishment must be proportionate to the crime (Locke II, §8), it is not clear how this claim can be systematically defended from his position. These three objections point to the claims that theories of punishment that take deterrence as their aim cannot provide a plausible theory of punishment, because they are unable to rule out unfairness, disproportionality, and punishment of innocents.

Instead of replying to each of them individually, these objections can be countered systematically by distinguishing between the justification of punishment as a system and the justification of the distribution of punishment. The main idea of such a 'mixed theory' response is that the theory of deterrence applies to the first, and some kind of retributive argument applies to the latter justification.[19] H. L. A. Hart, John Rawls, and, according to Sharon Byrd, perhaps surprisingly, Immanuel Kant all make similar versions of an argument that provides a rebuttal to those objections. The heart of mixed theories is twofold: first, it is the consequentialist thesis that crimes are prevented through the threat of punishment. This is the justifying aim of punishment. Second, retribution enters the picture when we shift the focus from the question of what the justifying aim of punishment is to the question of how punishment should be distributed.

[19] Locke does not follow this path, although it does fit with the general spirit of his position. In fact, Locke sometimes implicitly sounds like a mixed-theory proponent because he uses both consequentialist and retributivist language, for example in Locke II, §8: 'only to retribute him, so far as calm reason and conscience dictates, what is proportionate to his transgression, which is so much as may serve for reparation and restraint' (Locke II, §8). Simmons argues that the most plausible interpretation of the superstructure of Locke's conception of morality is to attribute to him a rule-consequentialist view. But unlike utilitarians, he does not think that the common good (often described as happiness) must be maximized. Instead, he conceives the common good in a distributive fashion (Simmons 1992, 57).

Sharon Byrd attributes such a view to Immanuel Kant (Byrd 1989). In a 'groundbreaking article' (Ripstein 2009, 300), she argues for a novel interpretation of Kant's theory of punishment. Her main point is that Kant is not the hardcore retributivist that he is usually taken for, an interpretation that relies mainly on passages like the one where he argues that every last criminal must be executed before society dissolves itself.[20] Byrd argues that Kant's systematic position was less drastically retributivist and included elements of consequentialism: while deterrence is effective in the general pursuance of not violating rights, retribution is a constraint on the treatment of individuals, so that they do not become an instrument of social policy. She claims that the purpose of Kant's 'mixed theory' of criminal law was to secure individual rights through threatening punishment to deter their violation (Byrd 1989, 184). Punishment is thus instrumental in nature for Kant, because its purpose is to protect the social order, where the social order is a system of universal external freedom (Byrd 1989, 154). The just treatment of the offender may not be affected by social considerations, and institutions must secure this just treatment with respect to the individual. But punishing the innocent and not punishing the guilty are both suspect and to be avoided (Byrd 1989, 197).

Similarly, H. L. A. Hart makes a distinction between the question of what justifies punishment as a systematic practice and how punishment should be distributed. The justification of the whole practice relies on the consequentialist principle of deterrence, while the distribution relies on a retributive principle, perhaps fairness or fittingness (Hart 1968). Thirteen years earlier, Rawls makes a similar point (Rawls 1955). Rawls argues that the principles justifying a practice can be distinct from the principle justifying a particular action under the practice (Rawls 1955, 3): 'one must distinguish between justifying a practice as a system of rules to be applied and enforced, and justifying a particular action which falls under these rules; utilitarian arguments are appropriate with regard to

[20] Kant writes that

> Even if a civil society were dissolved through the unanimous vote of its members, (e.g., if an island society decided to dissolve with its members spreading themselves over the rest of the earth), the last murderer within its prison first must be executed so that he experiences what his own deeds are worth and the bloodguilt does not cling to the society that did not insist on this punishment: since, if so, it can be seen as having participated in that public violations of justice. (Kant MM, 333)

questions about practices, while retributive arguments fit the application of particular rules to particular cases' (Rawls 1955, 5).

The justifying aim does not explain every action within the practice, but only the system of rules that guide the practice as a whole. Rawls argues that the reason why consequentialist arguments are often thought to be justifying aggregative utilitarianism is because the logical status of rules can be placed within consequentialist theories in two ways. The 'summary view' of the logical status of rules is the view that rules are devised by aggregating past applications of the utilitarian principle to particular cases, resulting in a 'rule', akin to a rule of thumb: using the rule (that rule reporting past experience) will guide decision-making and help decide cases more quickly. The decisions made in past experience are logically prior to the rule, meaning the rule is deduced from a number of past cases (Rawls 1955, 22f). In contrast to the summary view, there is the 'practice conception' of rules: in this view, rules *define* a practice. These types of rules are logically prior to particular cases (Rawls 1955, 23), which means that a specific action only falls under the practice because there is a rule that describes that particular action as part of the practice.

Consider the 'practice' of making a will. One has only 'made a will' if one has proceeded according to the rules that regulate the making of wills: if one has written the will down, signed it, had a witness, etc. If you had, for example, failed to write the will down, you have not 'made a will'. To engage in a practice then means to follow specific rules defining and regulating the practice, and the process of writing down how one's property shall be distributed can only be made sense of in reference to the practice of 'making a will'. We can explain the nature of the principle defining the practice by referring to its purpose.

But how do we explain that the principles that define and regulate the practice apply even in cases where a deviation from those principles would *better* serve the purpose of the practice? Why cannot an agent within the practice justify deviating from the rules by appealing to the purpose of the practice?[21] I think that two considerations matter in this

[21] Consider a game of football: there may be instrumental or aesthetic reasons that suggest changing the rules of the practice of football, but that does not mean that a player can appeal to those reasons while making a move during the game (Rawls 1955, 16). In a footnote, Rawls cracks a cricket-themed joke about the awkwardness of evaluating every single act in a practice according to the overall utility: 'A philosophical joke (in the mouth of Jeremy Bentham): "When I run to the other wicket after my partner has struck a good ball I do so because it is best on the whole."' (Rawls 1955, 27)

context. I discuss the second consideration in the next section. Rawls discusses the first consideration: he argues that the reason why not every agent within a practice has the discretion to appeal to the justifying principle of the practice for their actions is that this would destroy the capacity of the practice to coordinate behaviour in such a way that is conducive to the purpose of the practice. As a pragmatic matter, the deterrent function of systems of criminal punishment would most likely collapse because people could not avoid punishment under such a system of punishment. The point invoking deterrence as the justifying aim of a practice of punishment is based on the assumption that individuals rationally decide to forego criminal acts in the face of sanctions. But if they cannot control whether they will be punished or not (because they might be even if they are innocent if it furthers the justifying aim), it makes no sense for them to refrain from committing criminal acts. Being punished becomes a matter of luck, so you would have no incentive to obey the law, since this has no effect on the likelihood of being punished.

A system of punishment that worked like this would have as much of a point as a price system where you only learn of the price of something after you have agreed to buy it. Rawls's claim is that it does not make much sense to call this a price system at all, because the central function of a price system – helping you decide on a purchase by letting you know what amount of money you have to give up for it – is lost: such a system would give you no guidance in making your decision (Rawls 1955, 12). The purpose of a system of punishment is analogous: to guide people's actions by deterring them from committing crimes. A system is unable to provide such guidance if it applies the rules unevenly – that is, with the aim of maximizing deterrence – and would therefore be self-defeating because it could not guide our actions.

The distinction between justifying the practice and justifying its distribution gets us quite far in replying to the three objections. However, it can only explain why we *generally* should stick to the rules. It cannot explain why we should stick to the rules *every time*: it cannot explain why we think that every single person has a *right* against being sacrificed for a better overall outcome. Consider the objection that deterrence theories of punishment allow punishment of the innocent. According to the objection, a small number of innocents could be sacrificed for the greater good of security for a majority. Now, one could rebut this objection with the Rawlsian argument described above: a system with the purpose of protecting fundamental rights cannot achieve its purpose by violating fundamental rights – that would be self-defeating. The aim of the system is to protect exactly those rights, so why would it make sense to violate them? However, it could be argued that since we care about the consequences of actions, if violating *some* rights generates an overall better outcome without jeopardizing its stability and function, we should prefer it.

To avoid this conclusion, we need a second consideration, one that can explain why it is fair to apply the rules evenly, even if this leads to a less efficient outcome overall. Let me begin by pointing out that any objection of this 'sacrificing innocents' type assumes that the aggregative consequentialist principle itself must be invoked when justifying a system of individual rights. But this need not be so: consequentialist arguments about the good that a system of punishment produces can be understood either aggregatively or distributively. The aggregative view argues that the overall aggregative outcome matters, while the distributive interpretation argues that it matters how the overall outcome is distributed. The question thus becomes: why should we accept that the (egalitarian) distribution of the aggregated outcome matters? It will be difficult to explain that by again referring to a consequentialist argument, because it can then be objected that the consequentialist principle must be applied again: an (egalitarian) distribution is to be preferred only if it leads to better consequences overall. This does not solve the 'sacrificing innocents' objection.

Instead, I think that the most convincing answer to the objection has to do with our conception of the person and its relation to social institutions. For normative individualists, the notion that a good can be a good independently of its effect on individual persons does not make sense. As normative egalitarians – who believe in the fundamental equality of persons – we are also committed to the idea that unequal distributions must be justified to individuals, not to aggregates. But an unfair distribution cannot be justified towards the innocent who are punished for the sake of the greater good for the majority. Thus, making consequentialism and rights compatible has to invoke the idea that an unequal distribution of the benefits and burdens which an institution or a practice produces is incompatible with the position of normative individualism and egalitarianism.[22] This can explain why we usually recognize various constraints on the way in which social institutions may permissibly reach their aims. They must treat each person with the same respect, which implies that they cannot justify policies in

[22] This is the core of various attempts to make consequentialism compatible with rights. See, for example, Scanlon (1977) and Pettit (1988).

reference to a good that is independent of individual persons. The reason we should accept constraints on the behaviour of institutions in the form of individual rights is not because they make the institution more widely accepted, more stable, or more efficient. The reason we should accept them is that we are bound to the idea that goods only matter if they matter for *each individual* person. With this argument, we can now reply to the objection that a deterrence argument implies the permissibility of sacrificing innocents. It does so only under the assumption that the good that is to be maximized by the institution is thought of aggregatively, and not distributively. As normative individualists, we are bound to choose the distributive interpretation. Second, we can reply to the objection that the deterrence principle implies that only acts that do contribute to the deterrent climate should be punished, that as normative egalitarians, we must insist on an egalitarian distribution of the benefits and burdens that institutions generate. Any aberration from this normative egalitarianism can only be justified by considerations of desert, but not by the aim of the practice.[23]

The third objection against the deterrence idea is the criticism that there are aspects of punishment that will likely increase the deterrence effect of the principle. We might assume that the more severe the punishment, the more likely are persons deterred from committing the crime. This might lead us to think that an effective way of decreasing crime is to threaten severe punishments for relatively insignificant, but recurring crimes. Do we thus have reason to impose very severe punishments because they discourage crime more effectively?

One reply to this challenge is that empirical research indicates that the claim seems to be simply mistaken in this case: the severity of the punishment does not correlate with an increase in deterrence.[24] But most people also have the intuition that it would be morally *wrong* to impose harsh sentences for small crimes, *even if it did increase* deterrence. The intuition that the severity of punishment ought to reflect the gravity of the crime points toward a principle of 'fittingness' or proportionality.

[23] On the role that considerations of desert can possibly play in a theory of human rights, see Nickel's recent article (Nickel 2015) and Stemplowska's comment (Stemplowska 2015).

[24] Sometimes even the opposite is true: there is some indication that longer prison sentences produce the opposite effect because prisons are breeding grounds for criminal activity (Alexander 2012). Social research shows that instead of severity, the swiftness and likelihood of punishment are much better at deterring criminals (Nagin and Paternoster 1993; Nagin 1998; Wright and Sentencing Project (U.S.) 2010).

Although we have already established that punishments are to be distributed equally – according to the principle of desert and in the sense that like cases must be treated alike – we must now explain why 'light' crimes should be responded to with light sentences, and why severe crimes should be responded to with severe sentences.

At the same time, considering that persons normally have natural rights against being harmed – recall Locke's argument about how we have a general right to freedom from harm (Simmons 1992, 85) – we need to tell a story of how it is permissible that criminals are exposed to punishments, as punishments clearly constitute a kind of harm. How do we explain what happens to these rights when they commit a crime? In other words: we need an answer to the questions of why rights violations in the form of punishment are illegitimate *unless* it is a rights violation that responds to a previous crime, and why the rights violation in the form of punishment must fit the crime it responds to.

Christopher Wellman proposes a theory that explains the liability to punishment in terms of a forfeiture of rights (Wellman 2012, 2017). The idea is that just like someone can waive their right by choice, a person can also forfeit their right by guiltily harming someone. If you have violated my right to property, I can in turn violate your right to property because by violating my right to property you have forfeited your right to property.[25] Wellman distinguishes between two versions of the rights forfeiture theory. The weak version assumes that rights forfeiture is a necessary, but not a sufficient condition for punishment: another requirement would be that punishment achieves a valuable aim. The strong version assumes that rights forfeiture is both a necessary and a sufficient condition and requires no further aims or goals.

Wellman defends the stronger version: when a right has been forfeited, it ceases to exist, and we need not cite any other benefits that override that right – it simply plays no role in our moral world anymore. An objection against the strong version of the forfeiture view is one that we can call the 'accidental criminal' objection. Imagine that a toddler accidentally shoots a person in the leg. It would be strange to think that the toddler is liable to punishment; it did not know or control what it was doing. The reason why we think it would be strange is the same reason why we do not punish mentally ill persons who are not in control of their actions. For a person to be liable to punishment, that person must fulfil

[25] Carlos Nino defends a similar theory of punishment. He argues that those who commit crimes therefore consent to their punishment (Nino 1983).

the requirement of a 'guilty mind', of *mens rea*. The forfeiture theory has difficulties accommodating the idea of a guilty mind as a prerequisite for punishment.

One way to counter this objection is by saying that the violation of the right includes the *mens rea* requirement *per definitionem*. The answer would then be that if the *mens rea* requirement was not fulfilled, then it was also not a rights violation, but something else, perhaps unintended harm. But this seems to be an idiosyncratic definition of a rights violation because it would make true the claim that whether a harm was a rights violation depends on the state of mind of the offender, and not on the harm done to the victim. The mirror problem to the accidental criminal is the accidental innocent. The accidental innocent intends to commit a crime but by (bad) luck does not commit the crime. Think of a terrorist who planted a bomb, which failed to go off. Under Wellman's strong version of the rights forfeiture view, this person did not forfeit their rights.

These two problems imply that the forfeiture view is implausible, at least in its stronger version. A better explanation for the fact that we do not want to punish accidental criminals is one that disentangles the deed from the state of mind of the alleged criminal and treats both as necessary conditions for punishment. For example, a person can violate a right, but forfeits *their* right only when the second condition, the *mens rea* condition, is also fulfilled. This explains why the toddler does not forfeit its rights. The *mens rea* condition seems even more important when we think about whether we might want to punish accidental innocents: think again of the person who planned a terrorist attack but whose bomb did not go off. That person has not violated any rights but acted with the intention to do so.

In combination with a deterrence argument, the weaker version seems more plausible because it avoids the awkward consequences of the strong version of the rights forfeiture theory. In both versions, the forfeiture theory is built on a symmetry between the violated right and the forfeited right, and therefore naturally yields a tit-for-tat logic of punishment: if I violate your right to property, my right to property can in turn be violated as punishment; if I violated your right to life, my right to life can be violated in turn. On the one hand, this nicely explains the fittingness intuition. On the other hand, this might also be problematic for two reasons: do we really want violent crimes to be retributed with violent punishments? And what would fittingness mean in the context of massive human rights violations like the ones ICJ is concerned with? The rights forfeiture argument is unable to explain why a defendant responsible for thousands of murders gets 'only' a few decades (or even years) in prison.

I believe that there is no alternative to invoking pragmatic reasons for constraints on the severity and type of punishment any institution can impose. For example, the death penalty and very severe and harsh punishment should be excluded because we value the interests that are normally protected by fundamental rights so highly that we would want to design the system of punishment with the intention of protecting them as far as possible. Other pragmatic reasons might be that the death penalty should in principle be excluded because there is always the possibility of institutions having made a mistake – which they can never make up for if the convicted person is dead. It also gives offenders no chance of rehabilitation. Having alternative, serious punishment at our disposal, holding on to the death penalty just seems plainly irrational.

The aim of this chapter was to show that as a practice, punishment is morally permissible. I have begun the chapter by arguing that the main function of ICJ institutions is to prosecute and punish, and that is why we needed to examine whether punishment is morally permissible in the first place. I have then distinguished punishment from other, related concepts, and have elaborated on the different dimensions of punishment. I offered a systematic interpretation of the Lockean argument for a natural right to punish. In the state of nature, Locke argues that an equally distributed right to punish is an effective mechanism to discharge our non-optional moral duty to 'preserve humanity'. The existence of natural law implies that it must be enforced, and in the absence of common political institutions, this 'natural executive right' is possessed equally by everyone. The natural executive right grounds the right to punish, Locke argues, as punishment deters criminals from violating rights, and therefore helps enforce the natural law. I have then discussed three objections that could be made against the part of the argument that relies on the idea of deterrence. The objections can be rebutted by introducing a distinction between the justification of punishment as a practice, and the distribution of punishment. While the former indeed relies on deterrence, the latter relies on a mix of normative individualism, egalitarianism, rights forfeiture, and pragmatic reasons.

3

The Authority to Punish

3.1 Sovereignty and Human Rights

The purpose of the previous chapter was to show that the practice of punishment is morally permissible. The argument is that in the state of nature, persons have a natural executive right: they have a right to punish criminals by virtue of their moral duty to protect humanity. I will now tie this argument back to the main theme of the book, which is the question of how we explain the authority of institutions exercising *international* criminal justice. In this chapter, I argue that the natural executive right argument extends to criminals in states that systematically violate fundamental human rights. This is so because states that systematically violate fundamental human rights, or allow systematic fundamental human rights violations, are illegitimate. To support this argument, I defend a post-Westphalian conception of sovereignty that makes the legitimacy of states – and hence their right to be free from interference – dependent on their ability *and* their willingness to protect their citizens from mass violations of their basic human rights.

Tying the legitimacy of a state to fundamental human rights is a relatively uncontroversial position in the contemporary debate.[1] For example, John Rawls defends this position by arguing that fundamental human rights are 'necessary conditions of any kind of social cooperation' (Rawls 2003). Societies, Rawls argues, are 'systems of social cooperation over time from one generation to the next' (Rawls 2001, 5), and a system of social cooperation that disrespects those rights is not normatively justified in wielding power over its citizens.[2] Social cooperation is distinguished from mere coordination by the existence of publicly accepted rules and procedures that guide the actions of those participating in the

[1] See, for example, the work of Altman and Wellman (2009), Buchanan (2004), and Dworkin (2013, 17).

[2] I lay out this interpretation of Rawls in more detail elsewhere (Müller 2017, 2022).

system. In that sense, social cooperation includes the idea that the terms on which citizens participate in the system conform to some ideal of fairness (Rawls 2001, 6) and are in that way connected to the common good of a society. Basic human rights, Rawls argues, are the minimal conditions of any ideal of fairness – and their fulfilment is 'sufficient to exclude justified and forceful intervention by other peoples' (Rawls 2003, 80). Rawls thus ties the legitimacy of the state to its ability and willingness to protect the minimal conditions for a genuine system of social cooperation, which is the enjoyment of basic human rights for all. Only states that are legitimate in this sense have a justified claim to sovereignty and thus to freedom from outside interference.

Notice that Rawls does not embrace the full list of human rights from the Universal Declaration of Human Rights. Instead, he distinguishes between what he calls 'human rights proper' and liberal aspirations. Articles 3 (right to life, liberty, and security of person) and 5 (prohibition of torture or cruel, degrading treatment or punishment) are examples of human rights proper, while Articles 22 (right to social security) and 23 (right to equal pay for equal work) are examples of liberal aspirations. To Rawls, Articles 3–18 of the Universal Declaration of Human Rights and, as 'obvious implications', the special conventions on genocide (1948) and apartheid (1973) are human rights proper. I adopt Rawls's distinction for the purpose of my argument in this book. What he calls human rights proper, I shall call 'basic human rights' henceforth.

Any state that enables, allows, or engages in widespread and systematic violations of these rights loses its claim to non-interference. Among those basic human rights are the right to life, liberty, and security of the person, the right not to be deprived of one's subsistence, the right not to be held in servitude or slavery, the prohibition of slave trade, the right against torture or cruel, inhuman, or degrading behaviour, and the right not to be arbitrarily arrested, detained, or exiled. Those rather general rights can be specified by cashing them out in terms of what constitutes a violation of those rights. The formulation of those more specific violations is shaped by historical experience, for example: the prohibition of genocide by killing or by causing serious bodily or mental harm, or by deliberately inflicting conditions of life calculated to bring about physical destruction, or by imposing measures intended to prevent births, or by forcibly transferring children; crimes against humanity such as killing, extermination, enslavement, deportation, imprisonment, torture, rape, sexual slavery, enforced prostitution, forced pregnancy, enforced sterilization, sexual violence, persecution, enforced disappearance of persons, apartheid, and other inhumane acts; the prohibition of war crimes such as wilful killing, torture, inhuman treatment, biological experiments, wilfully causing great suffering, unnecessary destruction and appropriation of property, compelling service in hostile forces or compelling participation in military operations, denial of a fair trial, unlawful deportation and transfer, unlawful confinement, taking of hostages, attacking civilians, attacking personnel involved in humanitarian assistance or peacekeeping mission, excessive incidental death, injury, or damage, attacking undefended places, killing or wounding *hors de combat*, mutilation, coercive medical experiments of persons, pillaging, employing poison, employing prohibited gases, liquids, materials, devices, bullets and weapons, conscripting or enlisting children, starvation as a method of warfare, and other outrages upon personal dignity.[3]

What is important to note is that these basic human rights need no justification through a democratic procedure, but are *morally* justified, as Stefan Gosepath argues (2004, 333, 347). Although I will exclusively focus on basic human rights, let me emphasize that they do not exhaust the category of human rights. But many human rights beyond the basic human rights have to be specified in concrete political communities and interpreted in light of their political traditions.[4] Note that my remarks do not imply that human rights are somehow divisible or that a state has done enough if it has satisfied only the basic human rights.[5] I merely claim that the reasons for action that human rights violations give us are distinct in cases of basic human rights. Indeed, there is a wide range of

3 These examples of more specific descriptions of rights and their violations are taken from the Rome Statute, Elements of Crimes of the International Criminal Court; see International Criminal Court publication, RC/11. There is a sophisticated debate on what conceptually explains international crimes (Boghossian 2010; Luban 2004; May 2005, 2008, 2010; Renzo 2012; Vernon 2002, 2013), although, as Schabas argues, '[p]robably no single explanation accounts completely for inclusion in or exclusion from the list of international crimes' (Schabas 2012, 45). The Rome Statute also lists the crime of aggression (Article 8), inserted post hoc in 2010 by Resolution RC/Res.6 (11 June 2010). A human-rights-based argument like the one I defend cannot easily account for the crime of aggression, as this is primarily an act against another state, rather than against individuals.

4 Meckled-Garcia calls this argument the democratic specification argument and offers a critique of it (Meckled-Garcia 2015, 301).

5 I will not comment on the desirability of campaigning politically for those human rights that lie beyond fundamental rights. Whether we or our governments should criticize or shun states for unfair labour rights or discrimination and whether we or our governments should campaign for primary education everywhere are difficult questions that I do not take up here.

human rights that may even include a human right to democracy; but only some – which I call basic human rights – are enforceable in principle by third-party coercion and intervention. The account of human rights I stipulate for this matter will be acceptable, I believe, because whatever other human rights there are, those rights I call basic human rights are certainly included.

States that allow, enable, or engage in mass violations of basic human rights lose their normative claim to sovereignty and therewith their right to non-interference (Altman and Wellman 2009). Altman and Wellman argue that states are primarily justified by carrying out their requisite political functions,[6] defined as the ability and willingness to secure human rights (Altman and Wellman 2009, 3). Only then do states gain the right to exercise power, on which their sovereign right is dependent. Altman and Wellman understand sovereignty as a bundle of five powers: making, enforcing, and adjudicating legal rules; waging war in self-defence; entering into treaties; being free from external interference; and having territorial integrity (Altman and Wellman 2009, 4). Those powers are only granted to states that fulfil their political function of securing human rights. This means that a state's sovereignty depends on its legitimacy, which in turn depends on its performance in its task to protect human rights reasonably well, a view we have already encountered in its Rawlsian interpretation above.

In their view then, basic human rights violations potentially trigger the loss of sovereignty of the violating state, making them liable to interference by others. But note that a state's incompetence to protect basic human rights or even its intentional violation of basic human rights does not automatically justify other states to intervene according to their will: while basic human rights violations, in this picture, make the respective state *liable* to interference, they do not prima facie justify *any kind of* interference.[7] The intervention itself must be morally permissible. Take the example of military intervention: humanitarian military intervention and military presence are both supposed to halt aggression and massive human rights violations by military means. But because military force

[6] I discuss Wellman's account of state legitimacy (Wellman 2005) in more detail in Chapter 5.

[7] For this view, see also Rawls (2003), Viehoff (2013), Raz (2013), and Quong (2015). Raz attributes to Rawls an ignorance concerning the point that human rights violations are not sufficient for interference, but he does so mistakenly in my view. For an argument why Rawls is not guilty of this mistake, see my interpretation of Rawls's conception of human rights (Müller 2017).

almost always results in civilian casualties, the destruction of property and infrastructure, and the deep disruption of social and cultural life, among other consequences, its use is highly constrained by considerations of these side effects. Thus, the violation of basic human rights is a necessary, but not a sufficient condition for justified military intervention. All things considered, any potential intervention must satisfy a variety of other criteria: it must have a justifiable aim (such as halting the human rights violations), and, among other things, it must have a reasonable chance of succeeding. This means that even in those cases in which states are liable to interference, the type of interference must be shown to be morally permissible on independent grounds.[8]

The type of interference we are concerned with in this book – punishment of individuals – is indeed morally permissible, or so I have argued in the preceding chapter. But that does not mean that *any agent* who intends to punish may permissibly interfere in rights-violating states. We still lack an explanation as to *who* has authority to interfere by prosecuting and punishing individuals. When the defendant in the dock asks: 'By what right do *you* try me?', we need to be able to give an argument not only why the defendant is being rightfully prosecuted, but also, why he is being prosecuted *by that particular institution*. Importantly, this involves explaining how the institution came to possess a rightful claim to punish the defendant, or, in other words, how the institution that prosecutes the defendant came to possess the political authority to punish the defendant. In the remainder of the chapter, I present and discuss two positions that claim to provide such an explanation: first, the *international harm principle* and, then, a position I call the *duty view*.

3.2 Jurisdictional Authority and the International Harm Principle

In answer to the defendant's question – by what right do *you* try me? – Larry May defends a position that centres on a principle he calls the 'international harm principle' (May 2005). The basic idea of the international harm principle is that some crimes 'cross borders' and 'harm the whole of humanity'. Therefore, the international community is permitted to pierce the sovereignty of the state committing or allowing such

[8] For an overview and discussion of the reasons for military interference, see Seth Lazars excellent entry in the *Stanford Encyclopedia of Philosophy* (Lazar 2020), especially section 3 ('Jus ad Bellum').

'international' crimes, and prosecute its perpetrators. May's position is a sophisticated philosophical explication of an intuition that we find in some of the founding documents of international criminal courts and tribunals. For example, in the Preamble of the Rome Statute – the founding treaty of the International Criminal Court – the parties to the statute recognize that 'millions of children, women and men have been victims of unimaginable atrocities that deeply shock the conscience of humanity' and that these international crimes 'threaten the peace, security and well-being of the world'. The idea that some atrocities shock the conscience of all of humanity and that they threaten not only the victims, but the world, and everyone in it, corresponds to the argument May presents: namely, that committing international crimes harms not only the immediate victims, but also harms the interests of everyone else in the world, even when they are not directly affected.

May argues that there are two principles that can normatively justify international criminal law. The 'security principle' explains the limits of state sovereignty: where the security of the persons living in a state is threatened, the state's claim to sovereignty is no longer morally justified. Here is how May formulates the security principle:

> If a State deprives its subjects of physical security or subsistence, or is unable or unwilling to protect its subjects from harms to security or subsistence, (a) then the State has no right to prevent international bodies from "crossing its borders" in order to protect those subjects or remedy their harms; (b) and then international bodies may be justified in "crossing the borders" of a sovereign State when genuinely acting to protect those subjects. (May 2005, 68)

May derives the security principle from Thomas Hobbes (May 2005, 72). In his interpretation of Hobbes, rational individuals give up their natural right to self-defence in exchange for a life of security. Only a powerful sovereign, in Hobbes's picture, is capable of enforcing the mutual agreement between all persons in the state; and their claim to authority is therefore dependent on them providing security for all. Security has two dimensions: the 'security of existence' covers the bare preservation of one's life and the 'security of welfare or well-being' covers the unhindered pursuit of one's life plan (May 2005, 73). Here, May is more minimal than Hobbes, because he thinks that the second dimension of security – 'that one not be subjected to danger in ways that disrupt one's pursuit of contentment or happiness' (May 2005, 73) – is too low a threshold for external intervention in a state's sovereignty: 'Failing to provide for the broad contentment of the members of a State should not be given equal weight to the risk to liberty that is involved in international criminal prosecution' (May 2005, 73).

Although May does not use the language of human rights, the human interests that his security principle protects are reasonably co-extensive with what I have called basic human rights. If a state is not willing or not able to protect those fundamental interests of its citizens, it loses its right against external intervention. We can therefore see that May's security principle and the Rawlsian human-rights-based position of state sovereignty play analogous roles. Similarly, the way May conceives of the normative nexus between basic human rights and state sovereignty bears resemblance to the Rawlsian view I discussed above: May also thinks that while the security principle is a *necessary* condition for the authority of international criminal justice, it is not a *sufficient* condition. It does not follow from the security principle that any international body has the right to intervene: specific intrusions to prosecute certain crimes will require an additional principle (May 2005, 63ff), which in this case, May argues, is the international harm principle. Only then can we explain why international bodies have jurisdiction over certain crimes: because some crimes are so egregious that they not only harm the victims, but are a harm to humanity as a whole. May's position is that international courts have authority to prosecute individuals for international crimes *only when both principles* are satisfied.

To summarize, May's argument is that international crimes harm all of humanity and are therefore punishable by all of humanity. But what does harm mean in this case, and how do we know humanity has been harmed? May defines harm as a setback of interests (May 2005, 67), so we need to know how humanity's interests are set back by international crimes. To determine if harm to humanity has occurred, May argues that one of the two following conditions (and ideally both) must be met: either the individual is harmed because of that individual's group membership or other non-individualized characteristic, or the harm occurs due to the involvement of a group such as a state (May 2005, 83). The distinction between domestic and international crimes thus depends on the community whose interests are set back. If it is a *state community's* interests that are set back by a crime, a *domestic* crime has occurred. If *humanity's* interests are set back by a crime, an *international* crime has occurred.

There are two ways we can know whether the international community is harmed by a crime: either the crime is committed against an individual *because* that individual is a member of a specific group (e.g.

Bosnian or Jewish) or it is committed *by* a state or collective entity. The harm principle thus can be satisfied either from the victims' side or from the perpetrators' side. Ideally, both the victims' side and the perpetrators' side exhibit this group characteristic, but May permits cases where only one of the sides fulfils the group condition (May 2005, 83). Why does the fact that an individual was targeted because they belong to a group make the crime a special one – one that harms all of humanity? May observes that '(i)f an individual person is treated according to group-characteristics that are out of that person's control, there is a straightforward assault on that person's humanity. It is as if the individuality of the person were being ignored, and the person were being treated as a mere representative of a group that the person has not chosen to join in' (May 2005, 85).[9] The idea is that committing a crime against someone simply because that person is a member of a social group amounts to treating that person in a way that is inconsistent with their personhood, their humanness – because being a person requires that others treat me as an individual, and not as a token of some unchosen identity.

May's position is sophisticated, but it has problems that render it ultimately unconvincing. It will turn out that it does not give us a convincing justification for why the jurisdictional authority is allocated to the international community. Massimo Renzo points out that it is unclear why only crimes committed because of the victim's *non-voluntary* group membership – 'group-characteristics that are out of that person's control' – should constitute a humanity-harming crime. A crime committed against a person who has voluntarily become a member of a group – like a church – seems just as ignorant of that person's humanity, making it arbitrary to not also consider this a crime against humanity (Renzo 2010, 273). Another concern about May's international harm principle is the following objection. May argues that the group character is necessary to identify a crime as a crime against humanity because if a person is harmed by virtue of their group membership, their individuality is ignored and therefore their humanity is assaulted. But why should the motivation of those who perpetrate the

[9] 'Humanity' has two meanings in May's argument: humanity as the community of all humans; and humanity as an innate feature of all humans and a positive trait of character, meaning treating others according to their humanness. In the quote above, and when he discusses the group argument, May uses the first meaning, humanity as an innate feature of all persons ('there is a straightforward assault on that person's humanity'). In other contexts, when he discusses the international harm principle, the meaning of humanity as a community is used.

crime lead to international, rather than domestic, jurisdiction? Why should we, *as members of humanity*, be more worried about crimes committed out of group-based hatred than about crimes committed out of other motivations, for example greed?

Imagine a village that is located close to some site of exploitable natural resource. A paramilitary group that wants to control and exploit this site of natural resource to keep a steady influx of financial means into the group massacres all inhabitants of the village, enabling the group to fully control the natural resource without interference. The victims of the massacre are not targeted because of their group identity; rather, they are perceived as an inconvenience that potentially threatens the economic operations of the paramilitary group. Do the perpetrators of these crimes not also ignore their victim's humanity? In this case, the victims also *have not chosen* to interfere by living close to a resource that the paramilitary deems to be important for their economic operations; rather, they *simply happened* to live in proximity to a useful resource. In that sense, their murderers also ignore their humanity – and would that then not also count as a harm to all of humanity?

On the other hand, we might ask why domestic hate crimes – crimes in which the victim is targeted because of their group membership – should *not* trigger international jurisdiction: after all, they too fulfil the group condition. The reason the international harm principle is unable to provide a principled distinction between hate crimes and crimes against humanity lies in the opacity of the idea that a person's humanity can be assaulted in this specific way. Recall May's argument that if a person is harmed because of their group-based characteristics, the perpetrator ignores their individuality. Not taking a person's individuality seriously constitutes a harm to their humanity because the perpetrator attacks a characteristic that they share with all, or many, others (May 2005, 83). The human community has an interest that its members are not harmed, so if one of them is harmed, it constitutes a setback to their interests. When May argues that the victim's individuality is ignored when assaulted because of their group membership, how does that make it 'an assault on their humanity'? While I see how the victim is harmed and how the group the victim belongs to is harmed (because it does seem to imply a threat to the group as a whole), it is not clear what is meant by the idea that their humanity, and, by extension, all of humanity, is harmed (Altman 2006, 368; Altman and Wellman 2009, 75). Non-group-based harms equally ignore a person's individuality: the person is not being treated with the dignity and respect that they possess by virtue of being a human. It remains unclear why humanity's interests are set back *specifically* when the harm is group related. At least in this interpretation, the international harm principle is implausible and fails to explain why the authority to punish should be conferred on the international community.

Massimo Renzo discusses another interpretation of May's international harm principle (Renzo 2010, 274ff). In a consequentialist reading, the argument that some crimes harm all of humanity means that there are actual harmful consequences for other persons in other states. One could argue that some crimes threaten the peace and security of the world in the sense that they may, for example, trigger spillover effects of conflicts into other states, or that they unsettle the fragile peace in some regions of the world. When states other than those in which international crimes are perpetrated are in this way affected, external actors may legitimately prosecute them.

Renzo offers three plausible objections to the consequentialist reading of the international harm principle. First, he argues that under this interpretation, May cannot explain why crimes of the same nature, when committed in failed or failing states, would not fall under international jurisdiction. In a weak or failed state, murder, rape, and torture may occur in a widespread manner although no particular group is targeted (except those who are vulnerable) and no particular group is perpetrating the crimes. Still, because of a general lawlessness, many people seek refuge in neighbouring countries and the crimes spill over. Renzo argues that there is no reason to believe that this spillover effect would be less harming to the neighbouring states than group-based attacks. Thus, it is unclear why in this case the crimes should not be under international jurisdiction (Renzo 2010, 274). Another example that can be interpreted as a harm to the international community, but is not captured by the group-based explanation is when a crime is committed only to one individual, but the consequences are so severe that it sends the whole region into a crisis. Renzo imagines the murder of a political leader that sends the region into chaos. Where a single murder has grave consequences for the security of the whole region, it would have to be an international crime under the consequentialist interpretation (Renzo 2010, 275). These two examples show that on the consequentialist reading, May's international harm principle is under-inclusive, because the group-based account cannot explain all cases that are a threat to international peace and security.

A third argument Renzo presents is the following: whether, under the consequentialist reading of the international harm principle, a specific crime is an international crime may possibly depend on random facts. Consider his example where a criminal gang eliminates or tortures a group of people because they are in the way of their criminal activities, for example, because they live near a natural resource the criminal gang wants to exploit. Now, if they live in a border region, then the risk that the violence may spill over is high; however, if they live in a remote area in the middle of the state, the risk that the violence will affect neighbouring countries is almost zero (Renzo 2010, 276). In the first case then, these are crimes against humanity, but in the second they are not. Renzo admits that this is a coherent position, but would it not be an injustice if the first case was properly adjudicated by an international tribunal, while the second case was left to a dysfunctional domestic system? Considering all three points that Renzo makes, the consequentialist interpretation of the international harm principle is an equally implausible justification for the triggering of international criminal tribunals.

Note that the objections I just discussed concern how the international harm principle can be satisfied from the victims' side. Recall that it can also be satisfied from the perpetrators' side. A crime can still be a crime against humanity even if the victims are not attacked because of their group membership, but because the perpetrators act *as a group*, or *on behalf of a group* that is a state or a state-like entity. The rationale for this condition is different – it obviously cannot refer to the victim's individuality being denied, or humanity being assaulted because the perpetrator acts on behalf of a group. Instead, the rationale is that the involvement of the state (or a similar group) makes crimes systematic and invidious in their nature (May 2005, 88).[10] If a state is the perpetrator *and* the prosecutor at the same time, it faces a conflict of interests due to its double role – which makes it improbable that its own violence will be prosecuted fairly.

This argument is entirely plausible: it is indeed paradoxical to let the perpetrator prosecute itself by a system controlled by the perpetrator – and expect a fair trial. In all likelihood, the perpetrator will choose to act in its own interest as a perpetrator, rather than in the interest of the victims. That has certainly been one of the reasons why the Allied powers

[10] Notice that the problem is not that the perpetrator acts on behalf of just *any* group, but that they act on behalf of *the state* – precisely that entity which is supposed to protect the people on that particular territory. So, it is not the fact that the crime is committed on behalf of a group, but on behalf of the state; it is not the 'groupness' of the perpetrator, but the state-ness or state-likeness of the perpetrator.

could not leave the criminal prosecution of Nazis to the German state. Doing so also violates the security principle: recall that the state's legitimacy depends on state institutions respecting and protecting their citizens' security. But then why does May not simply rely on the security principle alone? Because the international harm principle plays a special role in his argument. While the security principle shows that a state's sovereignty may be pierced under certain circumstances, the international harm principle explains why some crimes fall under the jurisdiction of the international community. May argues that the security principle alone does not suffice for justifying international prosecution because 'violations of the security principle may not be serious enough to warrant international prosecutions of individuals' (May 2005, 70). The international harm principle justifies the *international* prosecution of the defendant: 'What the security principle does is to make potentially justifiable what would otherwise be considered an unjustified violation of a State's sovereignty when its borders is crossed, but does not yet justify a particular prosecution' (May 2005, 70). The reasoning is that just because a state loses its claim to full sovereignty by violating the security principle, it is not implied that any other institution may meddle with its criminal system and single out high officials for trials and a potential compensation or imprisonment.[11] The *particular* prosecution requires fulfilment of the harm principle.[12] The international harm principle thus accounts for the permissibility of the prosecution being done by the international community (May 2005, 81). It is a principle that *allocates jurisdictional authority* to the international community: it determines *who* is permitted to prosecute and punish.

In that sense, it is now clear why May uses the group criterion to satisfy the international harm principle from the perpetrators' side: if it is the case that the perpetrator and the prosecutor are the same agent, it is (practically) necessary that some other agent is given the responsibility to prosecute the crimes. But it is not clear that it does the work May intends it to do: because the fact that the state as a perpetrator is unfit to prosecute international crimes does not imply that the responsibility to prosecute falls on the international community. At least it does not do so without an argument why. We need an additional argument to fill the

[11] Massimo Renzo makes a similar point by using Hohfeld's analytical system of rights, arguing that a state's exclusive jurisdiction can be described as a claim-right (Renzo 2010, 270).

[12] I am grateful to Larry May for clarifying this in personal communication.

gap, and we saw that the argument that May provides – that humanity has a right to prosecute because it is harmed by international crimes – is unconvincing. Hence, we still need a story about why the international community acquires the right to punish international crimes.

3.3 Authority and the Natural Duty View

I have argued above that on any of the two interpretations, the international harm principle is implausible. Now that we know what role it plays in the justification of international criminal justice, we can see that dropping the harm principle would leave May without a justification for why the jurisdictional authority lies with the international community. Two of May's critics, Altman and Wellman (2009), argue that the reason for this gap in justification is that the security principle mischaracterizes the nature of sovereignty. They criticize May's position for holding on to an outdated and unhelpful Westphalian conception of the state. Coupling the authority of international criminal justice institutions to a metaphorical border crossing is only necessary, they argue, if you believe in the idea that states may do as they like within their borders in the first place. The Westphalian dictum of 'the absolute dominion of a state over its territory and its members' (Altman and Wellman 2009, 4) must thus be jettisoned in favour of a human-rights-based view of sovereignty. The preposterousness of the idea that you can impose moral constraints on the external behaviour of states so that other states can pursue immoral aims internally is indeed obvious and should be dismissed from international relations altogether.[13]

But their criticism of May as a defender of the Westphalian conception seems a little unfair; after all, it is precisely the role of the security principle to *disallow* states to do as they like, Westphalian-style, and instead to ensure that they guarantee the minimal security of their citizens. In May's picture, states must also fulfil their requisite political function to retain their sovereignty, namely providing security and protection of the fundamental human interests. What is more, we have seen that May *does* think that if states do as they like within their own territory and therefore violate the rights to life and security of their citizens, then they are liable to punishment by the international community. Similarly,

[13] This point is paradigmatically formulated by Charles Beitz: 'More generally, one might ask why a principle which defends a state's ability to pursue an immoral end is to count as a moral principle imposing a requirement of justice on other states.' (Beitz 1979, 365)

there is not much of a difference in terms of *what* a state must do in order to retain its sovereignty in May's theory in comparison with Altman's and Wellman's theory that I discussed earlier: May insists that the point of states is to provide their citizens with security and protect their human interests, while Altman and Wellman insist that the point of states is to provide their citizens with fundamental human rights, which are mostly rights to life and bodily integrity.[14]

Altman and Wellman argue that once states lose their sovereignty because they are neither willing nor able to protect their citizens' human rights, any third party of the international community may step in and take over the criminal prosecution. In contrast to May, who argues that the international community must have been harmed to acquire the authority to prosecute and punish perpetrators of international crimes, Altman and Wellman seem to believe that no extra argument to determine who holds the authority to punish is needed: when human rights violations are widespread and systematic, whoever comes first (and is effectively able to do so) may punish. But we have seen in the preceding sections that even though the practice of punishment may be morally permissible, that does not imply that *just any* third party has acquired the authority to do so. We still need an answer to the criminals' challenge: by what right do *you* try me?

To provide such an answer in the context of international criminal justice, I defend a duty-centred view, for which I make use of the Lockean natural duty 'to preserve mankind' that we encountered in Chapter 2. The duty-centred view is similar to Altman's and Wellman's view in many respects – it is based on the idea that a state's sovereignty is dependent on its function of securing basic human rights – but it goes beyond their argument in explaining how third parties from the international community *acquire* the authority to punish. We will later see that this has to do with a problem that comes into view with the exercise of the natural executive right: that moral equals will inevitably, and unjustifiably, subordinate one another in the state of nature. This problem gives them reasons to exit the state of nature and subject themselves to international institutions.

The duty view begins with a Lockean idea we encountered already earlier, which is that all persons have a natural moral duty to preserve humanity. We usually discharge this duty by supporting states that enact

[14] Altman and Wellman cite Articles 3–20 and Articles 25–26 as capturing 'reasonably well' what they mean by fundamental human rights (Altman and Wellman 2009, 3).

just laws.[15] The relation between states, human rights, and individuals with natural moral duties is well explained by a theory that Robert Goodin and others[16] have called the moral division of labour theory (Goodin 1988; Jacob 2014; Ladwig 2013). States perform the function of discharging the general obligations that everyone has against everyone else worldwide. In that picture, 'our fellow countrymen and -women' are not special in the sense that their 'specialness' – having the same culture or being 'of a kind' – can be a source of special obligations, but because they are simply those persons with whom we happen to share a delineated territory. Goodin compares his argument with the intuitively plausible idea of one doctor being assigned one patient instead of all doctors being assigned 1/n of their time to n patients: surely the doctor has general obligations towards all who need their help, but it does make sense to assign a specific number of persons to their responsibility while assigning other persons to other doctors' responsibilities. In this story, the source of the obligation towards the specific patient is not a special relation between the doctor and the specific patient, but rather the fact that the doctor has been assigned – somewhat arbitrarily – responsibility for that specific patient. The reason that we do have 'special' obligations towards our compatriots is merely that we have been assigned responsibility for that group, and not for another.

The moral division of labour theory supports the view that basic human rights must be secured for all and that the duty to secure them justifies political institutions like the state: it makes sense of the

[15] The *locus classicus* for this argument is Rawls's *A Theory of Justice* (Rawls 1999, 293). See Simmons's *Moral Principles and Political Obligations* (Simmons 1979), especially chapter 6, for an almost equally classical rejection of the Rawlsian version of the natural duty view.

[16] There are several other theorists who can be classified as adherents to a position with similarities to the moral division of labour theory. For example, the late Ronald Dworkin argues that: 'People around the world believe they have – and they do have – a moral responsibility to help protect people in other nations from war crimes, genocide, and other violations of human rights. Their government falls short of its duty to help them acquit their moral responsibilities when it accedes to definitions of sovereignty that prevent it from intervening to prevent such crimes or to ameliorate their disastrous effects' (Dworkin 2013, 17). Sinja Graf attributes a moral division of labour-type view to John Locke: 'Once the normative relationship between individual action and the preservation of mankind eludes judgement, the sole way forward to re-create law-governed and free communal life is to partition mankind into separate peoples under sovereign governments that deliver secure normative knowledge of the law and of property relations as well as the monopolized authority to resolve disputes definitively.' (Graf 2018, 577f)

assumption that states are the primary holders of responsibility for human rights on their designated territory. The fundamental idea is supported by the fact that states are in principle extraordinarily well equipped to uphold a human rights regime within their territory: they operate sophisticated legal systems that ensure access to rights and remedies, they operate a police force to help enforce them, and they often provide the relevant political channels for debate and improvement. States are also capable of integrating abstract rights into the social, cultural, political, and religious reality of a given society by transforming human rights into robust civil rights. They are – if they are sufficiently just – capable of realizing a common and reasonable conception of justice 'in a historically and culturally adjusted form', which deserves toleration (Ladwig 2013, 12).

However, those simple moral division of labour theories[17] are at pains to explain the current unequal distribution of territory and arbitrary drawing of boundaries (Ladwig 2013, 10). The fact that some states occupy large territories and other states occupy small territories, the fact that some territories are rich in natural resources and others are not, and the fact that some states are in landlocked locations while others have access to the sea, or other accessible (trading) routes, are a matter of chance. Nevertheless, these facts influence – sometimes dramatically – the capacity of states to provide their citizens with the human rights protection they are owed by the state.

Ladwig therefore modifies the moral division of labour theory so that it does a better job at explaining the current distribution of territory. The idea of his 'moral path dependency argument' is this: although some facts have no original moral relevance, they gain moral relevance in the course of history (Ladwig 2013, 11). This argument applies to the current system of states: although it is the result of non-moral – and sometimes plainly immoral – practices such as forced marriages, post-feudal warfare, and colonial boundary-drawing, it has generated societies that have instantiated universal moral claims and principles of justice which they made their own by interpreting them in a concrete way. The concrete instantiations of those principles and claims partly are, as Ladwig points out, 'responses to historically specific challenges and experiences' (Ladwig 2013, 11).

Ladwig emphasizes that the instantiations of claims and principles of justice in different territories are not merely a function of efficiency: the justification of the particular interpretations of justice in distinct states

[17] For an argument why moral division of labour theories cannot be used as an argument against the global scope of justice, see Gosepath (2001, 147).

does not only rest upon the functional desirability of an efficient division of labour as opposed to an inefficient world welfare state. There is moral value in the distinct 'paths to justice', as political communities provide space for deliberating and determining the distribution of goods and the ordering and internal relation of values that are important for leading a life in dignity. Reasonable pluralism, that is, pluralism about justice, within the bounds of what can reasonably be considered as just, is a fact that does not have any value per se. But the distinct interpretations of justice that make up this reasonable pluralism do have moral value. This, of course, not only applies to distributive justice, but also to criminal justice. Within reasonable limits, the degree of criminalization, the type and severity of punishments and compensations, and the procedural principles of guilt determination are likely influenced by and determined through the ordering and interpretation of more abstract values. Questions such as 'What is the conception and degree of autonomy that we value?' or 'How important is socio-economic equality for the chances that a person's life will go well?' will have an impact on the degree to which we think persons are responsible for wrongdoing, or on the type of punishment that we find appropriate for a crime.

Theories that rely on the idea of a moral division of labour with its moral path dependency modification can accommodate the claim that there are a great deal of other justice-related questions besides the protection of fundamental human rights that need to be specified in the relevant contexts and in light of particular experiences.[18] But this kind of theory can also tell us a convincing story about what happens when states become unable or unwilling to discharge our moral duties through their political institutions. To illustrate this point, we can return to the doctor–patient analogy: if a person is admitted to hospital with acute illness and for some administrative mistake, they have not been assigned a doctor (or an incompetent doctor), the 'residual responsibility' to care for that patient falls back to the present hospital staff.

The same is true of persons whose 'protector state' is absent, dysfunctional, or takes up the role of the predator itself: when states cease to fulfil their responsibility, the moral duty to preserve humanity falls back on everyone in the international community. After all, the moral value of a

[18] There are different reasons why one might think it is important that other justice-related questions should be specified in the respective communities. For example, Altman and Wellman emphasize that states have a moral right to self-determination, a collective right to settle a group's own affairs (Altman and Wellman 2009, 11ff).

particular path to justice is dependent on that path being *a* path to *justice* in the first place. Hence, the duty view argues that while normally, our moral duty to preserve others is discharged through our just states, it falls back to us when a state becomes unjust; that is, when it becomes unwilling or unable to protect the basic human rights of its citizens. When states fail in that respect, they lose their claim to legitimate sovereignty, and the international community is back in a state of nature in relation to that state. In such a case, persons must discharge their moral duty to preserve humankind in another way. And as the Lockean argument in the preceding chapter has shown, this is when the natural executive right – that is derived from their duty to preserve humankind – kicks in: persons acquire the right to punish perpetrators of human rights crimes, and this right is equally distributed between all individuals in the state of nature.

3.4 Leaving the State of Nature

The purpose of this section is to show why punishment in the state of nature is suboptimal, and why that gives us reason to exit the state of nature. I will also indicate what follows from these problems in terms of our setting up institutions that avoid the defects of competitive punishment in the state of nature. In the first step of the argument, I discuss what reasons we have for leaving the state of nature. The question thus is: Why is political authority – rightful coercion – preferable to the state of nature? My answer centres on the urgent moral necessity of protecting fundamental human rights and the capacity of institutions to do so fairly and without subordination.[19] Two reasons speak in favour of exiting the state of nature. The first reason has to do with the nature of persons: they do not always punish justly because they tend to be biased towards themselves and their friends. The second reason has to do with the nature of the laws: they are abstract, which means that their application requires complex interpretation and specification. It is unlikely that all will come to the same judgements, and this will lead to conflict. Both problems are a feature of any state in which there is no common judge with authority to whom the conflicting parties can turn. Therefore, we

[19] While some political theorists, for example Graf (2018), have interpreted the Lockean state of nature with focus on his conception of private property, my interpretation of the defects of the state of nature centres on Locke's theory of punishment, rather than on his labour theory of property – a decision explained by the topic of my study.

have reasons to leave the state of nature and transfer our natural executive right to an institution that is able to coordinate our actions so as to ensure that we make good of our moral duty to preserve humanity. Recall that the natural executive right is competitive because in the state of nature, nobody has political authority over anyone else; all persons are moral equals. Because people are biased when they punish and because their interpretation of the correct way to enforce the natural law will vary, we need an institution that authoritatively solves these problems. So, while we individually do have the right to enforce basic human rights, and punishment is a morally permissible means to do so, there are compelling reasons to abandon the state-of-nature-practice of competitive punishment. In what follows, I discuss this argument in more detail.

As I have already said, the fundamental reason for leaving the state of nature is that of competitive punishment. But we need to be more precise: what is it about competitive punishment that is problematic? Consider the following argument: if punishment is justified by its function to preserve humanity, then everyone has the right to punish everyone. Would not that, David Lyons asks, result in a situation where a wrongdoer is punished over and over again by different people for the same crime (Lyons 1976, 210)?

With Locke, we can reply to the problem of competitive and never-ending punishment in the following way: criminals cannot be punished over and over again because there is a definite and appropriate amount of punishment for them, and persons in the state of nature can know what that appropriate punishment is. Recall that Locke argues that all rational persons in the state of nature have only *derivative* authority to enforce the natural law because they are authorized by God to enforce His law. The natural law is that part of the moral law which is discoverable by the use of reason or, as Rawls puts it, by looking at the order of nature (Rawls 2007, 109f). In his 'Essay on the Law of Nature', Locke says that the natural law is 'the decree of the divine will be discernible by the light of nature and indicating what is and what is not in conformity with rational nature' (Locke, ELN, 111). The other part of the moral law is the divine or positive law, that law that is revealed in the Bible (Simmons 1992, 16f).

Hence, the enforcement of law is not the same as the decision on what the law is or authoritatively deciding on a person's guilt. Persons in the state of nature do not have the authority to determine *according to their will* whether a person is guilty. There are objective standards of guilt, given by the natural law. Even if a person does their best to find out whether another is guilty but reaches the wrong conclusion and punishes an innocent person, the punisher has acted wrongly on Locke's account, precisely because they neither have the authority to set the law according to their will, nor have they the authority to declare someone guilty. Only if that person is guilty *by the objective standards of natural law* is the punisher allowed to enforce the law. Only God has authority to lay down law and determine guilt; persons in the state of nature are justified in punishing offenders only by virtue of their role as enforcers of the natural law.

Locke's position is thus conceptually coherent, but is it plausible? The claim that individuals are only permitted to *execute* the law, but not determine it, does not solve the problem that it is not obvious what punishments are appropriate for each crime. There will be persistent disagreements about what constitutes proper enforcement. Even if it was true that what constitutes a punishable crime is always clear – if they were moral evils whose wrongness depends on an objective criterion – individuals will likely disagree on appropriate punishments. Hence, while punishment is conceivable in the state of nature, we need procedures that arbitrate between different judgements about the appropriate measures of punishment. And in the absence of a publicly recognized system of punishment that determines the correct amount and form of punishment to each crime, and that provides a procedure that distinguishes legitimate from illegitimate punishment, many cases of punishment will be contentious, leading to fractionalization and rivalry and at worst triggering a spiral of violence.

Although this problem does not render the whole idea of the natural executive right unintelligible, it points towards the reasons individuals have for transitioning from the state of nature to the civil condition. It is important to keep in mind that the natural executive right is only given *in the state of nature*, so during a time when persons are not members of a legitimate political society. This may be in times of civil war, after the collapse of government, and before we have consented to being a member of a political society (Simmons 1992, 125, 129), but also under an effective, but illegitimate, government (Simmons 1993, 16). Also, only persons who have reached adulthood and are in control of their cognitive capabilities possess the natural executive right (Simmons 1992, 129).

Furthermore, the natural executive right is not unbounded: punishment must be a reasonable response to a violation of a natural right. Locke stresses that punishment must be meted out calmly and reasonably and in proportion to the gravity of the rule transgression. While murder can be punished with capital punishment, other, less grave breaches of the law must be punished less severely (Locke II, §8–12). And finally, Locke does not insist that *only* private punishment is morally justified; he merely claims that a natural right to punish is the *origin* of the state's right to punish. But is that plausible? I now turn to an objection to the claim that the natural executive right in the state of nature can help explain – or even be the foundation – of an institution's right to punish.

Hanna (2012) has a fundamental worry about the Lockean project of taking the natural executive right from the state of nature and transferring it to government. He objects that although a natural executive might make sense in the state of nature, the reasons that speak in its favour in the state of nature are absent in the civil condition. In other words, the natural executive right does not survive the transition from the state of nature to the civil state. Punishment, as you recall, is an effective enforcement mechanism in the state of nature. And although this might be true, he argues, it is far from obvious that this is still true in the civil condition: creating a state 'substantially broadens the enforcement options and may thereby eliminate the basis for the right' (Hanna 2012, 599). He argues that natural rights theorists of punishment underestimate the institutional, non-punitive enforcement alternatives to punishment and that is why the natural executive right cannot be the origin of the state's right to punish.

Hanna's argument, I argue, fails, because he overestimates what he is able to show with his claim that there are non-punitive institutional alternatives. More specifically, my objection is that the fact that there are non-punitive alternatives does not imply that punishment becomes impermissible. The plausibility of Hanna's argument depends in large part on the question of whether one accepts his definition of punishment, which essentially includes the intent to harm. He argues that an action is to count as punishment *only* if it 'is performed in order to harm' (Hanna 2012, 603). Consequently, he claims that confinement, probation, community service, and imprisonment are not necessarily punishments because they can be inflicted without the intention to harm (Hanna 2012, 604). But it is not clear why, if someone did not intend to harm, that person would want to put prisoners in confinement at all. That is to say, the point of confinement *is* to punish. Furthermore, Hanna's definition is somewhat idiosyncratic: all of the above, but especially imprisonment, seem to be paradigmatic instances of punishment; indeed, if imprisonment is not to count as punishment, then what is? Here, the definition of what constitutes punishment seems to conflict with what most people think punishment constitutes. Of course, that does not mean that Hanna's definition must be wrong; but it does indicate that it might have problems. Let us look more closely to see what they are.

Hanna comes to his position because he defines, as we have seen, punishment as *intending* to harm (Hanna 2012, 603). And although imprisonment can be intended to harm, it does not *have to be* intended to harm (Hanna 2012, 604). It could also be intending to incapacitate, for example. If we accepted Hanna's argument that punishment is punishment only if it served no other purpose than intending to harm, then any kind of justification for punishment that relies on a deterrence-based theory must then also be considered non-punitive, as the intention of its infliction is not to harm, but to deter. That, indeed, is the point of deterrence-based theories of punishment. But this would mean that only actions that are inflicted with a retributive intent are considered genuine punishment. Excluding a justification for punishment by defining punishment in a way that only allows retribution as a justification is implausible, but more importantly, it does not fit Locke's deterrence-based account of punishment in the first place. Even if it was true that none of the things people do to each other in the state of nature in reaction to breaching a law counts as punishment, because they can also be inflicted without punitive intent – a claim I find implausible, as I argued further above – then there are enough non-punitive alternatives to punishment even in the state of nature, so that there would be no justification for a natural right to punish in the first place. One might think this is true, but it must be for other reasons than those Hanna presents – since it would then be the case that the problem of the natural right to punish does not lie in the transition, but in the state of nature argument itself.

The second flaw in Hanna's argument is that he thinks that because under civil government, there are non-punitive alternatives to punishment, punishment is unjustified under civil government. But this does not follow. As I reconstruct Locke's argument, the moral permissibility of punishment does not follow from it being the *only* enforcement mechanism in the state of nature. Rather, it is justified by its function to preserve humanity, and by the argument that criminals forfeit their right not to be harmed if they commit a rights violation. Therefore, although our enforcement mechanisms seem to be substantially broadened under civil government – a claim we can agree on – it does not render punishment impermissible. If anything, it adds more options of enforcing the law, for example by taxing citizens to redistribute wealth or investing in policing.

Recall that the reason why the natural executive right is competitive is because in the state of nature all individuals are moral equals, which implies that nobody has natural political authority over anyone else. To solve the problem of competitive punishment, individuals leave the state of nature. Locke's story of political obligation – of how the state acquires political authority – is that persons in the state of nature have reasons to consent to political authority because the state of nature is suboptimal. The important point for us now is not how the transition works precisely – whether it requires consent or not – but what problems in the context of punishment prompt the transition. Understanding this will help us understand the problems of instrumental accounts of the authority of international criminal justice[20] on the one hand, and on the other hand, it will point us towards how an institution that evades these problems must be constituted.

Transitioning to the civil state is preferable because authoritative institutions provide 'improved procedures for punishment' (Simmons 1992, 127).[21] But what problems do those improved procedures of punishment of the civil state solve? Jeffrie Murphy claims there is a paradox at the heart of Locke's theory of punishment. Locke's argument for the right to punish is incoherent, he argues, because it oscillates between two positions that logically exclude each other: either, he argues, persons in the state of nature are rational, all-knowing, and all-good – then they may punish because they will do so justly. But if it was the case that all persons in the state of nature are like that, then they do not need civil government in the first place. But if they do need civil government, how come they could possibly possess a natural right to punish, given they would exercise it unjustly? Locke, he argues, cannot coherently defend both arguments. Murphy therefore concludes that punishment is conceptually impossible in the state of nature (Murphy 1969, 257). Minimally, punishment requires three conditions: 'a system of rules, authorities to apply

[20] I discuss instrumental accounts in Chapter 5.

[21] For Locke, an institution – the state in his case – gains the exclusive right to punish by the voluntary transfer of the natural executive right from individuals. There is disagreement in the Locke scholarship just how voluntary this transition is. A. John Simmons thinks that the consent of the subjects is still the more important condition for civil government than the urgency of solving the authority problem (Simmons 1979, 2000). Hanna Pitkin, on the other hand, argues that the concept of consent plays a mostly hypothetical role (Pitkin 1965, 1966). We can sidestep the debate about the correct interpretation of the role of consent in Locke's theory. More important for our purpose is to understand what problems prompt the transition from the state of nature to the state.

these rules, and authorities to enforce sanctions for breaches of these rules' (Murphy 1969, 261).

Is Murphy right in claiming that Locke is being incoherent here? To address Murphy's challenge, we need to understand the origin of the problems in the state of nature. We have seen earlier that Locke believes the natural law is clear to every reasonable person: Everyone *knows what the rules are*. Locke writes that:

> Man being born, as has been proved, with a title to perfect freedom, and uncontrolled enjoyment of all the rights and privileges of the law of nature, equally with any other man, or number of men in the world, hath by nature a power, not only to preserve his property, that is, his life, liberty, and estate, against the injuries and attempts of other men; but *to judge of* and punish breaches of that law in others, *as he is persuaded the offence deserves*, even with death itself, in crimes where the heinousness of the fact, *in his opinion*, requires it. . . . But though every man who has entered into civil society, and has become a member of any commonwealth, has thereby quitted his power to punish offences against the law of nature, in prosecution of *his own private judgement* . . . (Locke II, §87–88, my emphases).

In this quote, it is clear that Locke did not think that the appropriate punishment is discoverable by reason alone as part of the law of nature, but that persons punish according to their own private judgement, as they see fit. People judge and punish breaches of the natural law *in accordance with their own interpretation* of the law of nature (Otsuka 2005, 57). But if people have the right to punish according to their interpretation, this means that they can issue binding judgments and rightfully carry them out. But at the same time, Murphy points out, judgments of punishment will have to be evaluative in character – and radical disagreement is possible with respect to evaluative judgements (Murphy 1969, 263).

We can see how this becomes a problem in the state of nature: if everyone has an equal right to punish by virtue of their equal status, but each has their own interpretation of what adequate punishment is, then there will necessarily be conflicts between individuals who have an equal claim to authority. Some interpretations will prevail over others, and thus some individuals will be subordinated to the will of others. But that is incompatible with the equal moral status in the state of nature. Civil government can solve this problem because it has the power to legislate and judge crimes and punishments:[22] 'And thus the commonwealth

[22] I am grateful to Jim Nickel for directing my attention to this point.

comes by a power to set down what punishment shall belong to the several transgressions which they think worthy of it, committed amongst the members of that society, (which is the power of making laws) . . .' (Locke II, §88). Locke needs an authority that interprets the law without subjecting individuals with equal status to one another.

Notice that this argument is not in tension with the earlier point about the clarity of the natural law: although the law might be clear in saying what not to do, it needs authoritative interpretation, so that equals in the state of nature do not subordinate one another. Murphy argues that the only circumstance under which a natural right to punish would make sense is in a state of nature where persons are fully rational, all-knowing, and all-good. But – and this is the paradox – in such a state of nature persons do not need civil government. In fact, they might not even need a right to punish: either because nobody would trespass against the law or because punishment would always be meted out proportionally and justly. But if persons in the state of nature are irrational, not thoroughly good, and not all-knowing, then they cannot have a natural executive right, because they cannot authoritatively apply and enforce punishments. It is either the one or the other; Locke 'cannot have it both ways', as Murphy points out (Murphy 1969, 257).

This is indeed a paradox, but I do not think it merits the strong conclusion that Murphy draws from it, which is that 'where everyone is said to be an authority, the concept of authority operates without sense' (Murphy 1969, 263). It is certainly conceptually possible for multiple authorities to be in conflict. This is not a *conceptual* problem; it is a *practical* problem, to which Locke offers a *practical* solution: he introduces a higher authority to which we render our judgement. While Muphy's observation about the instability of Locke's state of nature does not defeat Locke's argument, it is nevertheless insightful for our purpose. It shows why Locke wants a legislator and a judge: precisely because of this *practical* problem that persons need an authoritative interpretation of the laws of nature in order to preserve the equal status of all.

From Murphy's challenge, and my reply, we can now identify the two practical problems in the state of nature. The problem resides both in the *execution of the judgment* and in the *application of rules* to empirical situations, that is, in the practical judgments themselves (Otsuka 2005, 93). The first problem is that persons are imperfect. We have already seen that criminals put themselves above the law when they should not. But even those who are not criminals are imperfect. Even those who do not commit crimes tend to be partial and biased towards their family and friends (not to mention towards themselves!), and because they are also sometimes vengeful, they often over-punish, and they will sometimes punish even if there is no guilt at all. This inevitably invites a similar response by all the other equally irrational persons, and before long, 'confusion and disorder' (Locke II §13) – feuds, conflict, and war (Simmons 1992, 27) – follows.

The second problem in the state of nature is that the laws of nature are abstract, and their application warrants practical, complex, interpretive, and legislative judgement to specify the abstract natural laws. Not everyone will come to the same conclusion in all cases, and therefore they will disagree on at least some instances of the exercise of the natural executive right. Note, again, that the problem of interpretation concerns the rightful enforcement or application of the law, not the law itself. As I have argued in the section that introduced the natural right to punish, Locke thinks that the law itself is clear, and that the reason people violate it is *not* because they are confused about what the law is.

Thus, there are in fact two aspects of the natural executive right in the state of nature that warrant civil government. Both the abstractness of the laws of nature and the bias of persons prompt the necessity of transferring the natural right to punish to a civil government – because even though persons in the state of nature have a right to punish, it is impossible for them to exercise that right in accordance with the equal status of everyone else. What is needed is a third party that impartially arbitrates between the authorities claiming equal status: a common judge with authority (Simmons 1993, 27, 29),[23] where that authority implies executive and legislative competences.

Before I proceed to the next stage of my argument, let me summarize what I have argued so far. I began by reconstructing Locke's systematic justification for punishment. Locke begins with the idea that persons are moral equals and that we have a natural duty to preserve humanity. To exercise this duty, we have the right to punish those who attack humanity, thereby creating a deterrent climate. This is the conceptual part of Locke's systematic argument for punishment. Furthermore, his

[23] The addition 'with authority' is important, because some people might live in a society where there is a common judge, but one without authority. One example is an illegitimate government: as far as Locke is concerned, people who live under illegitimate governments still live in the state of nature. For a discussion of the relational character of the Lockean state of nature and its differences to the Hobbesian state of nature, see Simmons' *On the Edge of Anarchy* (Simmons 1993).

argument contains the consequentialist claim that to preserve everyone's rights, we are permitted to establish a deterrent climate by punishing criminals. A deterrent climate minimizes violations of the natural law and is a permissible mechanism to fulfil our natural duty to preserve humanity. Because the state of nature lacks political and judicial institutions, and all are equals to one another, each must have the same 'natural executive right' to enforce the law.

I then argued that we normally discharge our natural duty to preserve humanity through the state system that divides up the moral labour of protecting those rights among territorially defined states. The reason that speaks in favour of a system of territorially defined states is that having territorially bounded institutions is most effective in protecting fundamental human rights. Furthermore, there is also value in realizing differing conceptions of justice as an expression of the distinct historical, political, and cultural experiences of groups. I have argued for this position – which I called the duty view – by contrasting it to Larry May's harm principle, where the international community acquires the authority to prosecute and punish criminals by virtue of the harm they have suffered by international crimes. As I hope my discussion has shown, the international harm principle is ultimately unconvincing for a number of reasons; the most basic problem being that it is incapable of explaining how international crimes are special and how they harm the international community. In contrast, the duty view relies on the idea that persons have basic human rights that deserve protection from everyone else as a matter of natural duty. This implies that if states fail to protect basic human rights, the duty goes back to the international community. We are back in the state of nature vis-à-vis that state and retain the natural executive right.

The final step of the argument thus far was to show that we have reasons to exit that state of nature. Locke argues that there are several problems that result from the fact that we each have an equal claim to punish, and that this might cause conflict. I have emphasized that the core of the problem Locke worries about is not necessarily that we will be at each other's throats all the time – although disorder will definitely ensue – but that we cannot avoid subordinating one another, which goes against our status as equals. In other words: the natural executive right in the state of nature is a problem because it leaves us *no choice but to violate* each other's equal standing. We need an independent party that executes the law for us while preserving our equal status; that is, without subordinating some over others. But who can that independent party be?

This reasoning naturally implies that *institutions of international criminal justice* are the obvious choice for an impartial authority and may rightfully claim political authority. The work that is left for the rest of the argument is now to understand under which conditions institutions of international criminal justice are legitimized to prosecute and punish individuals.

4

Legitimate Authority and International Institutions

4.1 Institutional Legitimacy beyond the State

We have seen that an equally distributed right to punish generates practical problems in a state of nature. We therefore have reason to leave that state and submit our natural right to punish to an authority that can effectively solve those problems without subordinating some over others. This argument seems to speak in favour of creating an independent and international court that has the capacity to punish perpetrators of international crimes. Exercising the capacity to punish implies that such a court would naturally be coercive: it coerces both the defendants who are prosecuted and punished, and other agents, for example other states, by coercively excluding them from prosecuting or punishing criminals. But in contrast to states that obviously are coercive and therefore have the capacity to exercise the function of punishment, it is not clear that international institutions are equally so. The purpose of this chapter is twofold: first, I argue that some international institutions can be understood as coercive. But claiming to possess a right to punish, and to exercise it using coercion, if necessary, requires a special justification from those that claim it: it requires that those institutions satisfy standards that certify their *legitimate holding* of this right. So the second aim of the chapter is to understand what makes international institutions a legitimate holder of such a right. A prominent position in the literature is that international institutions are legitimate in exercising political authority when states have consented to them. As I will argue towards the end of this chapter, this is true for some international institutions, but not for all: in particular, international institutions that prosecute and punish international crimes are not dependent on state consent for their legitimacy.

The legitimacy of institutions can be regarded from different points of view: we can research whether they are effective (when they do what they say they do), whether they are perceived as justified (when people think they are allowed to do what they are supposed to do), whether they are stable over time, or whether they form part of a political culture, among other things. All of those are *descriptive* research agendas: they revolve around the question of what people *believe* makes an institution legitimate.[1] But we can also look at them from a *prescriptive* perspective: we want to understand under what circumstances institutions are normatively justified in doing what they do. Most contributors to the debate in political philosophy use legitimacy in the second, normative sense. Here, the question is not about whether people *believe* that institutions are legitimate, but whether they *actually are* legitimate in doing what they do by objective normative standards.

What gives institutions the legitimacy to impose coercion or coercive rules on others? This is a persistent question in political philosophy, with most of the literature focusing on the institution of the state. But new institutions beyond the state have emerged in the aftermath of the Second World War. Their most distinctive mark is that in contrast to states, they have no unified governance structure.[2] International institutions, designed to coordinate action and regulate cooperation between states, have started to play an increasingly important role in both domestic and international politics. International institutions facilitate the collective coordination of problems that transcend national borders, and they do so by providing a system of rules that enable relatively stable patterns of human activity. Institutions coordinate actions by specifying certain forms of action as permissible or impermissible, designating offices, procedures, and roles, and defining penalties. Therefore, they generate expectations of behaviour that are usually so stable as to make joint action possible through their coordination.

[1] The distinction between a descriptive conception and a prescriptive conception of legitimacy is widespread in the literature, see, for example, right at the beginning of Buchanan's and Keohane's seminal discussion (Buchanan and Keohane 2006, 405).

[2] There is a growing literature on the idea of global constitutionalism, which may be taken as a counterclaim to the notion that international institutions do not constitute a unified governance structure. However, global constitutionalists only claim that there is an increased interplay between different institutions beyond the state, which is bracketed by a unified rule system, consisting of human rights and the rule of law. This claim is compatible with what I argue, but for lack of space I will not be able to pursue these issues further. One of the claims I defend in this chapter is that the lack of a unified structure results in a necessity to judge the particular institutions on their own terms and, importantly, according to the purpose they have, instead of evaluating all international institutions by the same standard. There is no *one* model that can explain the legitimacy of *all* international institutions.

The practical role of the concept of legitimacy refers to this coordinative function of institutions: in the face of disagreement about what the right, or just, course of action is, legitimacy assessments are useful for evaluating the scope and the kind of political power that institutions may exercise to solve coordination problems. Allen Buchanan calls this position the 'Metacoordination View' about legitimacy (Buchanan 2013, 189). For an effective exercise of political power, institutions need to have a certain standing, that is, they must be acceptable to (or accepted by) all subjects even when they produce decisions or policies that some of the subjects do not consider fully just. In that sense, the concept of legitimacy is distinct from the concept of justice as a standard of normative evaluation; both relate to distinct domains (Rawls 2005). Importantly, legitimacy is not simply a less demanding version of justice.[3] Rather, it is a standard of evaluation that becomes salient when there is disagreement about what justice requires. Therefore, a justification of the legitimate status of institutions requires more than a reference to the justice of institutional decisions. Under conditions of reasonable disagreement (Rawls 2005) about what justice requires, some will always consider any substantial outcome not fully just. Therefore, we need a different standard to determine whether we must nevertheless comply with the institution's rule.

As institutions impose their rule on their subjects, they are required to justify their rule as legitimate. But if legitimacy really is about metacoordination, an important question arises: how can their rule be justified without invoking the *justice* of their rule? We often use legitimacy as an evaluative standard in two different interpretations: in some instances, the notion that something is legitimate means that its existence is morally justified. The conditions for legitimacy in this sense often include only a minimal 'do-no-harm' requirement. Think about someone who sets up a business or a charity. As long as these entities comply with whatever rules and regulations are in place, they are morally justified in doing what they are set up to do. In this case, we need not necessarily consider their actions *just* to tolerate them. It suffices that they do no harm.

But this general sense of legitimacy as 'morally justified' is of limited interest in our context, simply because prima facie – and unlike political institutions like the state – the existence and operations of morally justified actors and organizations do not pose much of a challenge to the moral liberty of persons. Third parties may have reasons not to

3 For a discussion on whether legitimacy requires full justice, see Wellman (2023).

interfere with the actions of actors that are legitimate in this general sense. But they have no obligations to do what those actors tell them either. That is, the reasons third parties have for not interfering with the legitimate actions of actors stem from considerations of general stability, courtesy, or respect, or the value of the actor's aims.

An example from the international world is non-governmental organizations (NGOs). The World Wide Fund for Nature (WWF)[4] has a morally justified aim – preserving wilderness and reducing human impact on the environment – and insofar as it refrains from harming third parties, it can be considered legitimate in the general sense of 'morally justified'. If you agree that wild animals should enjoy protection, you might think you have reasons to give money to their organization and not interfere with their work. Or you might not care about the animals, but find it admirable that people pursue projects dedicated to preserving and promoting what they value, and therefore you owe it to them not to interfere with their projects. In any case, institutions such as the WWF pose no serious threat to anyone's liberty, and the reason is that they do not wield (coercive) power and do not limit a person's fundamental liberty in the same way, and as significantly, as coercive institutions do.

In other instances, applying the term legitimacy to institutions means that not only is the institution morally permitted to exist and to act in the world, but that it can generate decisions and rules that are positively binding towards their subjects. When this is the case, an institution has legitimate *authority*.[5] An institution has legitimate authority when the reasons for actions its decisions generate for those who are recipients of the decisions are not merely optional, but prima facie obligatory. This, to add, does not mean that *all* decisions that an institution with legitimate authority makes are obligatory; if they violate other, more fundamental, or more important standards, then they are, or might be, all things considered not obligatory. But the important point is that legitimate institutions are viewed as the primary *source* of binding obligations: the reason I am bound by a specific duty is because the institution has

[4] Formerly known as 'World Wildlife Fund'.

[5] In her excellent entry in the *Stanford Encyclopedia of Philosophy*, Fabienne Peter argues that the view that connects legitimate authority is historically the dominant view, and most people still hold it (Peter 2017). Other views disentangle political authority from political obligation. See Applbaum for a particularly clearly argued example of such a view (Applbaum 2010).

decided I am. Joseph Raz has called this the content independence of reasons that originate from the rules issued by legitimate authorities (Raz 1986, 2006; Wellman and Simmons 2005, 95). For example, my obligation to drive my car on the right side of the street has no independent moral source other than the fact that my government said so. This does not imply that I necessarily owe the obligation *to* my government, as Buchanan and Wellman point out: I owe it to my co-citizen (Buchanan 2002; Wellman 2001).

This, in turn, does not mean that all our duties have their source in institutional authority. What Rawls calls 'natural duties' (Rawls 1999, 98) are our duties independent of whether an institution decrees them.[6] Besides, some rules and obligations are morally overdetermined, meaning that their bindingness has multiple sources, one of which can be a legitimate authority. For example, my obligation not to torture you does not only stem from the criminal code of the country I am a citizen of. There is also an *independent moral duty* not to torture you that originates in my natural duty not to harm you (because you are sentient, say, and a person with dignity). International crimes are some of the worst things people can do to one another, and they are overdetermined in precisely this way. They are overdetermined in the sense that they are prohibited from a natural duty view, from an international law view, and often from a domestic law view, too.[7] We have both content-independent and content-dependent reasons not to commit them.

The problem of legitimate authority – that is, the fact that legitimate institutions rule and therefore give their subjects a content-independent obligation – thus does not primarily concern your natural moral obligations to your fellow humans, but your obligation to obey the rule of that institution. Having legitimate authority in this more specific, political sense, as opposed to having legitimacy in the more *general* sense discussed above, means that an institution has the right to wield political power to enforce its rule (Buchanan 2002, 689). This raises, as Rawls observes, the question of the legitimacy of the use of coercion:

> political power is always coercive power backed by the government's use of sanctions, for government alone has the authority to use force in

6 Rawls gives the following examples for what natural duties there are: 'the duty of helping another when he is in need or jeopardy, provided that one can do so without excessive risk or loss to oneself; the duty not to harm or injure another; and the duty not to cause unnecessary suffering' (Rawls 1999, 98).

7 For example, Germany's 'Völkerstrafgesetzbuch' is part of the federal law.

> upholding its laws. ... This power is regularly imposed on citizens, ... some of whom may not accept the reasons widely said to justify the general structure of political authority ... or ... they may not regard as justified many of the statutes enacted by the legislature to which they are subject. ... This raises the question of the legitimacy of the general structure of authority. (Rawls 2005, 136)

The hard question about legitimacy thus is raised by the fact that institutions use coercion. Such institutions carry a stronger burden of justification that should refer to the necessity of the use of power or coercion. The state is the classic example of this: it uses coercion to enforce all kinds of their rules, from collecting taxes to restraining offenders. Justifying such institutions is a challenge, because they wield political power or use coercion and therefore constrain individuals' liberty, often very deeply. It is obvious that the state I live in can have an enormous influence on what I can and cannot do, primarily because it has the capacity to coerce me: it makes me do some things, like paying taxes, and keeps me from doing other things, like crossing their border without their permission. It structures my short- and long-term options, often dramatically, by allowing some of the options and forbidding others, for example, by making them very costly. Therefore, an institution only has legitimate authority when it is justified in wielding political power, where this includes the use of coercion.

What does it mean for an institution to possess legitimate authority? The practical role of metacoordination that legitimacy assessments play gives us some guidance in determining the kind of political power a legitimate institution has. Legitimacy – as the *right* to impose rules – is often conceptualized as one of the Hohfeldian types of rights.[8] The classical view holds that the right to rule is a claim right, which grounds the thesis that the addressees of institutions have a corresponding duty to obey (Simmons 1979). Another position views the right to rule as a liberty (Ladenson 1980; Wellman 1996, 2001).[9] Understanding the right to rule as a liberty implies that legitimate institutions are free to exercise (coercive) rule, but that the rule addressees have no corresponding obligation to follow the rule, at least not by virtue of the institution's right to rule. Some proponents of this view argue that the duty to obey can only be explained by reference to

[8] For a concise explanation of the Hohfeldian analytical system, see Leif Wenar's entry in the *Stanford Encyclopedia of Philosophy* (Wenar 2021).

[9] Liberties are also sometimes referred to as privileges (Wenar 2021).

another value, like fairness or the necessity of coordination (Wellman 2005). A third view understands the right to rule as a power to change the normative situation of the rule addressees (Buchanan 2002; Christiano 2012; Perry 2013; Enoch 2014). Those authors argue that institutions are legitimate insofar as their addressees are liable to the exercise of their political power.

But whether the right to rule is a claim, a liberty, or a power fundamentally depends on how we understand the purpose of the type of institution we are applying the concept to (Adams et al. 2020, 284). Equally, the standards of legitimacy are dependent on the function of the respective institution. This claim obviously presupposes that different institutions have different functions, which marks a substantial difference between international institutions and the state. While a state fulfils a variety of functions – it punishes, it legislates, it provides welfare, it organizes the economy and the market, it enforces laws, it interprets laws, and so on – international institutions are mostly focused on a narrow set of functions in one particular policy context. A variety of institutions regulate a variety of aims in different policy fields, such as health (World Health Organization), security (United Nations Security Council), trade (World Trade Organization), and, importantly for our purposes, criminal justice (International Criminal Court).

Allen Buchanan argues that the variation between different international institutions implies that we need to rethink the concept of legitimacy when we apply it to international institutions:

> [o]n the face of it, it is unlikely that a single substantive account of legitimacy could both cover the whole range of institutions to which the term is sensibly applied and at the same time be very informative as to what the criteria for legitimacy are, in the absence of information about the specific functions of the institution in question and the context in which it operates. (Buchanan 2013, 176)

Buchanan doubts that the legitimacy standards can be the same for institutions like states that rule robustly, international institutions like the World Trade Organization (WTO) that rule in a weak sense, and institutions like UN-based committees that, according to Buchanan, do not rule at all (Buchanan 2013, 176).

To Buchanan, this does not imply that the concept of legitimacy does not apply to international institutions. Rather, Buchanan criticizes the standard assumption that equates the term legitimacy with 'the right to rule'. Some international institutions, he argues, do not *rule*; some merely produce documents that states ratify or reject. Yet, it still makes sense, Buchanan points out, to ask whether these institutions are legitimate or not (Buchanan 2010, 84). Second, he argues that even though some international institutions do more than that – they can be said to 'rule' in a more robust way – they still do not rule *in the same way* that states rule. The difference between those two ways of ruling is, according to Buchanan, that both states and (some) international institutions rule by 'creating duties by issuing directives', but only states back those duties with coercion (Buchanan 2013, 176). It would be surprising, Buchanan thinks, if we found that one legitimacy conception fits both international institutions *and* states, simply because coercion is morally much more problematic than the mere creation of duties by issuing directives. Therefore, the legitimacy criteria for coercive institutions will be more demanding (Buchanan 2013, 176).

Buchanan thus argues that we need to distinguish between different legitimacy conceptions for different institutions: at the very least,[10] we need one for the state and a different one for international institutions. The legitimacy conception for the state is characterized by its robust standards for governance: institutions that are legitimate in this sense are not only justified in governing, but they are justified in using coercion to secure compliance, and they generate a moral obligation to obey their governance (Buchanan 2010, 82). This conception of legitimacy is, however, specific to the state; Buchanan argues that it is unsuitable for international institutions. To international institutions, a weaker conception of legitimacy applies: it includes that the institution is justified in issuing rules and seeking compliance through attaching costs and benefits to non-compliance and compliance, respectively. Although there is no moral obligation to obey the rules, international institutions generate a content-independent[11] obligation (or content-independent moral reasons) not to interfere, combined with content-independent moral reasons to comply with the governance for those towards whom the

[10] To be clear, Buchanan thinks that there is one general *concept* of legitimacy that applies to all institutions – what he calls the Metacoordination View – and that different *conceptions* of legitimacy, with different standards and in different contexts, are appropriate to specific institutions (Buchanan 2013, 188).

[11] The use of the Razian concept of content-dependent and content-independent reasons and obligations in the context of political legitimacy has proved useful in describing the origin of the action-guidingness of reasons and obligations. Content-dependent reasons are reasons that are action-guiding because of their content. Content-independent reasons are reasons that are action-guiding because of their origin (Raz 1986, 2006).

Table 4.1 *Comparison of Buchanan's two conceptions of legitimacy.*

	State	International institutions
Meaning of legitimacy	Justified in governing	Justified in governing
Reasons applying to subjects	Content-independent obligation to obey	Content-independent moral reasons to comply Content-independent moral reasons to support
Reasons applying to non-subjects	Obligation to not interfere	Moral reason to not interfere or moral obligation to not interfere
Mode of governance	Coercive	Attaching costs and benefits
Scope	Exclusive rule in one policy area	Not exclusive
Type of rules	Create duties by issuing directives and back them by coercion	Some create duties by issuing directives

governance is directed (member states for example) and with content-independent moral reasons for supporting the institution's effort to secure compliance for others (non-members and individual citizens of states).

Table 4.1 compares the two conceptions of legitimacy Buchanan describes.

Buchanan makes two arguments in support of his claims. The first argument is that, unlike the state, many international institutions do not claim an exclusive right to rule in a certain policy area. He argues that, for example, the WTO recognizes efforts of regional organizations to promote the liberalization of trade and the ICC allows for prosecution and punishment of criminals by their home states (Buchanan 2010, 84). And even when international institutions *do* claim the exclusive right to rule, they do not usually use coercion to exclude others from attempting to rule (Buchanan 2010, 84). Whether his argument is persuasive hinges on what specifically is meant by the notion 'exclusive right to rule'. There are two ways of understanding the idea: the exclusivity could refer to the idea that the institution is the *only* promulgator of rules. This would imply that the institution does not accept any other agents ruling in its respective policy area. If we accept this sense of 'exclusive right to rule', then it is true that international institutions do not exhibit this feature. To take an pertinent example: the ICC even *prefers* that individuals are prosecuted and punished by their own states. In line with the principle of complementarity, the ICC becomes active only when states fail to prosecute.

But states are not necessarily much different: they accept a variety of other agents that promulgate rules and they regularly hand competence and responsibility to other agents or units, for example in application of the principle of subsidiarity.[12] Just like the ICC, the state then only becomes active when these sub-institutions fail to carry out their purpose. Similarly, the United Nations and the Security Council welcome peacemaking efforts and other governance efforts at the regional level, but should those fail, the Security Council is justified in adopting a resolution concerning a situation irrespective of the fact that there is a regional organization that claims governance. In both international and domestic contexts, the principle of subsidiarity plays an important role in the governance structure. Other units – sub-federal units or supranational units – promulgate rules, and they often do so exclusively. In this respect, states and international institutions are more similar than dissimilar.

A more plausible interpretation of what it means to have the exclusive right to rule is when the institution is the *ultimate* authority, that is, the authority where the proverbial buck stops. If an institution is not the only rule promulgator, but the ultimate authority, it can accept other agents promulgating rules, while retaining the prerogative of intervention and ultimate decision. This interpretation seems much more appropriate in the case of states because it does a better job of modelling the complex authority relations within states. But if we apply this model, we will find that at least some international institutions function in the same way. A case in point is the United Nations Security Council. When a state or a regional organization fails to act in an appropriate manner in matters of peace or human rights, the Security Council has the authority to intervene and decide on an action.[13] An even more salient example for this

[12] The governance structure of states regularly involves giving other agents the right to promulgate rules: on the sub-federal level (e.g. Länder in Germany) or on the supranational level (e.g. the European Union). See Andreas Follesdal's survey article for a political theory discussion of the principle of subsidiarity (Follesdal 1998).

[13] See Articles 24 and 25 of the United Nations Charter.

book is the ICC: as Madeline Morris observes, it has superior authority in deciding whether a state has genuinely exercised jurisdiction over a case, making it a truly supranational authority rather than a mere delegate of states (Morris 2002, 594).

An important observation here is that not all international institutions are like that: many international institutions are in fact *not* the ultimate authority in their policy area. Further below, I argue that a neat way to distinguish those international institutions with ultimate authority from those international institutions that rule non-exclusively in this sense is to focus on the kinds of purpose or aim that they pursue.

4.2 Authority and Coercion

Another interesting aspect of international institutions is whether they use coercion in order to prevent other, illegitimate agents from ruling.[14] Allen Buchanan argues that they typically do not and that this is one significant difference between states and international institutions: international institutions do not seek 'to ensure compliance with rules through ... a credible threat of the use of physical force against non-compliers', while states do (Buchanan 2010, 84). We have seen above that the coercive nature of authorities is what raises the question of legitimacy in the more specific, political sense in the first place; therefore, if those authorities do not coerce, our worries about their legitimacy are less serious. Buchanan therefore thinks that international institutions have fundamentally different, less demanding legitimacy standards than states (Buchanan 2010, 85).

The purpose of this section is to reject Buchanan's argument that international institutions do not coerce. Against Buchanan's view, I do not argue that *all* international institutions coerce, but some – like the United Nations Security Council, or the ICC – in fact do. To successfully make my argument, I need to clarify in more detail what coercion can mean in the international context. I argue that the conception of coercion that Buchanan presupposes is unfit to capture what institutional or political coercion is. On a very general level, coercion is aimed at influencing a person's behaviour. I will discuss three conceptions of coercion in this section: (1) a narrow conception of coercion that merely covers sheer physical force, (2) the 'classical' pressure conception of coercion

[14] One could, for example, imagine that a regional terror organization wants to compete with a UN mission for bringing stability to a territory.

that focuses on the credible threat of physical force, and (3) the enforcement conception of coercion that focuses on a structural power differential that systematically alters the coerced's behaviour. In the section that follows this one, I argue that Buchanan relies on the pressure conception, which renders his argument ultimately unconvincing. Instead, the enforcement conception of coercion is most plausible in the context of political institutions. The discussion of coercion will help to distinguish different types of international institutions, which I will then group into two categories that differentiate the types according to their purpose. Each type of institution has a distinct standard for legitimate authority.

(1) According to the first conception, coercion equals brute force. When hearing the term 'the coercive power of the state', many people probably think of handcuffs, prison cells, and riot police. In situations in which, for example, a police officer handcuffs someone and physically throws them in a jail cell from which they cannot leave, the coercive power of the state is perhaps more clearly visible than in more subtle cases. In this very physical sense, the person in jail was 'coerced' into the cell. Call this the narrow conception of coercion. But this narrow conception of coercion is of limited use in the political world, at least when it comes in its exclusive form. It is unsuitable for political contexts, where coercion rarely works as bluntly. Of course, many citizens – legitimately or not – do come into contact with the physical coercive power of the state: they are imprisoned or taken into custody or handcuffed by the police. Nevertheless, the state is also coercive towards me if it does not do any of these things: the penalties I incur when I do not pay my taxes or when I speed, or the exclusion from the welfare system when I do not obey the directives from the government agency for employment – both are measures designed with the specific purpose of coercing me to obey a particular set of laws. Paradigmatically, coercion works in a much more encompassing and subtle fashion than the narrow conception presupposes. So even though we do want to capture those more drastic and physical cases, we also want to be able to understand the more subtle cases of coercion. The narrow conception is implausible because of its exclusive focus on drastic cases. We need a wider conception of coercion; one that can capture cases like speeding tickets or taxation as cases of coercion.

(2) On a wider conception of coercion, we can distinguish between two approaches to coercion: the pressure account and the enforcement account. As a proponent of the pressure approach, consider Robert

Nozick's seminal conception of coercion (Nozick 1974), which I present here in a simplified version that I take from Anderson (2011):

P coerces Q if (and only if):

1. P aims to keep Q from choosing to perform action φ
2. P communicates a claim to Q
3. P's claim indicates that if Q performs φ, then P will bring about some consequence that would make Q's φ-ing less desirable to Q than Q's not φ-ing
4. P's claim is credible to Q
5. Q does not φ
6. Part of Q's reason for not φ-ing is to lessen the likelihood that P will bring about the consequence announced in (3)

The standard case to illustrate this approach to coercion is the mugger who jumps at you on your way home, shows you their knife, and issues a threat: 'Your money or your life!' While the mugger is not physically coercing you in the narrow sense described in the first conception, to hand over your money – he is not grabbing your hand, and not physically wrestling the money from it – the mugger's actions do seem to qualify as coercing you. One might start explaining this case by saying that your options have been reduced dramatically by his threat. The options the mugger gives you – either give up your money or be prepared to lose your life – are both undesirable, but unless you are suicidal, the option of giving up your money is still better than losing your life. In contrast to the narrow conception of coercion, the coercer's role is largely communicative, instead of brutely physical: the mugger wants you to give up your money, he conveys this wish to you in the form of a threat, the knife he is flashing indicates to you that the threat is credible, and so you give up your money, for the reason that otherwise, he would make the threat true and attack you with the knife.[15]

One important feature that we can add to the pressure approach in order to distinguish between threats and offers is the idea that there is a moral baseline from which one can evaluate whether someone is better or worse off. If the mugger is in fact not a mugger, but someone offering you

[15] The pressure approach bears resemblance to John Austin's command theory of law (Austin 1995). H. L. A. Hart describes Austin's theory as 'a gunman writ large' (Hart 2012) because Austin understands laws in a legal system to be commands backed by threats.

a free cake if you do not φ, and part of the reason that you do not φ is because then you get the free cake, then technically, under the simple definition, this would be a threat. But it is an offer, and to understand it as such, we need to set some baseline representing the coerced's position before the threat or offer, respectively. If the 'proposal' leaves you better off than you were before, it is an offer; if it leaves you worse off, it is a threat.[16]

The pressure approach elegantly explains the mugger case, but it has serious problems. The first problem with the pressure approach is that it is under-inclusive. In contrast to the narrow conception that I described earlier, which can *only* explain brute force, the pressure approach can *only* explain threats, but not brute force (Anderson 2011). While the narrow approach captures brute force, but fails to explain other instances of coercion, the pressure approach captures the mugger case, but has difficulties explaining brute force. Consider again Nozick's argument above, especially claims 5 and 6. Q, who does not φ because P has threatened Q, has *acted*, albeit under circumstances with dramatically reduced options. Q made a decision and acted on it. This is not the case with physical force. Being handcuffed and thrown into a prison cell, or money being wrestled from your hand with physical force can hardly be understood as *acting* for a reason X (X being, for example, the threat). The handcuffed person is not acting at all but *acted upon*. Because of that, on the pressure approach, the handcuff example does not fall under the definition of coercion. Nevertheless, it seems counterintuitive to understand the handcuffed person as not being coerced. Although this kind of use of force is not the only case of coercion, and perhaps not even the paradigmatic case, we would nevertheless want to capture it in our approach because both cases clearly are instances of coercion.

I have just argued that the pressure approach is under-inclusive, but at the same time, it is also over-inclusive. Consider the following situation: a small environmental NGO threatens to make a multinational company, say IKEA, the subject of a 'naming and shaming campaign' unless they stop using wood from a particular source. Imagine further that IKEA wants to avoid the scandal, even though they would only be slightly worse off. But the main reason IKEA stops using the wood source is that they want to market themselves as a 'green' company and hope that

16 There is a large amount of literature on the baseline question; for a summary, see Anderson's excellent entry on coercion in the *Stanford Encyclopedia of Philosophy* (Anderson 2011).

announcing that they will stop using this wood will make the company more profitable with environmentally friendly-minded customers. In this case, it is true that part of the reason – even if it was only a small part – IKEA changes their wood production source is because the NGO has communicated a threat. But a large part of the reason they change their ways is because they perceive the change to be better for them anyway. It would now seem strange to say that the NGO has coerced IKEA into φ-ing, simply because although part of IKEA's reason for φ-ing was the threat, IKEA also chose to φ for independent reasons, namely the marketability of their new 'green' image. The NGO has exerted pressure on IKEA and apparently successfully so because IKEA has 'submitted' to the pressure. But one could hardly say that IKEA was *coerced* to change their source of wood by the NGO. Why not? It seems that IKEA is so powerful that it did have a real choice whether to bow to the pressure or not. The intention behind discussing this fictional case is to illustrate how coercion is dependent on the background structure of power, and, to be more precise, how coercion is dependent on there being a power asymmetry operating in the background that enables or disables one party to coerce another.

A second objection against the pressure approach is that the pressure approach makes the success of coercion dependent on altering the will of the coerced. In the way that Nozick presents it, coercion is a term whose nature depends on its success (Anderson 2011). If you decide not to hand over the money, you were not coerced, you were only threatened. But again, this seems counterintuitive, because in the context of political institutions, coercion seems to be depending not only on single, successful acts, but on structures. Consider a law that prohibits robbery and threatens non-compliance with incarceration. Such a law would be considered coercive under the pressure approach because it threatens the undesirable consequence of prison to anyone who commits a robbery. Now consider Anna, who would like to rob someone but is deterred by the law. The law acted positively coercive for her. But consider Benjamin, who has no intention whatsoever of robbing anyone ever. The law is not coercive for Benjamin because to him the threat of incarceration figures in no way in his decision not to commit a robbery. This then would not count as a case of coercion because it does not satisfy Nozick's condition that part of the reason for someone not φ-ing is to lessen the likelihood that another will bring about the announced consequence (as in 6).

As a third case, consider Charlie, who has robbed someone despite the law prohibiting it. He was *not* coerced because he defied the threat of punishment: it did not keep him from committing the robbery. Since the law did not keep Charlie from robbing, it did not coerce him. But this seems strange: surely if the law is coercive and general (meaning that it is applicable to everyone), it is just as coercive for Charlie as it is for Anna and Benjamin. The fact that Charlie now may be going to prison also does not count as coercion, because as we have seen above, the pressure approach has difficulties explaining brute force. It seems that what we want in a conception of coercion is that it can explain cases in which the institution is coercive even if some individuals defy its threats (like Charlie), and if some individuals refrain from φ-ing even though the threat against φ-ing plays no role in their reasons to do so (like Benjamin). Both the IKEA case and the robbery case cast doubt on the explanatory power of the pressure approach in the context of coercive political institutions.[17]

(3) More suitable to understanding what coercion is *in the context of political institutions* is what Scott Anderson has called the 'enforcement approach' of coercion. The enforcement approach holds that coercion is 'one agent's employing power suited to determine, through enforceable constraints, what another agent will or (more usually) will not do, where the sense of enforceability here is exemplified by the use of force, violence and the threats thereof to constrain, disable, harm or undermine an agent's liability to act' (Anderson 2010, 6). This approach centres on the idea of unequal power structures that *enable* some agents to be coercers. The idea is that those who have the power over the coerced (either by having created the power differential themselves or by using already existing unequal power structures) can influence the coerced's behaviour in two ways: they have the physical power to disrupt the ability of others to act, or, more typically, to leverage that ability by threatening them (Anderson 2010, 6f). The enforcement approach to coercion

> regards coercion as a kind of activity by a powerful agent who creates and then utilises a significant disparity in power over another in order to constrain or alter the latter's possibilities for action. This power differential may be used to put pressure on the coerced's will, but additionally it might work by simply interdicting or disabling agents, or disrupting various possibilities for action more systematically. Such systematic disruption can be achieved by incarceration or capital punishment, as well as

[17] These last two examples are a variation from examples given by Edmundson (1995).

> via longstanding threats that alter broad patterns of activity, and not just specific actions. This approach sees differential power relations as essential to coercion so, on this approach, some ways in which agents put pressure on other agents that do not arise from significant power differentials will not register as coercion. (Anderson 2010, 1)

Simply the fact that power structures are unequal between two agents will not suffice to determine that a situation is coercive. Imagine two people in a room: one is a tall strong woman with a black belt in karate, and the other is a weak old man in a wheelchair. Obviously, the woman has the potential to constrain the man, but this is not per se a coercive situation. We need to add another premise, which accounts for coercers as intentionally accumulating power needed to constrain others (for example by arming themselves) and implicitly or explicitly threatening to use this power. This does not have to be a physical threat; it can also be done in the mode of attaching costs and benefits to actions. The point is that the agent in the power position is *actively structuring* the options of agency for others. This explains why instead of pressure being the main mode of coercion, under the enforcement approach coercion is typically achieved by prevention (Anderson 2010, 9).[18] Coercion, on this account, is not a success term, but a structural situation: rebuffing or neutralizing the threat of coercion will have to involve neutralizing the very power structure that made the coercive attempt possible in the first place. This interpretation of coercion is useful because it can explain how handcuffing a person and throwing them in prison is coercive, but it can also explain how making a person do something without employing physical force is coercive. Moreover, it can explain why laws with attached penalties or punishment are coercive, because, unlike under the pressure approach, their coerciveness does not depend on the pressure they exert in every instance on every person. Rather, their coerciveness depends on the coercive structure that makes the coerced liable or vulnerable to the coercer's actions or threats.

Without wanting to dismiss the pressure approach altogether, the advantage of the enforcement approach over the pressure approach is that the enforcement approach does a better job of explaining cases of physical restraint, such as cases involving handcuffs and prisons or involving muggers wrestling money out from their victim's hands, and of criminalizing certain behaviour, such as robberies. This is significant:

[18] On this point, see also Kolodny (2016, 42).

the enforcement approach makes better sense of political and institutional contexts by emphasizing the *structural* dimension of coercion. But it does not only capture what the state does when it makes me observe the speed limit or makes me participate in re-employment strategies, but also captures what international institutions do when they attach penalties to a state limiting imports – or indeed, when they issue an arrest warrant for a head of state. With this approach to coercion, we can make sense of the idea that coercion is a gradual concept that covers a range of actions that can be classified as coercive: from military intervention, to setting strong incentives, and from criminalizing certain actions, to imposing penalties.

Recall that the reason I discuss the different conceptions of coercion is to show that under the enforcement approach, at least some international institutions can be conceptualized as coercive. Having said that, I do believe that there is a type of international organization that paradigmatically does not act through coercion. At the beginning of the chapter, I have said that the term 'legitimate' is also sometimes applied meaning 'morally justified' in a general sense. This sense of 'legitimate' arguably applies to some agents in the international sphere. We can use the analysis of coercion discussed above to make a general distinction between international institutions that use coercion and those that do not use coercion. NGOs, like the WWF, do not use coercion. They do not operate in a structure that is balanced to their advantage; as in the IKEA example above, they might pressure other agents to do something, but that does not make them coercive. Rather, their purpose is to promote values and aims. These organizations are legitimate in the weak sense: because they are not coercive, they are justified in doing what they do as long as they do not harm others and have morally acceptable aims. Instead of coercing others, they pursue their agenda by persuasion and pressure. Importantly, they do not generate content-*independent* reasons to obey their demands or requests, even if they promote morally important values. The fact that something has value does not imply that one has or should accept corresponding obligations (Wellman and Simmons 2005, 147). Note how, in the context of these kinds of institutions, the inadequacy of the pressure approach to coercion becomes clear: in this case, accepting the pressure approach would mean accepting the idea that NGOs are coercive because they try to influence state behaviour by conducting naming and shaming campaigns, for example. But that seems wrong, and the enforcement approach can explain why: because they lack the capacity to structurally enforce their aims. Only when organizations find themselves in structures that enable them to enforce their pressure (or threats), they can plausibly be called coercive.[19]

In this chapter, my main interest is institutions that *do* use coercion, so I will leave these cases aside now. Contrary to Buchanan, who argues that only states coerce while international institutions do not coerce, I argue that coercive international institutions do exist. Under the enforcement approach to coercion, many international institutions can be plausibly thought of as coercive, and this matters for understanding what standards of legitimacy apply to them. The way that both states and international institutions usually ensure compliance is by structuring the actions of their subjects – for example by attaching costs and benefits to those actions – in a way that makes the threat of physical coercion a last resort measure, rather than the paradigmatic manner of enforcing their rules. If we conceive of coercion in this more plausible way – as enforcement rather than pressure – it becomes clear that the way in which some international institutions coerce is very similar to the way in which states coerce. Adopting the enforcement approach to explain coercion means that international institutions are coercive if they structure background conditions in such a way that leaves some liable to their actions or threats. Some international institutions use the threat of enforcement as a mechanism to ensure compliance: for example, the issuing of an arrest warrant by the ICC Prosecutor leaves the respective suspect in a vulnerable position, because ICC member states are now under an obligation to arrest the suspect on their territory. Like states, some international institutions use the threat of physical coercion as a last resort measure: for example, when the Security Council decides on a humanitarian intervention.

But there is another mode of coercion that some institutions apply: they use the threat of *coercive exclusion* from the institution to enforce compliance. This, under the enforcement approach, is also properly called coercion, although it only applies to those members of an institution who are dependent on that institution for advantages. Hence, the relevant distinction is between institutions that only coerce their member states and institutions that are coercive towards all. In his posthumously

19 The Catholic Church in the Middle Ages would have been classified as coercive back then because of their immense structural power and political influence. Nowadays, transnational organizations of faith such as the Catholic Church have lost that structural power and are plausibly classified as a non-coercive interest or pressure group, maybe powerful still, but certainly a whole dimension apart from their old structural influence.

published 'A New Philosophy of International Law', Dworkin (2013) argues that there is a morally salient distinction between international treaties that set out a conception of a legitimate world order and include the UN Charter, the Genocide Convention, the Geneva Conventions, and the Rome Treaty for the ICC, and international treaties that are designed for only a limited club with expressly admitted members, such as the European Union (EU) and the WTO. In particular, Dworkin argues that the distinction lies in the force of these treaties: the rules of the first type of international treaties are not dependent on whether a state has consented to them, but bind all governments (Dworkin 2013, 21). The reason they are binding is that states are morally obligated to improve the moral quality of the international state system (Dworkin 2013, 19). But in the case of legal rules for limited clubs with expressly admitted members, such as the EU and the WTO, institutional rules 'cannot sensibly be used outside that club' (Dworkin 2013, 21).

I believe Dworkin is right to make this fundamental distinction, and I argue that this distinction explains the different scopes of coercion of international institutions, which finally affect what standards of legitimacy apply to their rule. Most international organizations can sanction their members, and some can even go so far as to exclude them (Rittberger et al. 2012, 123f). This does not necessarily come in the form of specific threats, like the pressure approach would presume, but in the form of a systematic effort to discount some options while shaping behavioural patterns through longstanding sanction structures to make them comply with the rule of the institution. Hence, while those international organizations do have coercive power over their members, the ultimate form of coercion for them is the exclusion of the members from their institution. This is different from the coercive power of the Security Council, which potentially uses coercion against *all* parties.

But the deeper point behind the question of whether international institutions can be plausibly thought of as coercive is whether they are *rightfully* coercive. Whether institutions do coerce does not always imply that they are justified in doing so. The permissibility of coercion depends on whether the institution therefore enforces justified, prior obligations. Coercing persons to φ without them having an obligation to φ is in tension with the moral autonomy of persons and can only be justified in a limited set of circumstances.

I argue that to determine whether institutions are permitted to use coercion, against whom they are permitted to use coercion, and, finally, what their institutional scope is – that is, over whom they have a right to rule – we need to refer to the different types of purposes or aims that institutions pursue. To better understand what makes international institutions legitimate and, more importantly, to understand what follows from their legitimacy, I argue that our concept of legitimacy should adequately mirror the diversity in purpose or aims between different international institutions. Consider the range of international institutions in reference to their distinct functions: there is, for example, the United Nations Security Council, charged with the responsibility to secure world peace. Then there is the EU, an organization that is constituted by nation states committed (some more, some less) to forming a close economic and political union, with the potential to create a common foreign policy, financial system, etc. Another example is the International Organization for Standardization (ISO), which has the function of harmonizing industrial standards. Then there are the WTO, which establishes rules for international trade, and the World Bank, which provides financial products. And lastly, and for this study most importantly, there is an international court that prosecutes international crimes (ICC).

Institutions fundamentally differ in terms of their purpose and their aims. Consider two of the examples, the United Nations Security Council and the ISO. Paradigmatically, the Security Council governs in matters of war and peace: they have the responsibility to maintain peace and security and are authorized to decide on several issues, for example whether to impose sanctions or whether to intervene in a state with military means. All member states are obligated to comply with the decisions of the Security Council. Consider, on the other hand, the ISO: their purpose is not to decide on matters of war and peace; rather, they govern norms and standard harmonization that facilitates the global transfer of products, information, and knowledge. The two institutions are established and designed to achieve fundamentally distinct aims and therefore potentially fulfil different purposes. While the ISO regulates a specific context with the aim of facilitating exchange to the advantage of all who are part of the institution, the Security Council rules to enforce the law of peace, justice, and human rights.

How does this difference translate into our concern with legitimacy? The different aims those institutions pursue can be categorized into either one of two functions: the protection of morally mandatory aims and the promotion of mutual advantages. Take the Security Council as a paradigmatic case of a category that we can call, in reference to Thomas Christiano, 'institutions with morally mandatory aims' (Christiano 2012). Their distinctive feature is, as the label indicates, that they facilitate international cooperation on morally mandatory aims. Those include, but are potentially not limited to, the protection of persons against fundamental and widespread human rights violations, the preservation of peace and security, the alleviation of severe poverty, and the avoidance of environmental catastrophe (Christiano 2012, 388). I want to concentrate here on the morally mandatory aim of fundamental human rights protection.[20] Recall that in Chapter 3, I have argued that all persons have a natural duty to help protect everyone's fundamental human rights. The duty to contribute to realizing these rights, we have seen, holds irrespective of special relations or consensual obligations: it is a natural duty. The point I want to make here is parallel to the justification of the state's legitimate authority: if states are justified through their capacity for effectively realizing those duties by protecting fundamental human rights, then international institutions that are capable of protecting fundamental human rights are legitimate *in the same sense*. Recall that according to the moral division of labour argument, the state system is justified by virtue of its capacity for effectively realizing our natural duty to protect human rights. The same is true for institutions with morally mandatory aims: their authority is justified by virtue of their capacity to realize morally mandatory aims and, in particular, the enforcement of basic human rights. An important caveat is that to be legitimate in this sense, institutions in this first category do not only aim at realizing morally mandatory aims, but they must be *reasonably capable* of realizing them, which usually requires reaching a critical threshold of state support and commitment.

The ISO is the paradigmatic case of a second category of institutions that promote mutual advantage. Institutions that promote mutual advantage are institutions that coordinate rules and that cooperate on non-mandatory aims, such as economic integration (e.g. the EU), harmonization of standards (e.g. the ISO), or trade (e.g. the WTO). Those institutions are designed as a club in which states may coordinate their behaviour on projects they have voluntarily taken on. The general reason to participate in such institutions is that participation and their aim are advantageous to states in some way. It is important to notice that producing advantages alone cannot make an institution binding. Institutions for mutual advantage do not create content-independent moral obligations for non-members: assume that being a member of

[20] Whether all morally mandatory aims that Christiano lists are capable of justifying *authoritative* institutions is subject to further discussion.

the local Rotary Club gives me career advantages. That means that I might have a reason to join. But it does not mean that the Rotary Club has any authorization to impose its rules on me and demand my obedience. Only when an institution helps realize aims that are morally mandatory do these institutions have a claim to be binding for all.

Mutual advantage through cooperation is only possible in a long-term and stable manner if the participants in the cooperative scheme follow the rules of cooperation on the one hand and refrain from free riding on the benefits on the other hand. Of course, *some* free riding does not endanger the whole enterprise. But because free riders will benefit from the advantages without taking on a portion of the costs, it will be rational for all to enforce rules that prevent (excessive) free riding. This is how such institutions can, and usually do, become coercive. But the difference in the institutions of the first category is that they are not coercive towards all, but only towards those that are voluntarily part of the cooperative scheme. Coercion in case of non-compliance would most paradigmatically take the form of attaching costs and benefits so as to structure and guide behaviour, but it might also take the form of threatening to exclude the non-compliant party from the organization. This use of coercion is legitimate, given that members have voluntarily agreed to the rules of the institution.

The proposal I have advanced so far differs from Buchanan's conception of legitimacy for international institutions that I introduced at the beginning of this chapter in the following way: while Buchanan argues that institutions coordinating morally non-mandatory aims generate content-independent moral reasons for all, my position is that they are the source of obligations for members and that they generate no content-independent reasons for non-members – although they might very well be the source of content-dependent reasons for non-members. To explain, consider again the Rotary Club example: I might have reason to join, but those reasons are prudential or strategic reasons (because I believe it will advance my career, for example), but it seems absurd to claim that I have a moral reason to join or a moral reason to comply with their governance. Specifically, the Rotary Club does not generate content-independent reasons for non-members. The same applies to institutions like the ISO: it might be good for states if they joined, and it might give them advantages, but the ISO does not exert content-independent moral reasons on non-members. It does exert content-independent moral obligations for members, but the source of those obligations is not the advantages that the institution produces, but the previous consent of the members that authorized the institution to coordinate member states' behaviour in order to achieve those advantages efficiently. Outsiders merely have content-dependent reasons not to interfere: for example, they might think that the ISO engages in useful work and therefore their activities should not be interfered with. But surely, they do not have content-independent moral reasons not to interfere with mutually advantageous institutions. For example, a state may permissibly try to persuade another state to leave an institution, and it is not clear to me just what would make the attempt at persuasion morally problematic. If some state tried to persuade other states to leave, for example the EU, they are not defeating a *moral* reason.

To summarize, I argue that coercive international institutions are usefully divided into two categories: institutions with morally mandatory aims and institutions for mutual advantage. This distinction between international institutions helps us understand the scope of their coercive power. The distinction also helps us understand what standards apply to them to count as legitimate authorities. The argument I seek to advance in the remainder of this chapter, and in the next, is that institutions for mutual advantage differ from institutions with morally mandatory aims in this regard, too. I claim that the legitimacy of institutions for mutual advantage is based on consent and therefore their scope is limited to those who have consented. But while consent is the right standard for institutions for mutual advantage, it is the wrong standard for institutions with morally mandatory aims: their legitimate authority – in other words, their right to rule – is not based on the consent of states that are subject to their rule, but on whether they do in fact realize those morally mandatory aims. Importantly, and in contrast to institutions for mutual advantage, their scope is thus not limited to members only. Because morally mandatory aims are morally mandatory for all, their authority extends globally, that is, to all states – whether they consented or not. Or so I show in the next section.

4.3 Morally Mandatory Aims and Consent

I finished the last section with the conclusion that there is a need to distinguish between institutions that realize morally mandatory aims and institutions for mutual advantage. I have argued that both kinds of institutions can be conceptualized as coercive. But what gives an institution the right to rule with coercion? In this section, I discuss an influential standard of legitimacy, namely, that international institutions claim a right to rule by virtue of the consent given by states. Under ideal conditions, the principle of state consent captures an important normative idea: states, as institutions that express the political will of their citizens, may submit to another institution's authority only if it is the will of the citizens. The normative point of consent is that it has this voluntary element: states can opt in, but more importantly, the opt-out option exists too. Only when a state has voluntarily decided to commit itself to some regional or international regime, by the binding power of the government's 'promise' may that regime impose rules on the state – provided, of course, that the government is reasonably representative of the state's constituency. For example, the bodies of the WTO may only impose their system of rules and sanctions on those states that have consented to them in the first place. Similarly, the ICC can normally only adjudicate cases of member states that have consented to the ICC's jurisdiction.

How far the consent theory is morally adequate for international institutions is the subject of an extensive debate in political philosophy. Some of those who interpret the practice of international law as a practice with room for moral reasoning to some degree[21] have criticized the consent principle as redundant. Allen Buchanan has argued that state consent, as a super-norm that has the capacity to justify the legitimacy of the international legal system, is neither necessary nor sufficient in this regard (Buchanan 2004, 301ff). Ronald Dworkin has proposed to eschew the principle of state consent in favour of what he calls the principle of salience (Dworkin 2013). In this section, I review some of their arguments. I argue that while the consent principle is not wholly redundant, its application is limited to the category of institutions that is defined by mutually advantageous cooperation. Consequently, the authority of international institutions that use consent as their standard of legitimacy only extends to those states that have consented to it. For institutions that realize morally mandatory aims, however, consent (even in its more complex version) is inadequate as a standard of legitimacy.

We can distinguish between a simple consent view and a complex consent view. The simple consent view claims that consent is a sufficient condition for an institution's legitimacy. This view treats international institutions akin to a contract between states: because the institution has only come into being by the voluntary consent of the states, it naturally derives its legitimacy from this consent. One powerful objection to this view is the argument that not all states represent the democratic will of

[21] As opposed to realists who deny that moral reasons should play a role in structuring international public law, see the introductory discussion in Buchanan (2004).

their citizens. States are not moral agents, at least not in the more familiar sense in which persons are moral agents. The only way they matter morally is by virtue of the individuals that make up the state. But it is obviously a false presumption that all states do in fact represent the democratic will of their citizens. This gives us reasons for modifying the consent view, so that only the consent of *sufficiently democratic states* can serve as a legitimacy standard for international institutions. The best version of the simple consent view encompasses the qualification that the consent of states is normatively valid when buttressed by internal democratic procedures that connect the state with its citizenry.

This version of the consent view is elegantly simple, and although it seems convincing at first glance, there are a number of problems with it that remain unresolved. First of all, many states either do not inform the public well enough about a given political decision so that their consent is not necessarily normatively meaningful; or, in a just as likely case, many states simply refuse the population any influence in the decision whether to consent or not. And even for those states that *are sufficiently democratic* in both of these senses, Allen Buchanan and Robert Keohane (Buchanan and Keohane 2006) point out that one grave problem is that the normative point of consent is not brought to bear in the case of state consent. This is due to the problem of bureaucratic discretion:

> The problem is that for a modern state to function, much of what state agents do will not be subject to democratic decisions and saying that the public has consented in some highly general way to whatever it is that state agents do is clearly inadequate. The difficulty is not in identifying chains of delegation stretching from the individual citizen to state agents, but rather that at some point the impact of the popular will on how political power is used becomes so attenuated as to be merely nominal. Given how problematic democratic authorisation is in the modern state and given that global governance institutions require lengthening the chain of delegation, democratic state consent is not sufficient for legitimacy. (Buchanan and Keohane 2006, 414f)

Other problems of the simple consent paradigm concern its own justification. One of them is that consent as a political decision procedure is itself subject to a voluntarist procedure. If the voluntary decision is so important in politics, then consent theorists cannot establish authoritatively that consent is the correct political decision procedure; instead, there needs to be a prior political decision procedure about the question of whether consent is what matters (Wellman 1996). Related to this point, there is the problem of open-ended consent. When states consent to something, what do they really consent to? Where are the limits to what the consent allows the institutions to do? The scope of consent – of what kind are the decisions to be determined by consent? – again is not self-explanatory: to determine them, we need a different political procedure, one that cannot be consent; otherwise, we will find ourselves in an infinite regress. The same is true for other procedural issues: what changes constitute a new policy needing to be affirmed by consent? All those decisions, again, would have to be subject to consent. These problems point towards the hypothesis that the consent principle only delivers on its normative promise when it is applied to contexts that are characterized by small-scale and face-to-face communication allowing natural and flexible deliberation. But the interaction between states and international institutions is not such a context.

Another avenue to defend the state consent principle is by 'negative argument', with the claim that despite its problems, state consent is justified by the fact that it is a decision procedure that prevents injustice. The idea is that what should concern us is how much more unjust international politics would be without it. Buchanan calls a version of this argument the predation prevention argument (Buchanan 2004, 192). In traditional consent theory, the idea of consent elegantly solves an important problem in political philosophy, namely the problem of how one can reconcile people's moral equality with political authority. The consent principle has a strong answer: in a society of moral equals, the only way by which some have greater political power over others is when those on whom the political power is imposed have given their consent to the power asymmetry. Persons are still moral equals to one another, but they can be subject to political power at the same time. Because they remain moral equals to the power holders, their consent is a powerful institutional quality control: should the political institution overstep or misuse the power, the consent can be retracted.

The predation prevention argument works in a similar way: it emphasizes that the principle of state consent can help keep in check overwhelmingly asymmetric power relations between states with stronger bargaining positions and states with weaker bargaining positions. When it comes to building institutions – especially if those institutions potentially pierce state sovereignty – states with weaker positions can withhold consent if they conceive of the terms proposed by the states in the stronger position as unjust. The idea is thus that any international system that allows a 'consent constraint' on the power of strong states prevents predation even where asymmetries of power are in place.

The predation prevention argument might be convincing if we view it in abstract isolation, but once we view it on the background of international relations, its problems become clear. Many states that are in a weak bargaining position are in fact so dependent on the cooperation or assistance of stronger states that they have virtually no choice *not* to consent. Vast economic inequalities translate into power inequalities, and this makes the independence normally needed for *genuinely voluntary* consent close to impossible. Against this objection, one might say that even if the power structures are so unequal that consent is not *always* voluntary, it might still be in *some* cases, and this justifies having a system based on the consent principle, all things considered. After all, the unequal power structures between states are not caused by the existence of the consent principle: they exist whether we have the consent principle or not. Better thus to have it, on balance.

But that counterargument ignores that predation does not only exist in the relations between states, but also a feature of citizen relations within states, or of the relations between states and their citizens. And in those cases, it *does* in fact matter whether we have the consent principle or not: when states internally prey on (some of) their citizens, to make the power of international institutions wholly dependent on consent *is* detrimental to the prevention of predation *of individuals*. A state that withholds consent to institutions that protect peace and human rights – for example when states do not let UN peacekeeping missions into their territory, when they veto a humanitarian intervention or assistance, or when they hinder international legal reforms for more progressive human rights protection – actually does contribute to the possibilities predatory states have. Predatory governments have an interest in vetoing rightful diplomatic, economic, or military intervention (e.g. as a response to slavery or genocide), because they fear intervention in their own states when they engage in the same kind of immoral behaviour. Hence, we might say that it makes the whole system more dangerous for individuals.

Considering these counterexamples, it is not clear how much state consent contributes to the prevention of predation. Evidently, because the 'negative' argument relies on a claim about state consent having advantages on balance, defenders of the predation prevention argument need to show that, on balance, simple state consent is still a good idea, even though it might encourage predation of individuals, and it might hinder progressive peacekeeping and rights protection mechanisms. But I am unsure whether this can be done, because as much as consent potentially hinders the illegitimate use of force, it might hinder the legitimate use of force too, as Ronald Dworkin points out: 'International law could not serve the purposes it must serve in the contemporary world – disciplining the threat some states offer to others, for example – unless it escaped the straitjacket of state-by-state consent' (Dworkin 2013, 7). There are other, less dangerous mechanisms available that might do just as well in protecting smaller states from predatory states, while at the same time avoiding the harmful side effects of the consent principle. A clearer and more concise content of the rules in international law is the first step. Regional organization or coalition-building within international institutions is another. In light of these better alternatives, the moral costs of the simple state consent theory may simply be too high.

Because there might be better ways of achieving the aim behind state consent, and considering the many problems that this theory has, we should dismiss the view, at least in its simple version. A complex version of the consent view is more promising. The idea here is that consent is a necessary, but not a sufficient condition for an institution's legitimacy. Thomas Christiano argues for such a complex version of the consent view (Christiano 2012). Although he denies that consenting to international institutions is entirely at the discretion of states, he does find that the possibility of reasonable disagreement over the way global problems should be dealt with, and how the benefits and burdens of cooperative efforts should be distributed, leaves room for a conception of international legitimacy that gives state consent an important role. As we have seen earlier, Christiano argues that for some international problems, there is a morally mandatory need for cooperation. States that refuse to cooperate in solving these problems may legitimately be subject to coercion:

> When a state refuses to participate in a cooperative venture for the pursuit of morally mandatory aims and has no adequate explanation, it may be subjected to some kind of sanction or coercion. States would be within their rights to contemplate noncooperation or even more coercive responses to those states that refuse to participate for unscrupulous, irrational or morally self-defeating motives. Hence there are severe limits to the moral liberty of states when it comes to morally mandatory aims. (Christiano 2012, 389)

Morally mandatory aims are such aims that, so Christiano argues, can be recognized as fundamental moral challenges 'on virtually any scheme of morality' (Christiano 2012, 388). We have seen in the earlier sections of this chapter that among them are the preservation of international security, the protection of persons against widespread and fundamental human rights violations, the avoidance of global environmental catastrophe, the alleviation of severe global poverty, and the establishment of a decent system of international trade. However, although states have a moral obligation to cooperate in order to confront these fundamental challenges, there is no single, straightforward best way of institutionalizing such cooperation. In other words: states may have different preferences as to how these problems are solved, and therefore should not be coerced to join particular institutions. Instead, Christiano argues that there should be room for experimentation in dealing with any of those problems. That is why it can be permissible, under special circumstances, for a state to exit the authority of international institutions. These include situations in which a group of states exits the authority of an international institution in order to set up their own institution to tackle morally mandatory aims, perhaps on a regional level: 'Experimentation within different regional associations as well as within competing global arrangements may be the best way to try to solve the problems we are facing' (Christiano 2012, 389).

As we have seen above, Christiano's complex consent view incorporates the idea – on the first level – that there are duties to which consent is irrelevant. The duty to tackle morally mandatory aims is 'natural' in the sense that it does not arise out of an agreement under which states subordinate their will. Our agreement to some mandatory aims is of no consequence because we are not at moral liberty to refuse it in the first place. But then we might as well ask, as Allen Buchanan does, if we can dispense with the notion of consent altogether (Buchanan 2004, 246). However, dismissal of consent on these grounds would be premature. Remember that we are not asking about consent to the norms themselves, but about consent to institutions that apply those norms. Even though one may think that some norms are non-derogatory, it seems to matter *who* enforces them. A usurper, for example in the form of a colonial government, may govern according to the highest human rights standards, but benevolent colonialism is nevertheless morally wrong.[22]

Christiano's approach is based on a similar thought: although the norms that are enforced are consent-independent, the enforcing institution *is* consent-dependent. In Christiano's complex consent view, two levels are separated: the level of mandatory cooperation, for which consent is irrelevant, and the level of institutionalization, for which consent does matter, at least in so far as states may have good reasons to withhold their consent. Christiano calls this kind of consent 'bounded consent'. The difference to the simple consent view is that states have

[22] For a debate on the particular wrongness of colonialism, see the contributions by Simmons (2016), Stilz (2015), and Ypi (2013).

these natural duties, but that they have discretion in how they choose to fulfil them. They have strong reasons for cooperating with other states, but Christiano also argues that states are allowed to withhold consent, provided that they have good reasons for withholding it. But, if they withhold consent for the wrong reasons, they may be coerced. Good reasons are reasons that show that despite withholding consent, the state tries to realize its duty to achieve morally mandatory aims. Wrong reasons are when states are withholding consent for egoistic or immoral reasons (Christiano 2012, 389).

This complex consent view is a major improvement vis-à-vis the simple consent view. Nevertheless, I have three worries about Christiano's proposal. First, I am not convinced that the notion of consent does much work in Christiano's argument. Recall that his version of consent is a version he calls 'bounded consent':

> In the cases of any treaty that attempts to realise a system of cooperation that is morally mandatory, the refusal to enter or exit from it would require an acceptable explanation that lays out the reasons for thinking that the treaty would not contribute to solving the problem and that some alternative might be superior. Exit or withdrawal is permissible but only with an adequate explanation. By "adequate explanation" I mean an explanation that is not irrational, unscrupulous or morally self-defeating and that displays a good-faith effort to solve the problem at hand. (Christiano 2012, 389)

But note that the idea of a 'heavily bounded system of consent and exit' (Christiano 2012, 390) leaves little room for the original normative point of consent: namely, that it is *voluntary*. The philosophical anarchist might argue that Christiano's version of consent does not have much to do with the original voluntarism that is essential to theories of consent. If a state cannot choose whether to consent to an institution or not, but only *which* institution it will subject itself to, it is not clear what role consent plays. With the introduction of bounded consent, Christiano's position effectively comes very close to a natural duty view like the one I introduced in Chapter 3. A natural duty view may or may not be plausible, but that is not the point; the point is that by introducing bounded consent, the complex consent view loses its voluntaristic element, namely, that states may determine according to their will what their preferred path to solve morally mandatory aims is.[23]

[23] The same criticism can be directed against – and also in the literature is directed against (Wellman and Simmons 2005, 117) – interpretations of Locke that understand consent as hypothetical consent, for example in Hanna Pitkin's interpretation (Pitkin 1965, 1966).

Second, and related to the first problem, is the idea that states may permissibly withdraw from institutions realizing morally mandatory aims for their own reasons in a way that replicates the problem for which Christiano has introduced international institutions in the first place: which is that international cooperation is necessary for many morally mandatory aims. The problem is that on Christiano's proposal states themselves may decide which institutions bind them – and which do not bind them. This is a problem because sometimes cooperation of all or most is needed in some cases to solve the problem. For example, if large polluters do not cooperate in climate change regimes, their non-cooperation can potentially cause the whole project to fall. The coordination effort that institutions are potentially capable of only works effectively if compliance reaches a reasonable threshold. Christiano cannot solve this issue by invoking the bounded consent idea, because the non-compliant states may cooperate on a different scheme (scheme B) to solve the same problem. They have a good reason to not cooperate in scheme A and are therefore permitted to not comply. But scheme A and scheme B might then *both* fail because none of them can generate enough compliance. Or they could even be non-commensurable, meaning that they generate conflicting solutions. Cooperation to achieve a particular aim often requires participation by almost everyone in the same scheme.

To alleviate this worry, Christiano maintains that if states refuse to cooperate and lack an adequate justification for their refusal, they may be coerced or sanctioned (Christiano 2012, 389). But what counts as a good reason will also be subject to disagreement: those states that do participate in the institution obviously do not agree that there is a good reason to exit; otherwise, they would do so as well. Consider the case of a morally self-defeating explanation, which, according to Christiano, is one 'that insists on a different coordination solution, defeating a coordination solution that in the circumstance advances everyone's aims' (Christiano 2012, 389). But state A cooperates in the institution *precisely because* it believes that one particular coordination solution will advance the respective morally mandatory aim. But if state A has this belief, how likely is it that at the same time it will believe that state B genuinely thinks that the particular coordination solution *will not* advance the morally mandatory aim? Moreover, if state A and its collaborators are then justified in sanctioning or coercing state B, the disagreement might easily turn into a conflict. This type of problem can be avoided by introducing an authority that judges whether states are justified in refraining from cooperation. But the idea of qualified consent just takes the problem up a notch: what counts as justified qualification of one's consent is itself a matter of disagreement.

Third, I believe that Christiano misjudges the overall costs of exiting existing institutions and building new ones.[24] Recall that Christiano argues that under some circumstances, states are permitted to deny cooperation in existing institutions that realize morally mandatory aims. One such circumstance is when states want to build an alternative international institution to tackle those aims. Not only does that invite misusing this as an excuse to ignore the duty to cooperate for morally mandatory aims, but it misjudges the significant costs that exiting existing institutions on the one hand and building new institutions on the other hand bring. The costs range from financial costs, to loss and costly transfer of technical and legal knowledge, and to political costs that arise out of the necessity to build trust in the authority of institutions. Besides these three worries, some of the objections against the simple consent view also apply to Christiano's complex consent view. It would need to be worked out how consent to an institution is determined, how often it has to be renewed, and how to solve the problem of bureaucratic discretion.

In conclusion, the complex consent view fares better than the simple consent view, but precisely because it introduces elements that qualify consent, it effectively comes closer to a natural duty view. Furthermore, as such, it cannot solve problems of coordination and disagreement, which is the point of joining institutions in the first place. If one thinks that institutions are necessary for morally mandatory aims, then one would do so precisely *because* of their capacity to solve such coordination and disagreement problems. Hence, consent conceptions of legitimacy are less convincing, at least not for morally mandatory aims. We need to look beyond consent for understanding the legitimate authority of such institutions.

To summarize the argument I have made in this chapter: I have argued against the position that only states use coercion when they rule. Instead, I have suggested an approach to coercion – the enforcement approach – that captures paradigmatic instances of coercion in the political context. This helped us understand how international institutions can be plausibly thought of as coercive. However, I have then distinguished two different modes of coercion that international

[24] I owe this point to Bernd Ladwig.

institutions employ: some coerce by threatening enforcement with physical force, while others coerce by threatening exclusion from the institution. The first type are institutions that realize morally mandatory aims, while the second type are institutions that coordinate for mutual advantage. I have then discussed which standards of legitimacy apply to these institutions. Consent approaches argue that only the consent of the governed can justify political legitimacy. As a standard of legitimacy, consent is useful for institutions that coordinate mutual advantage. For morally mandatory aims, consent is less useful, and I have argued that even complex versions of consent are problematic. One important consequence of the argument I am making is that I reject the distinction between stronger conceptions of legitimacy for state institutions and weaker conceptions of legitimacy for international institutions. This distinction is drawn along the wrong boundary, as it were. Instead, it is more convincing to draw a distinction between mutually advantageous and morally mandatory institutions. This means affirming *one* conception for all human rights protecting political institutions, be they domestic or international. If an international institution's legitimacy is justified by the same ground as a state's legitimacy – the protection of human rights – and thus fulfils the same function, they ought to share the same conception of legitimacy.

5

Fairness, Equality, and Democratic Authority

5.1 Fairness in Trials

Let me now tie the arguments from the preceding chapters in with international criminal justice (ICJ). I have argued that when states fail to fulfil their responsibility to protect the basic human rights of their citizens, they become liable to interference by the international community. Everyone is back in the state of nature vis-à-vis that state. But once we all then have an equal right to punish mass human rights violations, we have reason to relinquish our natural executive right to an institution that coordinates punishment precisely because the equal distribution of the right to punish leads to practical problems. Thus, we need an institution of criminal justice that evades the problems of the state of nature. But the other argument I pursued was that institutions with morally mandatory aims – and recall that enforcing basic human rights *is* such a morally mandatory aim – are justified in wielding coercive political power even if states did not consent to them, because consent is the wrong standard of legitimacy for such institutions. The question that remains for this chapter is thus the following: under what conditions may ICJ institutions justifiably wield coercive political power? What standards must they conform to if they possess legitimate authority? While it is fairly obvious that an ICJ institution must not itself violate fundamental rights – that would contradict its justification – what *other conditions* apply to its exercise of authority is an open question. In the remainder of the chapter, I introduce and discuss two conditions: fairness and equality.

That institutions that prosecute and punish individuals should do so in procedures that are fair is almost obvious. Fairness implies rigorous procedures that reconstruct and establish whether the defendant is legally guilty. The function of the procedures is not merely to find an answer to this question, but to find an answer which is fair to all who are subject to the institution. What does this mean? Fairness requires trial-governing rules that enable each party to present their case, strong rights for the defendants, including access to free legal counsel, and other rules of 'natural procedural justice'. Parties that undergo criminal investigation and prosecution must have the chance to produce evidence to support their version of the events during the trial. The question now is: what sets of rules should govern this trial to ensure its fairness?

What constitutes fairness varies according to the context. What set of rules makes a football match fair is different from the set of rules that would make an election fair. What kind of set of rules should apply to institutions that prosecute and punish international crimes? We need a set of rules that aims at a procedure with which the course of events and the role of the defendant – and therefore their guilt – can be established as accurately as possible. The value that the process attempts to achieve is truth, a criterion for the right result that is independent of the rules of the procedure (Rawls 1999, 75). This means that the rules can be designed with the aim of approximating this value: by making the rules so as to make the procedure of guilt determination as impartial as possible and avoid distortions that are results of unequal power relations. But it also means that it is impossible to design the procedure in a way that always leads to the truth, making a trial a case of imperfect procedural justice (Rawls 1999, 75). Rawls argues that cases of imperfect procedural justice are paradigmatically such cases where 'there is an independent criterion for the correct outcome', but 'no feasible procedure which is sure to lead to it' (Rawls 1999, 75). The reason is that the rules must aim at truth but be consistent with our other ends and ideals. For example, we might prefer to err on the side of acquitting some of those who are guilty, rather than convicting some of those who are not.[1] The reason for this seems to be that it would be more of a burden for an innocent person to go to prison for a crime they did not commit than it would be for the rest of society to have a guilty person among them who has been acquitted.

The rules that allow for all of this do not need to be invented from scratch. We have plenty of experience in domestic criminal law that we can use. The rules include the basic procedural rights that are in some form recognized in most systems of criminal law. They address defendants and court staff and are formulated as rights or prohibitions. Let us call the requirement of observing those rules the fairness condition. Institutions that fulfil the fairness condition ensure that the course of

[1] That is, we prefer false negatives (guilty persons going free) to false positives (innocent persons being indicted).

events and thus the guilt of the defendant are established as accurately as possible while at the same time giving a fair hearing to all sides.

The fairness condition applies to all criminal courts. Among those 'procedural due process' rules are: the prohibition of punishment without law and the prohibition of crime without law, the right to appear before a court, the right to an impartial trial that bases its decision solely on the evidence presented, the right to make a statement before a decision is made, the right to fair notice and to have time to prepare a defence, the right to be informed of the charges in a manner that the defendant understands and in writing, the right to confront witnesses against him or her and present witnesses for one's case, the right to professional counsel, the ban on double jeopardy (that a person may not be subjected to criminal prosecution for the same crime twice), the right to appeal, and the prohibition of using forcefully extorted confessions. These rules are complemented by some more rules that help ensure the fair treatment of the defendant in accordance with their human rights, like the right to humane punishment and the right to humane conditions of confinement, including, for example, medical treatment when needed.

Is this fairness condition sufficient to establish the conditions under which ICJ institutions have authority? Instrumental accounts of ICJ institutions, including those that defend the principle of universal jurisdiction, argue for something along these lines: as long as the procedures by which the criminals are convicted are fair, any court – be it an international ad hoc tribunal, a permanent court, or national courts exercising universal jurisdiction – may legitimately prosecute persons who have committed international crimes. I discuss three positions, and while each position presents a distinct justification for ICJ, they share a common core: namely the argument that fairness and perhaps the importance of the goals of ICJ ultimately suffice for the rightful exercise of ICJ institutions' authority. I argue that this argument does not succeed, because none of the justifications have a satisfactory reply to what Niko Kolodny calls the *subordination complaint* (Kolodny 2016). The idea behind the subordination complaint is that political rule constitutes a special type of relation that puts one below another individual against whom one has a claim to stand as an equal. This subordination consists 'in being exposed to the greater power and de facto authority of another individual' (Kolodny 2016, 36). A successful justification of authority can address the subordination complaint by explaining how the political rule does not undermine that equal standing. As I argue in the remainder of this chapter, purely instrumental accounts of ICJ institutions' authority fail to provide such an explanation.

As we have seen above, the fairness condition applies to all systems of criminal law and punishment. Enforcing ICJ by punishment can be done in two ways. Either ICJ, including the punishment it prescribes, can be enforced by national courts – that is, courts that exercise authority over the crimes of international criminal law, but that are embedded in a national political structure – or it can be enforced by an international court – that is, a court that is made up of multiple members of the international community. I consider both options in turn by discussing Song's (2015) 'enforcement gap filling view' that justifies the principle of universal jurisdiction – this is the principle that authorizes *national* courts to exercise jurisdiction over *international* crimes – with an argument that invokes a right to filling the gaps of enforcement of criminal justice. To my mind, Song's enforcement gap filling view is the most compelling case made in the philosophical literature for universal jurisdiction.[2]

Universal jurisdiction is the legal principle that permits domestic criminal courts of states to prosecute and punish perpetrators for international crimes. Consider the following argument for the legitimacy of national courts exercising universal jurisdiction (Song 2015). Pointing to the historical beginnings of the principle, Song argues that universal jurisdiction was originally permissible because it provided a system in which *enforcement* gaps – rather than *jurisdictional* gaps – could be filled. Back in the day, pirates were labelled enemies of all mankind; not because robbery at sea was morally more heinous than robbery on land, but because piracy presented a coordination problem for the enforcement of the legal prohibition of robbery at sea. The question we should be asking ourselves is thus not how to justify that one state has *jurisdiction* over another state, but why one state may *enforce* universal laws on another state.

Adequate enforcement, as Song defines it, consists of two dimensions: it encompasses the *detection* of violations and an *adequate response* to the violation. A gap in enforcement is thus defined as a failure to detect a violation or a failure to respond (or to respond fairly) to a violation (Song 2015, 482). Note that universal jurisdiction is of limited practical use as a means to detect enforcement gaps. It simply seems unlikely that other states are able to detect a violation that the state in which the violation

[2] For a more detailed discussion of Song's view, see my 'Universal Jurisdiction, pirates and vigilantes' (Müller 2019).

took place has failed to do so. However, universal jurisdiction is useful to fill enforcement gaps when it comes to the second dimension of enforcement. A failure to respond to a violation will result in de facto impunity, and an unfair response – for example, a response that is too lenient – will be unjust. Enforcement gaps typically arise when the state in which the violations have occurred, or to which either the victim or the perpetrator belongs, is either unwilling or unable to adequately respond to a violation.

One problem in Song's approach is that it lacks an argument for punishment as the adequate form of enforcement in the first place. By using the term of 'enforcement' rather than criminal prosecution or punishment, Song circumvents the difficult question of whether criminal prosecution and punishment are in fact permissible (as a way of enforcing the prohibitions of international law). In the discussion of Locke's argument for punishment in Chapter 2, we have seen that enforcement does not necessarily imply punishment and that we need an additional argument – for example one about the deterrent value of punishment – to make sense of the connection between enforcement and punishment. Hence, the claim that legal prohibitions must be *enforced* does not automatically get us to the claim that domestic courts can try and *punish* perpetrators of international crimes.

The reason Song provides that might be used as a justification for punishment is that punishment is owed to the victims: she says that they are entitled to legal redress (Song 2015, 489). Under normal circumstances, she argues, states are expected (and permitted) to choose their own means of enforcing international criminal law within their territory. Delegating the responsibility for the enforcement to the state is the normal way of enforcing international law domestically (Song 2015, 483). But if the respective state fails to do so for whatever reason, it is unjustifiable towards the victims to complain about foreign states prosecuting the crimes on their behalf: someone *owes* it to the victims to prosecute and punish the perpetrators. While I remain unconvinced of this particular justification for punishment, we can nevertheless assume that there is an adequate argument in favour of punishment as the adequate mode of law enforcement. Song's important point is this: the law must be enforced, punishment is one permissible way of enforcing it, and every state has jurisdiction over these crimes, which leads us to the conclusion that the enforcement of the law may be carried out by everyone.

Readers will be reminded of Locke's natural executive right by the structure of Song's argument. Recall that Locke's idea is that in the state of nature, all rational persons have the right to enforce the law by punishing criminals. This is the same reasoning that Song reconstructs for justifying universal jurisdiction: because there is no overarching political authority, the enforcement of the law may legitimately be carried out by individual states. Locke then introduced government because he thought that one of the problems that result from the natural executive right in the state of nature is that it would lead to unfair punishment: without a central authority, the decision to prosecute and punish is left to the responsibility of agents acting on their own and punishing according to their own judgement. The first of Locke's concerns about this was the uneven distribution and partial application of punishment in a 'private' penal system. Even reasonable individuals are sometimes 'partial to themselves and their friends' (Locke II, §13): they tend to privilege their own and their friends' well-being when it comes to exercising their right to punish. They might also fail to exercise the punishment calmly and within reason.

At first sight, one might think that this concern is reproduced in Song's proposal: states will exercise universal jurisdiction as a 'private' penal system, acting on their own and punishing criminals according to their private judgement. This would disqualify a system of universal jurisdiction as an adequate way of enforcing basic human rights. But notice that there is a structural dissimilarity: in the case of universal jurisdiction, states exercise their right to punish *through* domestic courts that – ideally – fulfil the fairness condition discussed above. Thus, Song's universal jurisdiction argument does not fall prey to the problems in the state of nature in Locke's argument. While the agents in the Lockean state of nature are individuals who are biased, the agents that execute international law are not individuals, but national courts. Since the fairness condition applies to *all* criminal courts, the danger of bias and unjustified privileging of friends is thus considerably less virulent than it was if agents executing the law were private individuals. Individuals who blatantly punish the innocent cease to be of concern when fair courts punish, because the rules regulating the trial minimize the danger of bias.

Luban (Luban 2010) might object to Song's universal jurisdiction principle that national courts do not always deliver fairness of the kind of quality that is to be expected for international crimes. He argues that in fact, only international institutions like the ICC or international ad hoc tribunals are likely to reach an adequately high standard of fairness. The legitimacy of ICJ institutions, he proposes, depends on the high standards of the trials that ICJ institutions provide: 'Tribunals bootstrap themselves into legitimacy by the quality of justice they deliver; their rightness depends on their fairness' (Luban 2010, 579). If ICJ institutions strictly adhere to procedural fairness and deliver 'champagne-quality' due process in their trials, so Luban argues, they can generate or 'earn' their authority that way, instead of having to rely on state authorization or state consent. He argues that this 'bottom-up' legitimacy approach is the best we can hope for in a world that lacks a world government that could potentially authorize ICJ institutions. The underlying rationale of this argument is instrumental: the authority of the institution depends on the quality of the outcome, that is, on the fairness of the trial and the subsequent punishment.[3]

It would be a mistake to think that Luban's proposal is simply a story of how actual ICJ institutions became legitimate in the sociological sense. Of course, it is plausible to suggest that how people come to think of ICJ institutions depends strongly on how well those institutions can build trust in their institutional efficiency, impartiality, and discipline between the public and the institution. But Luban's point is a different one: he claims that ICJ institutions gain *normative* legitimacy when they provide an outcome of high quality – in other words: when they provide an impeccable performance and deliver justice of a high quality. Contrast this claim with the consent approach: while the consent approach to legitimacy emphasizes the derivation of legitimacy from its origin – the subject that consents to it – Luban's instrumental approach emphasizes the derivation of legitimacy from its performance (or outcome), measured in 'trial fairness'.

One might object that if the authority of an ICJ institution does in fact depend on its performance, then why not have FIFA or the International

[3] For a similar view, see Aaron Fichtelberg's liberal conception of the ICC's legitimacy (Fichtelberg 2006). Fichtelberg argues in response to Morris (2002) that democratic conceptions of legitimacy are misguided because democratic decision-making often undermines basic liberal rights, and he is particularly concerned about the right to a fair trial. I agree with the latter, but not with the former point. As will become clear in the subsequent sections, I argue that the trials themselves, and hence their fairness, ought not be subject to democratic decision-making (and neither does Morris, I believe). But fairness is only one of two conditions that ICJ institutions must fulfil when they claim to exercise their authority legitimately. Democratic decision-making is important when it comes to legislative issues: many rules of international criminal law require application and interpretation, which ought to be deliberated and decided on in fora of democratic decision-making. In contrast to Fichtelberg, I understand the legitimacy of democratic decision-making in reference to the capacity to ensure non-subordination between democratic equals, rather than to the capacity to protect fundamental rights, like Fichtelberg does (Fichtelberg 2006, 776). This explains why it is indeed a problem that 'democratic states will be subject to a legal code that they had no hand in creating' (Fichtelberg 2006, 780).

Chess Federation prosecute mass human rights violations? After all, what really matters is whether they deliver high-quality trials. Luban's reply to this kind of (slightly stylized) objection is pragmatic: once we realize what it *actually takes* to deliver such high-quality trials, it is clear that the extremely stringent requirements for justice can only be met by tribunals that are authorized and supported by states: 'Evidence must be gathered from foreign war zones by trustworthy and impartial investigators, evidentiary chains of custody must be maintained, defence counsel and judges recruited and paid, defence witnesses subpoenaed across borders, appellate panels created and staffed, rules written, safe, humane prisons found, and long-time confinements monitored. Realistically, only states can carry out these tasks' (Luban 2010, 580).

Hence, although Luban thinks that the legitimacy of those tribunals does not arise from their political pedigree – for example state consent – in reality, the support of states will be instrumental in achieving fair outcomes. But is Luban's theory plausible? Can tribunals really 'bootstrap themselves into legitimacy by the quality of justice they deliver' (Luban 2010, 579), therefore 'self-generating' their authority? Note that Luban's argument for international criminal courts depends on the normative assumption that the fairness of a trial justifies the imposition of political power. In principle, there is then no reason to prefer international tribunals to national courts. The preference for international institutions is based on a pragmatic argument: only *they* can gain the factual support of states, which then enables them to provide fair trials. It follows that if the quality of the outcome ('champagne-quality trials' and 'fair, humane punishments') is what generates their authority, the argument for international judicial bodies, as opposed to domestic judicial bodies for example, is not an argument based on principle, but an empirical one: Whichever institution, national or international, does best in providing 'champagne-quality justice' has authority to prosecute and punish international crimes. As long as the trials meticulously abide by the principles of procedural fairness, it is in principle irrelevant whether they are an international body or a domestic body in any given state.

Duff (2010) responds to Luban that his account confuses two questions: one is the question of procedural fairness, and the other is the one of authority. Criminal courts usually make three claims in the context of their legitimacy to prosecute an alleged criminal: that the crime was a crime under a system of law that binds the criminal, that the court has the standing – the authority – to try the criminal, and that his guilt is proven by an impartial procedure (Duff 2010, 590). Duff argues that

Luban's strategy to ground the second claim in the third claim is ultimately unsuccessful: 'A defendant's challenge "By what right do you try me?" must be answered if the trial is to be legitimate; the answer "our procedures respect the demands of natural justice" is not an answer to that challenge' (Duff 2010, 591). Duff therefore denies what Luban suggests, which is that the authority of a court that prosecutes international crimes *does* depend on its performance, and that the origin of that authority – state authorization in this case – *is* irrelevant (Luban 2010, 580). But why would the fact that someone is good at something imply that that individual has authority? Recall that authority in the political context means that the authority holder may wield political power. The objection to Luban's argument is thus: just because international courts are good at delivering champagne-quality justice does not give them the right to use their ability to do so on anyone. The outcome of a procedure is by itself not sufficient to establish the legitimacy of an institution. Before we get to an explanation as to why that is, let us turn to a third and structurally similar account, defended in the literature by Christopher Wellman.

Wellman defends a Lockean natural executive right for human rights violations. But in contrast to the Lockean account of political legitimacy, Wellman argues that state institutions that punish are not authorized by the consent of the rule addressees, but by their extraordinary capacity to realize the aims of punishment – aims, which are of utmost importance. In his view, the primary aim of punishment is deterrence: not only is this the most important aim, but the capacity to deter future crimes is also sufficient in terms of justification (Wellman 2009, 428). His justification of the authority of state punishment thus consists of one normative claim – that the aims of punishment are of utmost importance because they protect the rights of the innocents – and one empirical claim – that the political institution of the state is uniquely capable of realizing the aims of punishment, much better than if everyone just punished wildly and without a system. In analogy to Locke, Wellman argues that the reason for this is that 'only in a system with an authoritative body which makes, enforces, and impartially adjudicates promulgated rules' (Wellman 2009, 428) can the important aims of punishment be realized. Taken together, these two claims yield the result that the state has the exclusive right to punish.

Notice how the authority of institutions that punish is justified by their instrumental value: they are only justified in punishing if it is in fact true that they are capable of realizing the aims of punishment better than, for example, a private system of punishment. What makes political institutions better at serving the aims of punishment? They have an institutionalized distribution of role obligations and a systematic procedure of processing claims; and they are more impartial, and thus fairer, than any uncoordinated system of punishment. This is why '(. . .) the state violates no rights in assuming executive control over the punitive process only because it is uniquely capable of adequately realizing the morally significant aims that a system of punishment can achieve' (Wellman 2009, 439).

But the fact alone that political institutions are better at realizing the aims of punishment does not suffice to allocate authority to them. We have already encountered this objection in response to Luban above: just because someone is better at doing something does not mean that the person has authority over the process. Wellman uses the analogy of tending a garden to make the point:

> The fact that others could do a decidedly better job of tending my garden or decorating my house does not give them the right to push me aside and take over these projects, for instance . . . we recognize that each person's moral dominion over her own life gives her the right to manage her affairs even when others might do so better. (Wellman 2009, 429)

But, he argues, while this is true in the case of tending a garden, it is different when we talk about securing innocent people's rights. Tending a garden is relatively unimportant, while securing innocent people's rights is of profound importance. If the aims of punishment were not enforced by a political institution, the consequences of an uncoordinated system of private punishment would cumulatively be so terrible that everyone's fundamental human rights would virtually be unprotected. The gravity of the consequences and the fact that not only *my* human rights go unprotected, but everyone else's too, give the institution the permission to rule authoritatively over matters of punishment.

To understand the subtle but important point of Wellman's position, compare Wellman's justification of punishment to A. John Simmons's justification of punishment. Wellman adopts Simmons's argument from Locke, but he diverges from it when it comes to the standard of *why* a political institution has authority. While Simmons 'sticks to his Lockean guns' (Wellman 2009, 427) and argues that only the consent of the governed can generate legitimate political authority, Wellman believes that the importance of the aims of punishment in combination with the precariousness of the situation without political authority can *functionally substitute consent* as the moral principle that closes the normative gap between the fundamental liberty of persons (expressed as the prohibition to interfere with their actions) and the coerciveness of political authority. It is important to understand how Simmons and Wellman differ here: Simmons sticks to a voluntaristic path, on which he ends up concluding that although states usually *claim* to have an exclusive right to punish, no existing state de facto holds the exclusive right to punish. The reason for this is that there is no state to which citizens have consented. Wellman avoids this conclusion by leaving the voluntaristic path. Instead, he invokes considerations of the dangerous consequences of leaving punishment in the hands of private individuals. This, Wellman argues, justifies the state to coerce their constituents to do what is necessary to save others from those dangerous consequences.

Wellman's argument is another version of the natural duty argument,[4] one that is buttressed by the duty to rescue others from peril. He puts it forward under the name 'Samaritanism' (Wellman 1996; 2001; 2005). In situations where there is an imminent threat of peril, agents are permitted to use coercion in order to fulfil their duty to rescue others from peril. Wellman develops his argument as a theory of state legitimacy, but it extends naturally to international institutions that punish. We have already seen in Chapter 3 that he also defends a 'post-Westphalian' view about the sovereignty of states: states are only legitimate when they reach a certain threshold of human rights protection. When they fail to achieve this threshold – when they fail to do a good enough job – they lose the right to govern their internal affairs exclusively (Wellman 2009, 428). If one accepts this post-Westphalian view, one might wonder whether the right to punish would not fall back into the hands of the citizens who then are permitted to take on the punishment of those who are guilty of international crimes. But the same reasoning that justifies state punishment then applies to international institutions: they are fairer and more effective – in terms of distributing the burdens justly – in punishing those criminals. Only when an authoritative body makes, enforces, and adjudicates the rules, the danger of chaos and of

[4] Wellman's argument is structurally similar to the argument I have been advancing; in particular, our duties to rescue people from peril and to enforce their basic human rights come to the same thing, as both are, as it were, morally mandatory aims. However, the Samaritan argument seems to explain primarily why the use of coercion is sometimes permitted in grave emergency situations. In the following sections, I argue that for stable institutions to exist over time, they must provide democratic mechanisms of decision-making in order to vindicate their legitimate authority, which has to do with the idea that institutions must govern in compliance with our equal democratic status.

succumbing to a 'horribly dangerous mess' (Wellman 2009, 428) can be averted. Because authoritative institutions are uniquely capable of realizing the aims of punishment, and because these aims are so important for the cumulative security and rights protection of persons, those institutions may coercively impose their authority on everyone. In fact, the institutions may even help themselves to private property to fund their 'Samaritan' punitive activities (Wellman 2009, 431). For Wellman, the jurisdictional authority of international institutions is dependent on the failure of the respective domestic institution: if a state fails to achieve the morally significant goals of punishment, it loses its exclusive right to punish and has no right to complain if other agents step in and punish perpetrators (Wellman 2009, 436). In those cases, international institutions may legitimately assume control over the punitive process.

While Luban's account locates the feature that justifies legitimate authority in the fairness of institutions, Wellman locates it in their effectiveness in avoiding peril. Despite this difference, notice the structural similarity in the accounts of Wellman and Luban: just like Luban, Wellman's argument seems to justify that *any agent* might have a right to enforce the natural duty to protect persons from peril. The idea that only international institutions should do so is justified by the fact that they just happen to be very good at it.

5.2 Instrumental Approaches and the Subordination Complaint

What the theories of Song, Luban, and Wellman share is that they all give a specific kind of answer to someone who would ask: by what right do *you* punish me? They all point to the fact that institutions are *really* good at remedying certain failures of coordinated action. Their justifications distinguish themselves merely in terms of their empirical assumptions. Song argues that institutions are permitted to fill enforcement gaps by prosecuting criminals through domestic courts under international law. Luban thinks that international institutions do a better job because in the face of global power structures, state authorization is needed for any trial to function properly. Wellman attributes the superior capacity of institutions to the fact that they are capable of carrying out the punitive process more impartially and more effectively, limiting the danger of chaos. The value attributed to institutions exercising the prosecution and punishment of massive human rights violations in all three approaches is instrumental: institutions simply do better when it comes to achieving the aims of punishment.

Therefore, one way of criticizing the approaches I just discussed is to attack their respective empirical claims. Is state authorization *really* needed for fair trials? And do international institutions *really* do a better job in achieving the aims of punishment? For example, one might think a mixed system of state punishment and private punishment works even better to achieve the aims of punishment than exclusive state punishment. Where criminals escape justice or innocents are convicted because of procedural errors or system bias, it seems quite plausible to assume that the ends of punishment are better served by letting vigilantes fill the gaps of institutional punishment. In any case, assessing the validity of these empirical claims certainly requires an extensive data-based analysis.

What about the normative claims that proponents of instrumental approaches make? In order to see what is normatively problematic about instrumental approaches such as Song's, Luban's, or Wellman's, let me invoke an objection that I call 'the just vigilante objection'. I submit that if we understand what is wrong with vigilantism, we might come closer to understanding what conditions apply for legitimate punishment beyond the state – over and above the fairness condition. Vigilantism describes a phenomenon in which private persons or groups of persons take it upon themselves to punish (whom they perceive to be) criminals. Vigilantism usually evokes ethical concerns. But what is it exactly that makes us uncomfortable about vigilante justice? Consider this thought experiment: imagine that there is a vigilante group operating in a society, and this group has taken it upon itself to render just punishment on criminals who have violated fundamental rights. One worry about vigilantism that comes to mind is that vigilante groups behave like mobsters: in exercising their punishment, they do not give the alleged criminals a chance to defend or excuse themselves, or they over-punish, punish inhumanely, or use torture. In short, they provide neither a fair trial nor a fair punishment, and that is what makes them normatively problematic.

But is it really the fairness condition that separates legitimate punishment from vigilantism? Besides the fact that sometimes state institutions punish unfairly and put a burden on persons – for example when they must let a criminal go because of some procedural error, for example, when the evidence was obtained illegally and is therefore banned from being introduced into the trial – we can imagine a vigilante group that delivers trials and punishments that observe the principles of natural procedural justice. That is, these just vigilantes give defendants the chance and the resources to defend themselves properly, they only use legitimate evidence, etc. The vigilantes also specify and lay out the rules, apply them evenly, and do not punish excessively; for example, they do not use capital punishment and their conditions of confinement are humane. In short, they have all the virtues of a proper criminal justice institution.

Is there a problem with such a just vigilante group? I submit that the group will strike most of us as somehow problematic, and my claim is that this is because *they put themselves above* the rest of us by putting themselves in charge of criminal punishment. Our imagined vigilante group is subject to what Niko Kolodny calls the 'subordination complaint': 'to be subject to political rule is to be put in relations of subordination or social inferiority to other individuals with whom one has a claim to stand as an equal' (Kolodny 2016, 63). Kolodny's argument is that the problem of political power – that we stand in relations in which some rule and others are ruled – is that it potentially threatens our status as equals (and not so much our autonomy or freedom). And my claim is that this is precisely what the problem is with the just vigilantes. The reason why we think that they behave like 'wannabe sovereigns' (Waldron 1999, 114) is that they impose their law without having been authorized to do so. The problem is *not* that their punishment is never fair, or always unjust, but that the vigilantes coerce group outsiders, who in turn have no voice or control over the punishers. This creates a (prima facie unjustified) relational asymmetry between those who punish, and those who receive punishments. It is difficult to reconcile the vigilantes' form of coercion with the view of persons as equals, when one person's or one group's decision over what people deserve in terms of criminal justice takes precedence over others. By asserting your right to punish me, you establish an asymmetry between you and me, which is a relation of subordination: 'At its core . . . subordination consists in being exposed to the greater power and de facto authority of another individual' (Kolodny 2016, 63).[5] Therefore, the vigilante group is liable to the subordination complaint; a claim I will try to make plausible for the remainder of this section.

Song's, Luban's, and Wellman's accounts of ICJ authority are liable to the just vigilante objection: they are unable to refute vigilantism, because they fail to see what it is that makes it fundamentally problematic. It is not necessarily the fact that vigilantes punish unfairly: sometimes, public

[5] It seems that the criticism that most of the ICC's prosecutions are in Africa is exactly that: a complaint about subordination, about a lack of respect for the equal status of African states.

institutions do too, and we can imagine a vigilante group that employs the same fairness safeguards as the state. The problem is that they uphold relations of subordination. Their failure to adequately respond to the subordination complaint is instructive for understanding what the deeper problem with instrumental accounts is. For instrumental accounts, the argument that explains by what right one authority, rather than another authority, may impose their coercion on agents refers to the institutional capacities to achieve a certain goal. For example, Wellman argues that a group is permitted to impose authority because it saves its subjects from peril. We have also seen that the goal must be extraordinarily important: it does not suffice that someone does something better than me; it must also be an important thing not just for me, but for everyone. By letting myself be ruled by an effective institution, I am contributing to fulfilling my duty to others that they be saved from peril. Now, my objection to Wellman is that the normative work that the argument that something is important actually fails to do the work he intends it to do. That is, if someone challenges me as to why I think I have the right to rule over them, then saying that the matter over which I rule is very important and that I am very good at ruling is simply the wrong kind of answer. Granted, it has some plausibility in emergency situations, but it is less convincing for justifying a stable institution like the state or an international court over time. In such cases, there still is a normative gap that is not closed by pointing to the importance of the goals.[6]

What is the nature of the normative gap? If it is true that we are one another's equals, then subjecting some to the rule of others prima facie requires an explanation that refers to how the fundamental equality between agents is maintained even though some rule and others are ruled. The importance of goals and the efficiency of institutions do not give us such an explanation. Similarly, the fact that some institutions offer extraordinarily fair procedures does not give us an explanation of how equals remain equals although some rule and others are ruled. And neither does the fact that institutions close enforcement gaps. While the fairness of procedures is a necessary condition for the rightful authority of international courts, it is not sufficient. Institutions to which all are subject must treat their subjects not only fairly, but also in accordance with their status as equals. This then gives us *two* conditions that make

[6] At this point it becomes clear why Simmons is better off sticking to his 'Lockean guns': consent can fill the normative gap that opens once we ask ourselves why agent A may impose its authority over agent B: because B has consented to A's authority.

their authority legitimate: a requirement of (procedural) fairness and a requirement of non-subordination.

But is the subordination complaint really what is problematic about the authority claims of ICJ institutions? You might think that I have missed the target, so to speak, by focusing on the wrong 'grievance'. Thus, an objection could be this: the decision for one conception of just punishment is arbitrary. Accounts of international criminal law such as Song's, Luban's, and Wellman's ignore that beyond procedural fairness, there can be *disagreement* about the way in which these international law prohibitions are enforced.[7] Call this the disagreement complaint. I will discuss this objection and argue two things: first, that the disagreement complaint can be countered with a principle of subsidiarity; and second, that if we look closely, we will find that what makes disagreement a problem is not that people with different views about justice have a right that their preferred view about justice is realized, but that some views might not be treated with the same amount of consideration. This, however, only strengthens the argument I made earlier: because what is morally wrong with vigilante-like enforcement of punishment is that it prioritizes one view (that is, the vigilante's view) about criminal justice over the others. It constitutes an unequal distribution of the way in which differing views are taken into account when institutionalizing punishment. In other words: the disagreement complaint effectively collapses into the subordination complaint.

Suppose all agents have agreed in good faith that they want an international system of criminal law and that its aim shall be the prosecution and punishment of international crimes for the sake of enforcing fundamental human rights. Nevertheless, there is a plethora of institutional paths to how they can realize this aim. The duty to protect human rights is under-determined in terms of what system of rules we must adopt, even if we have agreed that a system of punishment is the right institutional means. Different institutions vary in terms of procedures, rules, definitions of elements of crimes, and other issues of institutional and procedural design. In other words, the argument that an institution with the aim of deterring crime through a system of criminal punishment is legitimate does not show why a specific institution with a specific set of rules can rightfully claim authority. States, as well as persons within them, disagree

[7] I have defended such a view in my earlier work (Müller 2019), but I am not convinced anymore that I got the problem right back then: I think my mistake was to think that disagreement is merely a practical problem that needs solving; now I believe that it is a symptom of a normative problem that is encapsulated by the subordination complaint.

when it comes to the definition of just punishment. Moreover, they do not only disagree, but their views about how to adjudicate crimes and how to punish and compensate are often incompatible.

Following Rawls, I assume that at least part of the disagreement is due to what Rawls calls 'the burdens of judgement'. The burdens of judgement explain the source of the disagreements without having to refer to explanations such as ignorance, egoism, or the relentless pursuit of status and power gains. Some of the disagreements can be explained by the fact that agents weigh considerations differently, even if they agree on the underlying values, that many concepts rely on judgement and interpretation when it comes to hard cases, that empirical evidence is sometimes complex, difficult to assess, and conflicting, and there is no straightforward correct side of the issue, and that our judgements depend on our subjective experience of the world, and that with different experiences comes different judgement (Rawls 2005, 56f). In Jeremy Waldron's words, the 'difficulty of the issues – and the multiplicity of intelligences and diversity of perspectives brought to bear on them – are sufficient to explain why reasonable people disagree' (Waldron 1999, 112 f).

Rawls thought that the subject of disagreement is comprehensive doctrines, that is, doctrines that cover the religious, philosophical, and moral aspects of human life (Rawls 2005, 59). But as Waldron argues, disagreement also applies to the realm of law. He argues that not only are comprehensive doctrines, that is, ideas about the good, subject to disagreement; but he emphasizes that people disagree about social justice and therefore on the justice of laws and rights (Waldron 1999, 10). Although Rawls acknowledges that social justice can be subject to reasonable disagreement, he spends too little time on this significant point, in Waldron's opinion. The authority of the law can therefore not be extracted from the theoretical justice of laws but depends on democratic legislation. And social justice does not only encompass distributive justice, but also encompass retributive or criminal justice. Persons, as well as states, have their own interpretation of what they take to be a just criminal justice system. Understandings of criminal justice are shaped by a variety of overlapping factors, and the political and moral culture of a group is certainly one of them. Hence, there is disagreement about what criminal justice requires – procedurally, as well as substantially. Not all opinions on what justice requires are acceptable. There are limits on the scope of disagreement to 'reasonable disagreement' about justice. Not every conceivable position is one that must be taken seriously. The first limit is that of human rights. It is evident that a position that views stoning as a proper punishment for *genocidaires* runs against the entire human-rights-based argument that buttresses the idea of ICJ, as I have portrayed it thus far. The second factor is what Rawls calls the definition of reasonableness. To be reasonable means to be proposing terms of cooperation that are justifiable to all who are part of the cooperation. This implies the idea of reciprocity and thus the idea that persons are not in principle ready to violate the terms of cooperation once it seems expedient to them or the circumstances make it possible (Rawls 2005, 50). Reasonable agents recognize 'the independent validity of the claims of others' (Rawls 2005, 52). To allow only reasonable disagreement thus implies a degree of impartiality or fairness.

Hence, is the problem with my imagined vigilante group a problem of disagreement, rather than one of subordination? Here are two replies, which show that disagreement about justice per se is not a particularly troubling moral problem for ICJ institutions. First, there exists an institutional mechanism that ensures that under normal circumstances, states get to use their own criminal justice system to punish perpetrators of international crimes: that is the principle of subsidiarity. In short, the argument is: if you do not agree with the way criminal justice is administered in international courts, or domestic courts acting under international law, then you are free to prosecute and punish international criminals yourself. It is only when states are unable or unwilling to prosecute their citizens that international courts or other states step in. In cases where justice is sought out in earnest, political subjects *will* be judged according to their communities' standard of criminal justice.

The second reply is this: surely it is true that each reasonable view about justice is owed some respect, and, as Waldron argues, respect has to do with 'how we treat each other's beliefs about justice in circumstances where none of them is self-certifying' (Waldron 1999, 111). If you find yourself under the coercive power of criminal prosecution, you should have had the opportunity to have a say in the question of what a just system would look like. But the reason why the disagreeing parties each deserve a measure of consideration is not that each party has a right to be treated in accordance with their preferences. When it comes to disagreements of the kind described above, we might say that one solution is as good as the other, as long as it achieves a reasonable threshold of fairness. The criminal certainly has no right to demand that they be punished according to their preferences. The point is that disagreements have normative purchase because each party deserves an equal measure of respect by virtue of their equal status.

But this now turns the complaint about disagreement into a complaint about being treated unequally, and this brings us back to the subordination complaint: because what you are really saying when you complain about the fact that your opinion is not being treated with respect is that you want it to be treated with equal respect because you have a claim to have it treated equally to everyone else's claim in this regard. And the wrong that is committed against you is that other views are given more consideration than yours, which makes it the case that you are put into a position of subordination.

How can institutions achieve treating their subjects as the equals that they are? We have already briefly encountered one option: subjects choose to confer authority to an institution by consenting to it. This is the traditional way Locke addresses the subordination complaint. But we also saw that consent, both in its simple and complex versions, is ultimately unsuitable for international institutions that coordinate morally mandatory aims. The second option addressing how institutions can treat their subjects as equals is by providing and fostering democratic institutional structures that allow each subject an equal opportunity of influence over their decision-making process. This implies that an adequate response to the subordination complaint gives us a reason to prefer *international* institutions to exercise ICJ.[8] Importantly, the reason

[8] Miriam Gur-Arye and Alon Harel make an argument that also points in an internationalist direction (Gur-Arye and Harel 2016). They argue that international criminal law is often mistakenly conceived as a means to overcome deficiencies in national legal systems. Instead, it is normatively more convincing to view international criminal law as necessarily international because the values it promotes can only be provided by an international court. That means that international criminal justice is only justified when it is administered by either international institutions or domestic courts that act as if they were international institutions. Their view is that 'the judgement that an act is a wrong against the international community must be made by the international community (given that no state can make authoritative determinations that bind other states or the entire international community)' (Gur-Arye and Harel 2016, 234). Making their case for what they call 'robust internationalism', Gur-Arye and Harel base their argument on the idea that only international institutions embody the expressive function of international criminal law because international criminal law is what they call an agent-dependent enterprise: that is, an enterprise (or practice) whose success depends on the agent performing it. As such, it depends on the international community as an agent to perform its function of expressing public condemnation for international crimes. Only an institution that is superior to the states has the moral standing to express this kind of public condemnation; states lack this moral standing and therefore cannot 'make authoritative determinations that bind other states' (Gur-Arye and Harel 2016, 234). I find their argument brilliant and compelling, but I am not entirely convinced. Gur-Arye and Harel argue that the problem that robust internationalism solves is that unilaterally

is not contingent on those institutions really being able to work more fairly, or efficiently. Instead, the reason is a principled one: because international institutions can offer institutional structures that give each subject a say in the decision-making process and therefore treat those subjected to them as equals. One important implication of the democratic view I defend in the following sections is that it thus excludes the practice of universal jurisdiction. This is because national courts are unable to offer institutional democratic decision-making structures that are open to all parties subject to the court. As the point of universal jurisdiction is that it gives national courts exercising universal jurisdictions the right to rule over non-citizens without offering them a say in the decision-making processes in the institution, it falls short of satisfying the condition of treating them as equals – on the contrary, it subordinates them.

5.3 Equality as Non-subordination

I argued that we require an international institution through which we exercise our natural right to punish in order to counter the subordination complaint. Where no authority is naturally higher than another, those who are being ruled, or judged, have a reason to complain. They may ask: by what right do *you* try me? As equals, no one has a greater claim to authority than another.

If this is plausible, the subordination complaint already tells us what we look for in an institution capable of countering the complaint. Its constitution must reflect the fact that its subjects are equals to one another in the relevant sense, which is that no one may be subordinated to another. The final step in my argument is thus to discuss in what sense the requirement of equality as non-subordination can be institutionally reflected, so that it effectively counters the complaint. The position I defend in the remainder of this chapter is that the value of equality as non-subordination is best reflected in institutionalized democratic decision-making procedures, because '[t]he concern for democracy is rooted in a concern not to have anyone else above – or, for that matter,

determined punishments fail to convey that expressive dimension. But why would that be the case? As long as domestic courts prosecute and punish only international crimes, the expressive function of their punishment seems to remain intact. Rather, what is problematic about unilaterally determined punishments is that they subordinate some who have a claim to stand as equals.

below – one' (Kolodny 2014b, 287f). That is not to claim that democratic decision-making procedures are sufficient for achieving equality as non-subordination: in fact, equalizing informal power and authority may be just as important, or even more important.[9] But in line with the scope of my argument as outlined in Chapter 1, I am interested in how ICJ institutions must be formally designed or set up when they exercise political authority over their subjects.

The main thought is this: insofar as subjects are equal to one another from a moral point of view, the prevention of unequal power relations that allow more powerful actors to subordinate less powerful actors is to be avoided. This can be achieved when all subjects under the rule of an institution have some sort of *equal democratic control* over the institution. Equal democratic control is necessary for an institution to have legitimate political authority. This view is defended by a number of people when it comes to state legitimacy (Pettit 2010, 145; Viehoff 2014; Christiano 2008). The conclusion of this chapter will be that if ICJ institutions are said to have authority – if they have the right to punish – then that authority must be democratic in nature.

This might sound surprising at first glance: is it not counterintuitive to defend a *democratic* principle for the authority of a *court*? After all, courts are supposed to be impartial, and especially trials must not be open to influence, independent of the fact that it is democratic or not. In a way, that is obviously true, and by invoking the democratic principle, I do not mean to argue for any kind of politicized trial or that judges should be political activists.[10] The trials should guarantee the highest degree of impartiality when it comes to the reconstruction of crimes or the determination of criminal responsibility. For all legal decisions, the judicial officials should act independently, with their only orientation being the law. Rather, I invoke the democratic principle by virtue of its role in the non-judicial elements of ICJ institutions, because '[a]ll international criminal courts and tribunals make law', as Gallant observes (Gallant 2013, 572). Some examples are the definitions of the Elements of Crimes, the procedural rights of the Prosecutor and the Defence, or the institutional design of the Court.

[9] See also Kolodny (2014b, 288). Insofar as wealth disparities translate into relations of subordination, the argument might also imply that the staggering global economic inequalities must be remedied to achieve equality as non-subordination.

[10] This seems to be Martti Koskenniemi's vision for international human rights courts (Koskenniemi 2006).

The argument in the remainder of this chapter proceeds in two steps: first, I elaborate on the meaning of equality as non-subordination and argue that equality as non-subordination can be achieved through an institution over which its subjects exercise equal control. In a second step, I argue that there are two ways to institutionalize equal control: first, by connecting the court with a legislative assembly which gives subjects equal opportunities of influence, and second, by incorporating democratic accountability principles directly into the workings of the court. Both ways are important and should ideally work in tandem for ICJ institutions. The point here is that subjects who exercise equal control over an institution have reasons to comply with the decisions of that institution. Why? Because complying with democratically made rules is a means to uphold equal relations – relations of non-subordination – between subjects under a democratic institution.

The fundamental idea of the justification of democratic principles for authoritative institutions is that it matters that we exercise equal control over our shared world (Christiano 2008, 247; Brighouse 1996, 119). Equal control applies to the structure and character of relationships.[11] The argument that it matters that we exercise equal control over our shared world is grounded in a variety of reasons: for example, it expresses the importance of treating persons with equal respect. Others express a similar idea negatively, by arguing that relations marked by unequal power distributions threaten the equality of control over our shared world (Viehoff 2014, 353).

What does it mean to exercise equal control? In the context of my argument, equal control applies to our common institutions. The thought is familiar from the context of the state: one aspect of how we exercise equal control over our shared world is by being afforded equal opportunities to exercise democratic control over the state. But what does democratic control mean? Philip Pettit distinguishes three models (Pettit 2008). The first model explicates the idea that people have *causal influence* on government. The second model explicates the idea that

[11] I am relying here on a version of equality that has been developed in contrast to the literature of luck egalitarianism, and that often goes by the name of social, democratic, or relational egalitarianism. See the works of Anderson (1999), Gosepath (2015), Kolodny (2014a; 2014b), Scheffler (2003; 2015), Schemmel (2021), Viehoff (2014; 2019), and Wolff (1998).

people have *intentional direction* over government. While the first model is not demanding enough, because it does not guarantee that the government is actually responsive to the influence (Pettit 2008, 47), the second model is too demanding because it is resisted by 'the difficulties presented by elites and by the recalcitrance of bureaucratic, military and economic life' (Pettit 2008, 49). Pettit favours a third model in which persons have *institutional control.* The institutional control model can be interpreted in two ways: either by interpreting control through the ideal of a market, or by interpreting it through the ideal of a community of condominium owners. It is this last interpretation that Pettit deems most adequate as a model for democratic control:

> the sort of association exemplified by the condominium, in which the owners of apartments in the same building combine to run their affairs after what will intuitively count as an acceptable manner. The condominium will not usually operate as an assembly but will elect a committee they are bound to have an influence on how their common affairs are pursued and under common or at least readily imaginable arrangements, they will have an influence that promotes a very specific target. The target is that of forcing the committee to act according to terms of reference endorsed by the members as a whole. (Pettit 2008, 52)

Democratic control thus does not mean that the institution's subjects *direct* the will of those in the institution, and neither does it mean that they merely have a theoretical possibility to influence the institution. Instead, subjects can exercise meaningful control over those who staff the institution. The terms of reference that Pettit speaks of in the quote above will likely be the exclusive promotion of the institutional goals (those goals that 'are important from all points of view' (Pettit 2008, 52) and that the institution is set up for in the first place) and the promise that the institution will listen to all subjects equally and select 'policies that deal fairly' with everyone (Pettit 2008, 52).

To be sure, this model of democratic control is distinct from the idea of individual or collective autonomy and can sometimes be in tension with it. The idea of democratic control does imply that the autonomy of subjects, understood as the freedom to act, can be restricted when others make a collective decision that happens to go against the interests of some of the subjects. A straightforward illustration is majority voting. The fact that the votes are distributed equally does not guard those states in the minority from having to act on or comply with the majority decision and therefore having to act against their judgement or interest. This is how a subject's freedom or autonomy is restricted by equality as equal control. A commitment to equality explains why subjects must in principle yield to majority decisions.[12]

The concept of democratic control also has another implication that leads to an objection. If the goal of democratic control is to achieve equality as non-subjection, and if this is more important than self-rule, then there might not be a reason, at least in principle, why we should not simply subject decisions to an impartial third party. Having no control is compatible with having equal control: when every subject has zero control, they can be said to enjoy an equal amount of control. Does that mean that the best way to achieve equality as non-subordination would be to avoid that subjects exercise *any* control over the institution, perhaps leaving decisions to a third party? In theory, this would be an option that is aligned with the idea of equal control. But as a practical option, it is not obvious who that impartial third party would be. Any global institution that would act as an impartial third party has to be financed and staffed with actual persons, who in turn are citizens of states. This would then simply take the problem up a notch: one might then say that those who have control over staffing and institutional design issues exercise control.

A second option in the same vein would be an impartial decision procedure, such as flipping a coin or having a lottery to make decisions. Such aleatoric procedures[13] satisfy the equality requirement for democratic control for the same reasons an impartial third party does: the procedure defies *any* control by the affected parties. Such procedures have several advantages, two of which are of special importance in the context of the problem we are concerned with. First, (unweighted) aleatoric procedures are strictly egalitarian. They enable an equal distribution of decisions through a randomized procedure. Second, they are a neutral decision procedure and an efficient decision procedure in the context of stalemate situations. If we think that there is no one right way to do something, then there is no reason to object to tossing dice (or a similar randomized procedure) to reach a decision. Since aleatoric procedures are strictly egalitarian, all participants have the same chance of having their proposal chosen.

[12] For a similar point, see Buchanan (2002, 714).

[13] Aleatoric approaches to procedural decision-making have a long history. The Greeks have used a lottery to distribute public offices in Athenian democracy. The United States uses a lottery system to appoint a jury in criminal trials. During World War II, some states used a randomized distribution for the military draft.

Yet, there are two reasons why we might not want to rely on aleatoric procedures, at least not exclusively and for all decisions. Note that both reasons rely on pragmatic rather than principled argument because it is simply true that if we care about equal control, flipping a coin is an option to be taken seriously. But here are the pragmatic problems: the first issue with pure aleatoric procedures is that before we 'flip the coin', we need to reach an agreement about what the reasonable or equally good options are, since they are usually not self-evident in political contexts. But what equally reasonable options are is itself often subject to disagreement. So there seems to be some deliberation necessary prior to subjecting decisions to aleatoric procedures, even if it is just for the purpose of structuring the 'menu of options'.[14] So even if we had decided to use aleatoric decision procedures, we somehow need to structure the options, and this process again should be guided by the principle of equal control. If some parties in the procedure have much more control over the structuring of options, we can hardly call the subsequent coin flipping democratic in the sense of equal control.

The second problem of the aleatoric proposal is that deliberations prior to majority voting often contribute to technical and practical knowledge because they usually involve an exchange of reasons, aiming at the rational persuasion of others. Political deliberation contributes to successful learning processes.[15] These two replies indicate that democratic voting procedures do have one advantage over aleatoric procedures: they filter out objectively better from worse options, potentially leading to the elimination of 'bad' options and generating practical knowledge that enhances efficiency and legitimacy. Of course, these replies do not show that aleatoric procedures should *never* substitute for voting procedures: in stalemate situations with truly equally good options, or when we need to appoint someone, flipping a coin is no worse idea – or could even be a better idea – than holding a vote. But this is also the reason why the justified use of aleatoric procedures is limited in political contexts.

I have been using the term 'subject' so far because one important issue remains unresolved until this point, namely the issue of who – or what – the subjects to the democratic authority of ICJ institutions are. David Luban argues that in the absence of a world government that could

[14] See also Gosepath (2004, 317f).

[15] Keep in mind that deliberations do not only have useful consequences but can also reproduce or magnify inequality.

potentially authorize ICJ institutions (Luban 2010, 579), an instrumental account (like his fairness account) is our best option for conceptualizing the political authority of ICJ. The ideal of a world government authorizing the prosecution and punishment of international crimes indicates why democratic decision-making is valuable: the thought seems to be that an authorization procedure through a world government is normatively valuable *because* it would give each person an equal opportunity to exercise control over the institution and its institutional decisions. But although a world government might be the most ideal institution to govern ICJ, there is de facto no world parliament that could facilitate democratic decision-making on the global level. International political agency is primarily exercised through states. But that of course does not lessen the importance of equality as non-subordination. Rather, it gives us a reason to favour alternative institutional arrangements that realize the value of equality as non-subordination best. In contrast to Luban, I argue that we do not have to give up the value of equality in the absence of a world government. Instead, we still try to realize this value in a different institutional arrangement: by establishing an international court with the institutional capacity to incorporate democratic decision-making procedures.

But can the value of equality as non-subordination really be transmitted onto and realized in structures between individuals, states, and international institutions? The problem I see is this: while humans are ultimate moral agents in their own right – they are self-authenticating sources of valid claims (Rawls 2005, 72) – states are political constructs that, as mere institutions, carry no comparable intrinsic moral value in their own right. Their moral value, *if* they can be said to have any at all, is entirely dependent on the moral value of the people that the state is made up of. It is to the *persons* within the state that non-subordination is owed. Is it plausible to say that the political societies those persons are part of – as institutionalized in states – are *also* owed equality as non-subordination?

Two main issues appear: first, treating states as if they were perfectly representative of their citizens is misleading because many states are de facto undemocratic and thus hardly representative of (all of) their citizens. Second, even democratic states are not unconditionally representative of (all of) their citizens. Recall Buchanan's and Keohane's argument about the bureaucratic distance between diplomatic representatives and their citizens: in modern states, citizens are in fact so far removed from the state agents that the impact of their will on state agents is nominal at best (Buchanan and Keohane 2006, 414f). Treating states' agency in analogy to the agency of persons disguises these important caveats.

But discounting the role of states in the formation of a political identity and hence in the formation of a political culture that finds expression in their diplomats seems equally implausible. Understanding states as meaningful agents in moral theory does not mean treating them *as if* they were persons. Views that mirror the moral value of persons and states are inadequate for the reasons stated above. If states are owed non-subordination, then *only* by virtue of their citizens.[16] Following Stilz, I understand democratic states to be capable of being moral agents (Stilz 2011). They do more than simply realize duties impartially; they interpret and specify those duties. Naturally, this argument only holds under the condition that individuals meaningfully participate in their political society. What this would mean in practice is a difficult question, for example in terms of a threshold. Surely, it must be shown that individuals somehow are the ultimate subjects of legitimation of the decision-making process. I do not want to discount the possibility that political societies that are not liberal parliamentary democracies can allow meaningful participation. However, *some* form of democratic participation seems to be a necessary condition for a state's moral agency.

Another response to the worry that ICJ institutions are too removed from the democratic control of individuals for their authority to count as democratic is to point to complementarity. The combination of the moral division of labour logic with the idea of the remedial function of international institutions I have argued for naturally yields a principle of complementarity for ICJ. Recall that the system of states is justified by the states' capacity to realize our cosmopolitan duties and that responsibility for them only falls on the international community when a state is unable or unwilling to realize them. The principle of complementarity describes the idea that the states have the primary responsibility to prosecute international crimes. Given the argument I made in Chapter 3, namely that normally states assume the primary function of enforcing and

[16] Whatever states are owed refers to their political project and not so much to their heritage or national way of life: those are matters that individuals will and do disagree about, and that maybe require toleration, but not necessarily respect. But if they have a genuine common political project that realizes a common interpretation of justice, at least to some extent, they are owed respect. This argument is based on the same idea we already encountered in Ladwig's moral path dependency argument in Chapter 3.

specifying human rights in a moral division of labour, we can understand ICJ institutions to be complementing state efforts in cases where they are not genuine or sufficient.[17] Such a principle of complementarity allows states – in line with the idea of the moral significance of path dependency – to choose their own means of dealing with atrocities.[18]

It is important to note that complementarity does not necessarily describe a relation between a state and a centralized international court, but also allows, and in fact encourages, experimentation. In the interest of faster trials that are closer to the communities that are victims of international crimes, the principle of complementarity enables a division of labour that evades a massive backlog of cases. Moreover, the principle of complementarity is not merely grounded in pragmatism. Legal structures of smaller political communities are better capable of being controlled by the citizens who are subject to them than an international court, not least because we have seen before that national parliaments have been reasonably successful in representing the citizens. This gives us a principled reason to prefer national prosecution over international prosecution. All of this only holds, of course, where there is a genuine effort to initiate and go through with the prosecution and punishment. The question of whether a state has done so – whether it has indeed been genuine in its effort to prosecute and punish perpetrators of international crimes – might again be subject to disagreement, but that is why ICJ institutions are the holders of the ultimate authority. While states have reason to grant each other a 'margin of appreciation' with the principle of complementarity, they might also have reasons for introducing rules for what counts as a genuine effort at prosecuting international crimes.

[17] The first Prosecutor of the International Criminal Court (ICC), Luis Moreno-Ocampo, puts it like this: 'As a consequence of complementarity, the number of cases that reach the Court should not be a measure of its efficiency. On the contrary, the absence of trials before this Court, as a consequence of the regular functioning of national institutions, would be a major success.' Luis Moreno-Ocampo at the ceremony of his inauguration in the Peace Palace in The Hague, 16 June 2003. See www.iccnow.org/documents/MorenoOcampo16June03.pdf.

[18] For example, Philip Pettit proposes a procedure in which those responsible for crimes plead guilty and decide, together with the victims or their families, on the appropriate restorative measures instead of a criminal trial (Pettit 2014, 150). Examples from the real world are South Africa's Truth and Reconciliation Commission that was set up after the end of apartheid, or the Gacaca Court System in Rwanda after the genocide. Pettit makes the proposal in the context of non-ideal political circumstances, that is, contexts in which the circumstances of criminal justice are not satisfied.

5.4 Democratic Control, Equal Opportunity to Influence, and Accountability

How do we translate – or rather institutionalize – the value of equality as non-subordination into ICJ institutions? The ultimate sources of the institution's democratic authority are individuals, but states play an intermediary role and, given they are adequately representative of their citizens, can send deputies or proxies who represent the political project of the community that makes up the state. There are several ways in which ICJ institutions can be made to be under the democratic control of their subjects, and I discuss them in this section. Keep in mind that none of those options are *intrinsically* valuable; they are justified by virtue of their capacity to realize the value of equality as non-subordination. Therefore, it is reasonable to support each of those options insofar as they in fact help realize the value of non-subordination. Before I discuss the ways in which ICJ institutions can be made to be under the democratic control of their subjects, I will comment on three questions we need to get clarity on before we continue.

The first question we need to tackle here is: when we talk about democratic decisions, to what questions and decisions do they apply? What are the questions that are to be influenced politically in the context of an international criminal court? Here are some examples of possible legislative issues: How are the crimes defined? What actions fall under a definition of a crime?[19] How are the punishments determined? What punishments fit what crime? When are prison sentences appropriate, and how long should they be for each crime? Is there the option for parole? What should count as extenuating circumstances?[20] How are the victims compensated? What are the minimum and maximum of victim

[19] Take the example of sexual violence, a crime that has long not been recognized as a violent crime. Only during the International Criminal Tribunal for the Former Yugoslavia (ICTY) tenure has rape been recognized as a war crime, detailing the instances of what constitutes sexual violence, including the formerly ignored sexual mutilation or forced nudity.

[20] Take the example of the Erdemović case at the ICTY. Dražen Erdemović pleaded guilty for crimes against humanity, but cited physical and moral duress stemming from his military superiors. In the different legal systems, there are different provisions of how to deal with duress. According to Gur-Arye and Harel, most common law jurisdictions do not accept duress as a complete excuse when the defendant kills innocents in order to save his own life. Civil law jurisdictions, however, do regard duress as a complete excuse in such cases (Gur-Arye and Harel 2016). The Appeal Chamber of the ICTY ruled that duress is not a complete excuse.

compensation and how is compensation to be distributed? Under what circumstances and in what form do victims receive compensation? What is the extent to which monetary damages can be imposed?[21]

Beyond the potential disagreement about these substantive questions, people might also disagree about the design of the institutions that produces law. Rawls observes that 'a citizen must decide which constitutional arrangements are just for reconciling conflicting opinions of justice. We may think of the political process as a machine which makes social decisions .... A citizen will regard some ways of designing this machine as more just than others' (Rawls 1999, 171f). Rawls's argument is equally true for institutions such as courts. The way in which a decision-making process is institutionalized – that is, how the process is institutionally designed – makes a difference to the outcome. This means that agents may not only disagree about the justice of the policies and laws, but also on the justice of the decision-making process that leads to the legislation and application of these laws. A few examples are the distribution and the extent of the powers of the prosecutor and pre-trial chambers, the procedures of victim compensation, the extent to which the victims are involved in the court, and the standards of evidence. What are the procedures to initiate or dismiss an investigation? How is the role of the prosecutor defined and what kinds of powers do they have?[22] For example, Gallant argues that the ICC has a democratic deficit

[21] See Morris for more specific examples (Morris 2002, 597).

[22] One might argue that the decision whether to use the civil law tradition or the common law tradition is fundamental and will yield many practical differences. Consider the example of the introduction of evidence. In civil law, all evidence and witnesses will have to be introduced before the trial actually begins. The reason for this provision is that there are no surprise witnesses or evidences during the trial; this way, counsels cannot just introduce new evidence without giving the defendants enough time to review the evidence. The disadvantage is that if new evidence is discovered during the trial, even if it is crucial, there is almost no chance that either of the parties can use it for their position. In Anglo-Saxon law, however, new witnesses and evidence can be introduced during the trial. The advantage is obviously that once new evidence turns up during the trial, it can be considered for the case. The disadvantage is that the opposing party has no preparation time. Another example is the role of the judge during the trial. In the civil law tradition, the judge has a more prominent role: for example, they frequently question witnesses. In contrast to that, the common law tradition is characterized by cross-examination by the legal counsels. Another very prominent difference is the existence or absence of a civil jury in common law traditions, respectively in civil law traditions. Should there be a jury and, if yes, what role should it have during the trials? Then there are questions about the appointment procedures and terms of officials of the court. How many judges should there be and how are they appointed? Should a quota system be

insofar as it excludes the defence systematically from the lawmaking process because only the prosecution, a state party, or the judges may propose changes to the regulations of the court (Gallant 2013, 579).[23]

The second question is about the forum in which such questions of ICJ, its application, and the institutional design of the institutions exercising ICJ are deliberated and decided on. Such lawmaking does not necessarily have to happen in a world parliament. Rather, a legislative assembly can be formed with the limited assignment of making law only for the policy area of international crimes and punishment.[24] Here, I am taking inspiration from Reidar Maliks, who argues for a legislative assembly for international human rights courts based on Kantian theory. He claims that courts themselves do not have to be democratic because judges are supposed to apply the law, not make it. However, because international human rights law is ambiguous and needs to be dynamically developed, the 'solution, on the Kantian view is to develop international lawmaking institutions to match the courts, thereby decreasing the likelihood of a situation where courts faced with entrenched law cross the line from application to legislation' (Maliks 2013, 168). Since, as I argued earlier, the authority of ICJ institutions extends to all states irrespective of their consent, participation in the legislative assembly must in principle be open and offered to all.[25] One caveat of a state's participation might be that, as I argued in reference to Stilz's theory

used? Should there be an election? How long are the terms? What kind of qualification must they possess?

23 See also Kenneth Gallant's illuminating chapter on how to remedy this democratic deficit (Gallant 2013).

24 This idea builds on the existing assembly of state parties (ASP or 'Assembly') that is part of the ICC. Meeting once a year, the Rome Statute gives them the following functions: '(a) consider and adopt, as appropriate, recommendations of the Preparatory Commission; (b) provide management oversight to the Presidency, the Prosecutor and the Registrar regarding the administration of the Court; (c) consider the reports and activities of the Bureau of the ASP . . . and take appropriate action; (d) consider and decide the budget for the Court; (e) decide whether to alter, in accordance with the Statute's provision on the nomination, qualifications and elections of judges, the number of judges; (f) consider any question of the non-cooperation of State Parties with the Court; and (g) perform any other function consistent with the Statutes of the Rules of Procedure and Evidence.' See the Coalition for the International Criminal Court's website, URL: www.iccnow.org/?mod=asp.

25 Madeline Morris argues that '[t]he offer to non-party states cannot be: you enter into this new, majority-rule form of decision making with us – or, if you do not, then we will simply govern you without your consent or representation' (Morris 2002, 599). But this is precisely what my argument implies, and I hope I have shown why that should indeed be the offer to non-party states when it comes to morally mandatory aims.

earlier, they can be plausibly conceived of as representative of their states.[26]

Finally, I want to address a view that is sceptical of the idea that international institutions can be the locus for a democratic ideal at all. Robert Dahl worries that reality does not conform to the ideal world that supranational democracy theorists often describe, and believes that 'we should openly recognize that international decision-making will not be democratic' (Dahl 1999, 23). He argues that international institutions are not loci of democratic procedures, but of bureaucratic bargaining. Dahl's main worry seems to be the degree to which effective control is delegated by citizens to international policy elites (Dahl 1999, 32). The plausibility of his argument depends on what conception of democracy one thinks is relevant in this context. Not surprisingly, Dahl's conception is rather demanding, taking as its model a deliberative parliamentary interpretation of democracy.

I have two replies to Dahl's worry: first, recall Pettit's (2008) three ways in which citizens can exercise democratic control earlier in the chapter. There, we have already seen that democracy does not necessarily imply that individuals are the direct source of democratic decisions. In fact, in some contexts it is not even normatively desirable that they are, as is the case with the problem of outrage dynamics in the context of criminal legislation (Pettit 2002). Second, there is empirical evidence that the international sphere can be, and has been, the locus of normative argument and persuasion, rather than bureaucratic bargaining. For example, Thomas Risse shows that in world politics,

> processes of argumentation, deliberation, and persuasion constitute a distinct mode of social interaction to be differentiated from both strategic bargaining – the realm of rational choice – and rule-guided behaviour – the realm of sociological institutionalism. . . . human actors engage in truth seeking with the aim of reaching a mutual understanding based on a reasoned consensus (verständigungsorientiertes Handeln), challenging the validity claims involved in any communication. (Risse 2000, 1f)

Another example is offered by Nicole Deitelhoff, who shows how this was the case in the Rome negotiations that ultimately led to the establishment of the ICC (Deitelhoff 2009).

[26] Jamie Mayerfeld similarly argues that an ICC with only democratic states as members is better than an ICC 'flooded' with violent dictatorships (Mayerfeld 2004). He observes that little attention has been paid to how the ICC improves democracy at the national level by 'working through national institutions and reorienting those institutions in a democratic direction' (Mayerfeld 2004, 147).

A second issue Dahl worries about is the lack of a global demos. This leads to the impossibility of truly legitimate and efficient institutions that organize transnational cooperation. Against this view, Christian List and Mathias Koenig-Archibugi contend that the political procedure leading to the establishment of the ICC is an example for the argument that when an issue is perceived as affecting the international community as a whole, a kind of global demos that reaches decision by 'democratic' deliberation, rather than bureaucratic bargaining, is conceptually and empirically possible (List and Koenig-Archibugi 2010, 104ff).

I have argued earlier that non-subordination can be realized institutionally when subjects liable to the authority of an institution are able to exercise democratic control over the institution and when they can do so equally. It is important to note here that the mere fact that I am subject to democratic decisions is not a sign of me being subordinated, insofar as I can exercise democratic control that is equal to everyone else's.[27] Kolodny argues that an important component of relations of social equality is that individuals 'enjoy equal opportunities for influence over the political decisions to which they are subject' (Kolodny 2014b, 308). Disregarding democratically made decisions then means that I am 'depriving others of equal opportunity to influence this very decision', therefore 'relating to them as a social superior, at least in this instance' (Kolodny 2014b, 315). The reason for this is that I therefore take my own vote to be more important than someone else's, and that is a sign of subordination. Equal control can thus be achieved, among other ways that I turn to later in this section, by giving each subject an equal opportunity for political influence.[28]

Equal opportunity for influence is best interpreted as equal opportunity for *contributory*, rather than *decisive* influence[29] (Kolodny 2014b,

[27] See also Kolodny (2014b, 316). Note that Kolodny speaks of 'having power over' rather than 'having democratic control over'. As far as I understand Kolodny's view, the two concepts only differ in nuance.

[28] Harry Brighouse defends a similar principle, the principle of equal availability of political influence (EAPI): 'The amount of influence available to them is given by the probability we would assign to their getting their way . . .. EAPI is realised when equal means to affect the collective conditions of their shared social life are available to each citizen.' (Brighouse 1996, 119).

[29] To fill out this interpretation of contributory influence in more detail, Kolodny writes: 'by X-ing, I exercise equal contributory influence over a decision just when my X-ing *has equal a priori chances of being decisive over the decision*, that is, has equal chances of being decisive on the assumption that no pattern of X-ing by others is more likely than any other pattern' (Kolodny 2014b, 320f).

320). As such, it is, so Kolodny argues, characterized by five properties: first, having influence means that political decisions are sensitive to one's choices, but need not be in correspondence with those choices in the end. Second, having no influence over a political decision is not a problem per se; it is only a concern if *others have* influence, that is: if the influence is unequally distributed. Third, the value of influence does not lie in its exercise, but merely in having an *opportunity* to exercise it. A choice not to exercise the opportunity is not of moral concern, at least not for equality as non-subordination. Fourth, the influence subjects have an equal opportunity of should be equally *informed* influence if it is to evade power imbalances. And finally, fifth, not only should it be equally informed influence, but also equally *autonomous* influence, so as to avoid manipulation (Kolodny 2014b, 309f).

How do institutions ensure that each subject has an equal opportunity to influence decisions within that institution? As Kolodny argues, this need not suggest direct democratic procedures, like referenda, at all (Kolodny 2014b, 317). Instead, there are other ways of democratic decision-making aligned with the idea of equal opportunity for influence. Political representation is likely the most important avenue for ensuring equal influence on an institution. Delegating certain powers to a representative who then acts as an agent for the citizens does not imply any relation of subordination (Kolodny 2014b, 318), at least if it is the case that certain conditions that secure that the agent in fact acts in the interest, and on behalf, of the 'principal' are satisfied.[30]

Representation, in particular in parliaments, has been extraordinarily successful in establishing stable and reasonably democratic institutions. Beyond the state there are two avenues to political representation: the first is direct representation of individuals, where representatives would be elected directly by individuals and without an intermediary agent like a government. One could imagine a global campaign for the election of representatives into a legislative assembly of an ICJ institution. The second avenue to political representation beyond the state is indirect representation of individuals through representatives of their states, where an elected government appoints those representatives. This would be the more familiar process of an elected president, chancellor, or prime minister selecting an individual (or several individuals) who represent

[30] See Kolodny (2014b, 318) for a list and a specification of what conditions must be satisfied so that the delegation of power is not an instance of subordination.

the elected government within the legislative assembly of an ICJ institution.

At first glance, direct parliamentary representation of individuals seems superior in terms of its democratic credentials. But there are three reasons speaking against individual parliamentary representation. The first one is presented by Philip Pettit. He argues that criminal law legislation is regularly driven by an 'outrage dynamic' that explains a number of persistent features of criminal law politics, for example why heavy sentencing is so resilient (Pettit 2002). To be 'tough on crime' pays well with voters but rarely leads to reasonable criminal law. The main reason he identifies as working in favour of this dynamic is the combination of a sensationalist media and the sporadic occurrence of terrible crimes. How far is this dynamic at work in the context of ICJ? This is inevitably speculative, but it is certainly true that international crimes are particularly outrageous; this point needs no labouring. It is also true that indignation about the crimes seems to be amplified when the defendant is not perceived as 'one of us': the 'us' being a national community, or even the 'community of moral people'. But Pettit argues that 'few of us would want the criminal justice system to be shaped by the outrage dynamic' because the only thing it surely does is to satiate those who think of the criminal law mainly as an avenger. Those who are concerned about the degree and kind of the punishment, or the relative levels of punishment that are allocated across crimes, or of the effects of the punishment on defendant and victim – and here we can add concerns about reconciliation and democratization in war-torn and post-atrocity regions – have a good reason to evade the outrage dynamic that leads to unreasonable legislation (Pettit 2002, 440). All of this at least supports the assumption that the outrage dynamic would be reproduced within an institution that features representatives directly elected by individuals.

The outrage dynamic is a problem caused by the specific features of the kind of wrongdoing that the criminal law is supposed to regulate. But there are other, more general problems of representation of individuals that presumably apply to legislation in ICJ institutions too. One of them is a problem of representation that Christiano calls the problem of persistent minorities (Christiano 2008, 288ff). The problem of persistent minorities is that 'the minority rarely gets its way on any of the properties of the common world it shares with the majority' (Christiano 2008, 290). It is important to understand that the problem of persistent minorities does not arise out of dysfunctional democratic institutions, but may well appear within democratic institutions that function reasonably well, or even quite well. It simply is a structural problem that comes with democratic decision-making procedures, especially majority voting. Christiano argues that while this is already a problem that undercuts institutional authority with respect to minorities in the case of *state* authority, it would be even more problematic in an institution with a significantly larger constituency, because '(t)he larger the constituency, the larger the chances are that particular minorities would simply get lost in the democratic decision-making' (Christiano 2011, 76). Whether this problem would factually apply to decision-making in ICJ institutions is not entirely obvious. But we can at least imagine that it does: for example, there could be a group whose interests are not substantially represented. They might have an interest that ICJ institutions recognize a special crime that is of importance to them and that has not been recognized yet. Having no representation in the assembly because of their status as a persistent minority, the institution fails to enable the opportunity for equal influence for every subject.

Finally, a third problem might be caused by the large-scale application of democratic procedures that usually work reasonably well for a smaller-scope democracy. Christiano argues that the democratic quality of parliamentary representative democracy within states has not been reproduced beyond the state, and it is unlikely that this will happen anytime soon. The main reason for this, he thinks, is that the global civil society – if we can say that it exists in the first place – is incomparable to the civil society that exists in a reasonably well-ordered state; the former is less dense than the latter (Christiano 2010, 134). This last problem might again compel us to prefer indirect representation of individuals through representatives of their elected governments: it is precisely the unmatched quality of parliamentary democracy within states that serves as a reason to tie supranational democratic procedures to national democratic procedures.[31]

How can the other two problems I outlined above – the outrage dynamic problem and the problem of persistent minorities – be countered? It is important to be aware of such problems, and there are ways in which international institutions can mitigate them. While there may be no definitive procedure that solves these problems, taking them into account and trying to mitigate them institutionally we can minimize their acuteness. In response to the outrage dynamic problem, Pettit offers

[31] See also von Bogdandy and Venzke (2014, 201).

a mitigation proposal for the domestic sphere that works for international institutions too and that, again, speaks in favour of indirect representation. He argues in favour of creating a democratic body that operates 'at arm's length' from parliament, but stands under their control, consisting of parliamentary-appointed experts. Such a penal board or commission helps to keep in check the consequences of the outrage dynamic since it does not face the same pressures as democratically elected representatives, who often seek re-election. A penal board or commission can therefore operate more independently. It can be sent to represent states or other entities that might require special representation within the legislative assembly of the ICJ institution. To worries that such a penal board or committee is democratically unacceptable, Pettit replies that there are two desiderata, of which only one is desirable in the name of democracy. It is the desideratum that the electorate should be the ultimate arbiter of policy and therefore have the ultimate power. The second – questionable – desideratum is that the electorate should be the proximate source of policy (Pettit 2002, 448). It would be nothing short of 'rank populism', Pettit argues, to think that democracy is only satisfied when the electorate is the proximate source of policy. A penal board that operates close to and is controlled by an elected parliament fulfils the reasonable desideratum that the electorate is the ultimate arbiter of policy. Similarly, in reference to the persistent minority problem, a system that includes representatives of such minorities in the legislative assembly, perhaps elected by and organized in interest groups, might be created. This is to make sure the minority is not substantially disadvantaged in the democratic process. However, even though the existence of persistent minorities might produce substantially worse outcomes for those minorities, which is a problem in itself, it is not accurate to claim that they do not enjoy equal opportunities for influence. Kolodny shows that almost no one is ever electorally decisive, so that it does not matter for one's influence whether one is in the majority or in the minority (Kolodny 2014b, 328).

These arguments speak in favour of indirect representation of individuals through their states, and their elected or appointed representatives. In combination with my claim that the scope of the ICJ institutions' legitimate authority is global,[32] the implication is that every state has a claim to equal democratic control of ICJ institutions. To be fair, it could

[32] The scope of the existing ICC is also global in a sense, but only through the intermediary power of the Security Council. The Security Council can refer a situation to the ICC, and it then falls under its jurisdiction. The democratic deficit and the effectiveness problems

be objected that it is utopian to think that states will join those legislative assemblies, as joining implies a deep limitation of their sovereignty. But this objection overlooks both that many states have already joined such institutions[33] and that the limits on the sovereignty cannot be evaded by simply refusing to *make use* of one's equal opportunity for influence. The limits that ICJ institutions impose on state sovereignty do not depend on the will of states, but on their duty to protect human rights by creating a criminal justice system that deters mass human rights violations. The decision states can make in the face of this is merely whether they choose to have some degree of control over the content of these limits (Maliks 2013, 168f).

Now we have an idea of how to connect national parliaments and persistent minorities through representatives and penal commissions to the legislative assembly. The next question is how the idea of equal control can be realized *in the workings* of the legislative assembly. In practice, the idea of political representation points to either state unanimity or state majoritarian voting procedures. Majoritarianism is compatible with equal control because equal control is not outcome-oriented, but applies to the relationship that subjects find themselves in. A subject can be overruled, but nevertheless have equal control over an institution.[34] This might sound counterintuitive but consider this analogy. Anna, Betty, and Christina are deciding what to do on a Saturday night. There are two options, and after deliberation, they hold a vote. Christina is outvoted. Does she have less control over where to go on

of the Security Council are well known and need no repeating here. There is no principled argument that could possibly support the power of an unelected body of five states to refer or veto the jurisdiction of an international criminal court. The power to decide what situation warrants prosecutorial attention should be, I believe, entirely in the hand of the court, that is, the prosecutor and the judges. Only then can the court operate independently. However, I am also aware that this might not be possible in the near future, so there might be pragmatic reasons to leave the Security Council as an intermediary between non-member states and the ICC.

33 One hundred and twenty-four states have joined the ICC. For a comprehensive study that seeks to explain why states have joined an international court that severely curtails their sovereignty and therefore seemingly acts against their own interest, see the work of Deitelhoff (2009).

34 For a more complex elaboration of this argument in the context of equal opportunities for influence, see Kolodny's discussion (Kolodny 2014b, 320ff). The only exception might be if one agent is constantly overruled, as is the case when that agent is part of a persistent minority as I have discussed above. For a discussion on why the persistent minority problem is not as virulent for equality as non-subordination, also see Kolodny (2014b, 326f).

Saturday night? Presumably not: her being outvoted does not indicate that she had less control than Anna and Betty, illustrating the point that the criterion of equal control does not apply to outcomes.

But why not use the principle of unanimous state consent? This decision procedure does exist in international institutions. Think of how the Security Council works: decisions can only be made when all parties agree, or, for that matter, when many parties agree and the rest abstain from voting. The practical problems with such a procedure are painfully demonstrated each time there is a decision to be made that can be interpreted by some members of the Security Council as going against their perceived economic, security, or ideological interests. Once we accept the idea that international institutions must incorporate democratic procedures and that they must incorporate representatives of groups, the reason for choosing majoritarianism over unanimous consent is that unanimous consent renders any procedural progress difficult, if not impossible. In that context, unanimity as a standard for the democratic authority of institutional decisions would lead to paralysis – and any democratic institution needs to have some degree of effectiveness to function at all.

Allen Buchanan argues that the appeal of state majoritarianism lies in the idea that some states are more powerful and dominate weaker states and that majority voting ensures that all states are given an equal voice, regardless of their relative power position (Buchanan 2004, 197). But he notes that he, for one, 'would be much more comfortable if the members of the European Union had the power to determine the character of international law than if the UN General Assembly did' (Buchanan 2004, 197). The reason for this is that Buchanan thinks that democratic majoritarianism in general is supported by two arguments: first, it expresses equality for individuals, and second, democratic majoritarianism secures the protection of human rights. But Buchanan rejects that these reasons in fact support *state* majoritarianism. The idea that state majoritarianism expresses equality for individuals requires an implausible premise. The argument would only be successful if one could show that states' having an equal say in international lawmaking somehow produces equal consideration for individuals (Buchanan 2004, 199). But this premise is implausible, Buchanan argues, once one disregards nationalist fantasies about the identity of persons with their states. As to the second justification, Buchanan argues that the thought that state majoritarianism is the most reliable mechanism for protecting human rights is mistaken. In fact, it could well be that state majoritarianism *inhibits* progress in terms of international human rights protection. One can presume that whether state majoritarianism improves the protection of human rights in general is dependent on how committed the majority of states are to human rights (Buchanan 2004, 197f).

I am sympathetic to both worries: emphasizing that the ultimate subjects of democratic equality must always be individuals, and not states, is important. But his first objection distorts the complex nature of the relationship between individuals and the international equality of their political communities. It is possible to tie in respect for individuals with the idea of state representatives in international legislative assemblies. At the same time, it is obvious that strengthening the idea of democratic control over ICJ institutions implies that the internal democratization of states whose representatives are given an equal opportunity to influence politics in the legislative assembly is strongly desired. As I argued earlier, without some degree of democratic representation of individuals within the state, there is less of a moral reason that states should be granted a vote in majoritarian decision-making. Only if states themselves are democratic and reasonably representative of their people's interests will majority voting for state representatives make sense. There surely is no normative point in giving dictators more of a say in institutional contexts. But as Pettit has shown, the idea that the people must be the *direct* source of policy if representation of interests in deliberations about criminal law and punishment is to be taken seriously is also misleading (Pettit 2002; 2008). I do think that the link to national parliaments nevertheless implies that the democratization of states is a desirable aim for the democratic process at the ICJ institutions. Given how complicated and fragile processes of democratization are, other agents may merely encourage, but not enforce it. The dilemma certainly is: who decides who represents the interests of their constituents well enough? Who has sufficient democratic credentials? Who is entitled to make that call? I think that any active role that the ICJ institution itself can play in this context is limited.

Buchanan's second objection is that majoritarian democratic procedures are justified by their likelihood of securing human rights. But while human rights protection is certainly important, it is neither theoretically nor empirically the best argument for state majoritarianism. As I have shown in Chapters 3 and 4, basic human rights and the duty to protect them are the reason why we have coercive institutions in the first place. But even if it was true that majoritarian voting is generally reliable in protecting human rights – which is not at all obvious, as one can imagine a benevolent dictator who delivers much better rights protection as the majority[35]– it does not follow that those subjects must comply with the decision or can even be coerced because of a majority's decision. In a similar context, Kolodny calls this the Bridging Problem: if someone was able to bring about better rights protection by going *against* the majoritarian decision, why would they be bound not to do it (Kolodny 2014b, 291)? Presumably not because majoritarian decision-making secures human rights. Hence, justifying majoritarian voting procedures through their ability to protect human rights is unconvincing. And neither is it clear that it is the best case for majority voting empirically. Consider the case of democratic states, in which significant advances for rights protection have often been promoted by courts and held against the majority.[36] In summary, I doubt that majoritarianism can be plausibly justified in reference to better rights protection.

But what if majoritarianism does not improve human rights protection, but actively inhibits it? This is the crucial question in another variation of the argument that Buchanan advances against the importance of democratic equality between states. He argues that it is at least not obvious that the current inequality of states is really morally arbitrary. Perhaps the inequality between states can be justified if it results in moral progress – raising the human rights standards – in a 'deeply defective system' (Buchanan 2004, 199). This argument is a variation of the earlier claim that state majoritarianism does not improve respect for human rights. Perhaps *inequality* between states actually *advances* respect for human rights. Giving human-rights-violating states an equal measure of control might lead to a human-rights-undermining majority that blocks human-rights-friendly legislation. Giving states *equal* control over institutions might then actually *inhibit* human rights progress while state *inequality* can be expected to be *conducive* to progressive human rights policy.

Whether state majoritarianism hinders human rights protection can only be proven by empirical analysis, and as far as I am aware of the literature, there is no evidence as to whether and how state inequality improves human rights. But there are ways to design institutions that make it less likely that majoritarian decision-making procedures hinder

[35] For a similar argument, see Kolodny (2014b, 291).

[36] This seems to be true of several landmark decisions by the US Supreme Court, for example *Brown* v. *Board of Education*.

human rights protection: for example, by tying majoritarian procedures in with a constitution, or by limiting the scope of what can be decided by a majority. Apart from that, it sometimes works to include states that are human rights unfriendly in global human rights policy issues. With several case studies, Risse, Ropp, and Sikkink show that paradoxically, states sometimes end up in a 'human rights spiral': although they intend their superficial commitment to human rights – mere 'lip service' – to be only a tactical concession to domestic and international pressure to improve their record on human rights, they often end up *actually* improving their record on human rights (Risse et al. 1999).

To summarize the discussion: majoritarian voting procedures are an adequate way to ensure that states exercise equal control over ICJ institutions. They do not, however, necessarily ensure that *individuals* exercise equal control over ICJ institutions unless their states are reasonably democratic. To reiterate: the place of majoritarian voting is in the legislative assembly, not the trial. What evidence is admitted, whether the defendant is guilty, and which witnesses may be called are not matters state representatives can vote on during the trial. The trial is impartial, and as such, it is the prerogative of the judges and officials applying law.

But perhaps legislative assemblies are not even the only places in which lawmaking by representatives takes place. Like Gallant (2013, 572), Armin von Bogdandy and Ingo Venzke argue that international courts are mischaracterized when their function is merely viewed as the discovery of predetermined law, rather than the making of law (Bogdandy and Venzke 2014). We have encountered this idea already in Locke: enforcing the law means applying the law; and when law is applied, problems of interpretation appear. Ideally, problems of interpretation are solved by democratic legislation, one which gives the subjects an equal opportunity to influence the institution, and therefore, they exercise democratic control over it.

But realistically, judges inevitably contribute to developing the laws too. The cognitive paradigm – the view that law is discovered by courts, rather than made or developed by them – is an untenable position, not least because the vagueness of much international law compels judges to evaluate and interpret, rather than merely apply a norm. This is specifically observable in cases where courts interpret terms such as 'adequate', 'necessary', 'proportional', or 'appropriate'. But beyond the – often extensive – scope of interpretation of those standards, judgments themselves can be utilized as an argument within the legal argumentation of another case. Earlier judgments coin the future development of law significantly, and even more so when there is no legislative body that develops statutes. Past judgments generate legal normativity – and hence make or develop, rather than 'discover law' (Bogdandy and Venzke 2014, 136ff).

Whatever one thinks of the desirability of this kind of generation of legal normativity, Bogdandy and Venzke argue that it is inevitable. Of course, one of the reasons why this kind of judicial lawmaking is especially prominent in international law is that international courts are only loosely, and sometimes not at all, connected to legislative bodies. That does not mean that in international law, courts fully absorb the function of the political lawmaker. There are significant differences: legislative assemblies enjoy a much greater scope of liberty and creativity when it comes to law, whereas judicial lawmaking is more limited. Judicial lawmaking is best described with the term 'legal development' because it continually refers to past legal and judicial decisions. Judges have to consider that their judgment in turn will be used for future judgments (Bogdandy and Venzke 2014, 147ff; Schauer 1987). Bogdandy and Venzke argue that unlike political lawmaking, judicial lawmaking does not solely depend on *voluntas*, but also on *ratio* (Bogdandy and Venzke 2014, 147).

In the end, it seems that we must accept the fact that judicial lawmaking inevitably exists. Bogdandy and Venzke embrace this empirical fact and encourage that judicial lawmaking should be made more democratic or at least more democratically accountable. In a sense, I agree with them there. *Where* judicial lawmaking is inevitable, we should encourage mechanisms that facilitate its democratic accountability. But on the other hand, judicial lawmaking can be reduced by empowering *political* lawmaking. This is the position that Reidar Maliks defends: instead of embracing judicial lawmaking, he argues for a closer relation of international courts with legislative bodies (Maliks 2013). Even so, perhaps we need to recognize that judicial lawmaking can never be (fully) eliminated, but only fenced by specifying the law in legislative assemblies.

Beyond political representation in legislative assemblies and judicial lawmaking, Bogdandy and Venzke argue that courts can 'earn' their democratic legitimacy by using strategies such as transparency, victim participation, and dialogue (Bogdandy and Venzke 2014, 210). The main function of accountability principles is not to make courts more democratic in the representative sense, but to prevent courts from overstepping the boundaries of their judicial function, make sure they function properly, and take everyone's interests into account as best as they can. The notion of accountability is not independent of the notion of democratic representation. Iris Marion Young argues that representation is best understood as a dynamic relationship between authorization and accountability (Young 2010, 129). In this study, the authorization part takes the form of majoritarian voting among representatives of states, as I have developed it earlier in this chapter. The mechanism of accountability then complements this authorization mechanism, therefore adding another dimension to representation. Often, Young argues, the moment of being held accountable is when a representative is re-elected (Young 2010, 132). This mechanism is accountability by re-authorization. But the compulsions of re-election and the technical nature of the questions might be detrimental to the quality of governing specifically in matters of punishment. I have argued that appointments of delegates or penal commissions might better serve the requirements of legislating international criminal law.

But re-authorization by re-election is not the only accountability mechanism. Bogdandy and Venzke argue that there are several means that can increase the courts' democratic accountability vis-à-vis individuals. The key to these means are transparency, publicity, and deliberation and dialogue (Bogdandy and Venzke 2014, 210). A prior condition for activating these three modes of accountability is then an increased politicization (Bogdandy and Venzke 2014, 154).[37] Politicization is a term that describes the transportation of a previously unpolitical matter into the field of politics. The facilitation of social awareness of international institutions, its discussion within a political context, and the mobilization of demands, judgements, and interests relating to the institution, often through transnational interest and pressure groups or non-governmental organizations (NGOs), are indicators of politicization (Zürn et al. 2012, 77). Although an increase in politicization has to ultimately come from the global public itself, ICJ institutions can facilitate such processes institutionally. This would make the process of politicization a process of mutual reinforcement: the stronger the

[37] Zürn, Binder, and Ecker-Ehrhardt have shown that the de facto authority of international institutions has led to an increase in politicization, where politicization is not merely understood as protest, but also as utilization of international institutions by states and non-state actors when the international institution has reached a certain level of perceived legitimacy (Zürn et al. 2012, 71).

facilitation of the politicization process by means of institutional increase of accountability, the stronger the politicization, which in turn then reinforces the need for democratic accountability.

Here are some examples of how: transparency in the ICJ institutions' legal reasoning – the clear presentation of the assumptions, principles, and objections – allows for an increased public engagement with the courts and its decisions. Beyond that, the principle of collective judicial responsibility (*Kollegialprinzip*) requires that judicial decisions must be justified to the collegium, that is, to the other judges on the bench. This requirement ensures mutual control and accountability (Bogdandy and Venzke 2014, 268). Dialogue and inclusion of affected and interested individuals – for example victims or their families – can also make ICJ institutions more accountable to individuals. A paradigmatic example of this is the calling of victims and kin of victims as witnesses who are given space to share their stories. The inclusion of non-governmental advocacy groups, for example in the role of an amicus curiae, can also help to increase accountability to the general public. NGOs can and do act as an intermediary between the international courts and interested persons of the civil society. Besides enabling individuals and groups to participate in the court, they pool expertise and information and can push the interests of minorities or groups that are not sufficiently represented through their state (Bogdandy and Venzke 2014, 211). Another example is the fact that any person – any citizen of the world – may make a 'suggestion' for changes to the ICC's Rules of Procedures and Evidence or the Elements of Crimes (Gallant 2013, 582). Additionally, outreach programmes, such as the ones maintained by the International Criminal Tribunal for Rwanda and the ICC, help to make the court's proceedings more accessible to interested and affected parties (Glasius 2012, 50). Lastly, the publicity of the trials, their physical accessibility for individuals, and their broadcast on radio and the internet can connect individuals with what happens at the courts, increasing interest from and accountability to the public. Regarding the last mechanism in particular, it is important to consider with great care that the mechanisms are accessible to those who have been victimized, as those who have been victimized are often also marginalized in other ways and therefore especially vulnerable. Hence, it is important that participatory mechanisms reach those individuals too. Their exclusion would be particularly tragic.

Bogdandy and Venzke also propose a politicized appointment procedure for judges. Although they reject the idea that judges should run for office and be voted for by the public, they argue that a democracy-based approach to selecting judges is possible when it is aligned with parliamentary deliberation. Von Bogdandy and Venzke argue for procedures that take the parliamentary selection of domestic High Court judges as a model and warn against betting solely on the wisdom of governments in the selection of judges. Additionally, international institutions can contribute to the procedure by publicly specifying the criteria for judges and 'promote a discursive engagement' about the candidates (Bogdandy and Venzke 2014, 170).

Bogdandy and Venzke argue that such a 'politicization' of a court has democratic potential. While I believe that its democratic potential is more limited than what they argue, and above all, cannot substitute political lawmaking by a legislative assembly, it *can* deepen democratic control by making the institution more *democratically accountable*. Therefore, I propose a two-pronged approach. Legislative assemblies specify the laws of international criminal law and therefore reduce the need for judicial lawmaking. Additionally, principles of democratic accountability can make what happens in a courtroom more accessible to interested individuals of the public. Both spheres – political lawmaking and judicial lawmaking – are controlled in equal measures by the subjects of the institution. This implies that both individuals and adequately representative states are the subject of democratic equality: via democratic accountability to individuals as well as via democratic participation through state representation. Taking this perspective, we can avoid having to choose either one or the other, which I believe is a theoretical advantage in our non-ideal global order: on the one hand, because states are the most important agents in international law and individuals participate through their representation, and on the other hand, because idealizing their democratic representative capacity easily falls into the trap of being normatively blind to the dark side of oppressive state power.

These observations conclude the substantive part of the argument for the legitimate authority of ICJ institutions. I have argued that any authority that claims to have a right to punish international crimes must regard some rules that ensure a fair and impartial criminal justice process. But this 'fairness condition' is not sufficient to explain the political authority of ICJ institutions. As distinct as the three justifications for supranational punishment that I have discussed in this chapter may be, they all share a common argumentative structure and thus a common flaw. Luban, Song, and Wellman view institutions of supranational punishment in a specific instrumental way, in the sense that institutions are well equipped to prosecute and punish efficiently and fairly. But fairness is not sufficient for authority because it cannot answer the subordination complaint. Political rule constitutes an asymmetry between rulers and the ruled, and such a subordination of the ruled entails being exposed to the power of the rulers. This is incompatible with the status of persons as equal authorities.

The challenge for the final part of the argument was to find an adequate answer to the subordination complaint. The complaint becomes salient when authorities use coercion: they raise the question of *legitimate* coercion, that is, how the exercise of their right to punish can be justified towards all its subjects. I have argued that insofar as ICJ institutions have authority, that authority must be democratic. The reason for this is that the requirement to treat an institution's subjects as equals – so that none is in a subordinate position to another – requires those subjects to exercise equal control over the institution. To institutionalize equal control, I have proposed two mechanisms that promise to make ICJ institutions more representative of, and accountable to, individuals. The first suggestion I make is to supplement an ICJ institution with a legislative assembly in which national governments and, if necessary, persistent minority groups are represented. In these assemblies, the decisions should be taken by majority voting, provided that the representatives are sufficiently democratically representative of their states' citizens. The second suggested mechanism is an increase in democratic accountability to individuals from within the court. Because some degree of judicial lawmaking is inevitable, I have agreed with von Bogdandy and Venzke who argue for a variety of mechanisms that ensure that judges and court officials are accountable to the public.

6

Conclusion

Justice in the Real World

The most morally progressive rules are useless if they do not have any effect when applied to a social world that does not honour them. There is a scene in the WWII movie *A Bridge on the River Kwai* (1958) where the British officer Lieutenant Colonel Nicholson is being taken prisoner with his battalion at a Japanese prison camp in Burma. The Japanese commander Saito, who is running the camp, orders the British battalion, including the Lieutenant and his higher officers, to prison labour, building a bridge over the River Kwai. In an almost comic scene, the British officer takes out a copy of the Geneva Conventions from his tattered uniform, reminding Saito that according to the Geneva Conventions, the officers and the commanders of POW battalions are exempt from prison labour. He even reads out the respective passage, assuring Saito that he is willing to send his lower rank soldiers to work, but not his officers. He then hands the copy to Saito, offering to organize a Japanese translation, apparently convinced that the Japanese commander was simply unfamiliar with the rules, and would now realize his mistake. When he keeps on explaining what the code specifically states, Saito slaps the book across his face: 'Code? What code? It's the cowards' code!'

To my mind, this scene raises an important concern: how far can we rely on institutions that we might think of as authoritative in an ideal world – that we might think of as having the *right* to punish in an ideal world – when we in fact live in a non-ideal world? Some realist commentators believe that international criminal law is naive and headless activism that does not stand a chance to effect real change in a world that stubbornly resists moral argument.[1] Perhaps a more political form of justice – like justice by the firing squad – is needed for our non-ideal world after all. A related concern, but coming from a different perspective, is put forward by Catherine Lu: she argues that under conditions of

[1] Goldsmith and Krasner defend a variation of this view (Goldsmith and Krasner 2003), although their variant is less strong than the way I have put it here.

structural injustice, international criminal justice (ICJ) may not be an adequate response to what she calls 'political catastrophes' (Lu 2018). Others may doubt not only the efficacy of ICJ, but the intentions of its supporters: according to this view, ICJ is yet another way for strong states to police the internal affairs of weak states in the name of 'universal' values – but which is really a mere fig leaf for enforcing their interests. Or one may claim that criminal justice for atrocities is not necessarily a bad idea, but that it is not anyone's concern but the affected: states should deal with what happened on their own terms after political catastrophe has hit.

Supporters of ICJ often agree with that last point. That is why the principle of complementarity only allows the ICC to become active when the post-atrocity state is either unable or unwilling to deal with the crimes. But even in cases where states are unable or unwilling to prosecute – or to do *anything* for that matter – we might ask: is there anything wrong if we simply leave it be? Cornered by such scepticism, ICJ supporters sometimes resort to vague and metaphysical claims: that punishment is owed to the victims of atrocities, that humanity is harmed by war crimes, or that the moral equilibrium of the universe needs rectification. I am sympathetic to these metaphors, but they do not survive rigorous analytical examination. Instead, I hope to have developed a systematic argument that explores the conditions under which ICJ is morally permissible and politically legitimate. One important part of that systematic argument is a theory about the permissibility of the practice of punishment. But we saw that we also needed an argument that explains why prosecuting international crimes should be a matter of international concern and why we need international institutions to do so.

In the first chapter of this book, I have argued that the success of my argument for the political authority of ICJ institutions depends on whether it can be shown that punishment beyond the state is morally permissible and likely effective. In the final chapter of the book, I am going to discuss two ways in which my argument might founder in the face of the real world. The first way in which the argument may prove useless for our world is that while a democratic ICJ institution seems plausible in theory, our global state system is deeply hierarchical, and international institutions and international law operate under conditions of structural injustice, in which powerful states make use of such institutions to dominate and exploit powerless states. To be sure, international institutions are certainly not at fault because of this, but it does render their legitimacy dubitable. The second way in which my argument might be useless in the face of the real world is that the main justification of punishment as the function that I identified ICJ institutions are exercising – deterrence – does not withstand empirical scrutiny. Both are serious issues; and while they certainly warrant a more detailed discussion than I can offer here, I argue that they do not impugn my argument after all.

One may say that I have painted a picture of ICJ that is too rosy to be applicable to the real world.[2] As Catherine Lu observes, '[t]he ICC represents the approach of international criminal law and justice, which presupposes a fairly well-ordered and lawful international community with legitimate authority to punish' (Lu 2018, 98). A systematic argument for ICJ must respond to the worry that international criminal prosecution deepens problematic structures in a non-ideal world like ours: that is, in a world with steep power inequalities between states. Might not those institutions generate their own injustices when they operate in unjust conditions? The current distribution of punishment is evidently unfair: selective prosecution, specifically targeting African countries, while blatantly overlooking the crimes committed by those who have power in the international arena, has become a major criticism of the ICC. Although current international power structures do allow criminal prosecution by the ICC, they do so only very selectively.

This, the criticism goes, makes the whole project illegitimate as it stands: prosecuting some while leaving others free to commit atrocities of the same gravity is a gross injustice. One might object that an uneven distribution of punishment is not an especially troubling moral problem as long as *only* the guilty are punished: it surely would be better if all who are guilty are punished, but as far as the non-ideal world is concerned, those who *are* guilty can hardly complain *that* they are being punished for their crimes.[3] But I am not sure this reply gets to the heart of the criticism because the injustice does not necessarily concern individuals, but the international state system as a whole. Lu observes that '[s]ince its inception, ... enduring structural disparities between states have raised the question of whether the International Criminal Court risks becoming an International *Colonial* Court, or an instrument for already dominant

[2] For a comprehensive view on what the problems of the ICC operating in the African political context are, see Phil Clarke's book *Distant Justice* (Clarke 2018).

[3] For a discussion of this problem, see Altman's and Wellman's discussion (Altman and Wellman 2009, 91).

states to teach manners to the weak and marginalized, while remaining largely immune to such judgements in their own cases' (Lu 2018, 95). Lu also argues that both powerful and weak states[4] instrumentalize the ICC and often for reasons that contradict its normative foundations (Lu 2018, 89). This taints the legitimate authority of the ICC because instead of being an impartial arbitrator, the ICC becomes a tool in the hands of one of the factions, amounting to 'waging war by legalistic means' (Lu 2018, 97).[5]

Christopher Wellman joins those voicing concerns over the court's dysfunctional impartiality: he points out that instead of a genuinely global court that can address the worst rights violations in the world, 'we have constructed a regional mechanism largely funded by Europeans that will largely prosecute and punish Africans' (Wellman 2013, 940). Thomas Christiano argues that such selective prosecution seriously taints the legitimacy of ICJ (Christiano 2021). Instead of having global reach, the ICC may prosecute only those states that have submitted to the court, which in practice means that it has no jurisdiction over the world's most important military powers. Worse still, since the world's most important military powers – China, Russia, and the United States of America – are also permanent members of the United Nations Security Council, they can veto any referral of a situation to the ICC by the Security Council under Article 13 (b), as Christiano argues in a separate piece (Christiano 2020, 352). Hence, the issue of selective prosecution is not necessarily a consequence of bad or prejudiced prosecutorial practices, but seems to be a structural problem: its causes lie in the fact that the circumscription of the ICC's jurisdiction is arbitrary, which in turn is a consequence of the system of state consent (Christiano 2020).

On the position I defend in this book, the criticisms that I just recounted are not only valid, but *supported* by the arguments I offer for the authority of ICJ institutions. The problem I identified, and to which I argued that a democratic conception of authority is the solution, is that

4 For a political science perspective on how less powerful states use the ICC for their political aims, see also Ba (2020).

5 Lu also rightly observes that from an abolitionist perspective, the very concept of a crime is suspicious; abolitionists often prefer conflict resolution rather than prosecution and incarceration. While I share many of the criticisms that abolitionists have put forward, and the goals they defend, I tend to think that international crimes are one of the few cases in which criminal prosecution and incarceration are morally and politically justified. For a recent convincing and nuanced discussion of (prison) abolition, see Tommie Shelby's work (Shelby 2022).

a non-democratic ICJ institution wrongfully subordinates its subjects and therefore fails to treat them as equals. My sense is that this is exactly the normative issue that animates the criticisms of, and complaints against, the ICC that are being made by Lu, Wellman, and Christiano. In fact, I believe that the idea of non-subordination can give a plausible theoretical underpinning of the core normative problem expressed in the type of criticism that I just discussed. Hence, the analysis of legitimate authority I develop in this book is not obsolete in the face of reality; perhaps it is even urgently needed to identify the source of the ICC's normative defects in the real world.

And yet, perhaps not all hope is lost for the ICC. Consider some facts that we might interpret as 'contributory developments'[6] towards a fair distribution of prosecutions and a less arbitrary circumscription of the ICC's jurisdiction. It is certainly true that the most common mechanism of triggering the ICC's jurisdiction is when member states refer themselves or other member states to the ICC. That, of course, means that many human-rights-violating states remain beyond the reach of the ICC's jurisdiction, simply because they refuse to become a member of the institution. However, this does not mean that those states are *always* beyond the reach of ICJ: under Article 13 (b) of the Rome Statute, the United Nations Security Council may refer a situation to the ICC Chief Prosecutor, giving them jurisdiction over potential cases without the consent of the states that are connected to the crime through the personal or territorial principle. While Christiano is right that the most powerful military powers also sit on the Security Council and can veto any referral, the normative problem lies with the constitution of the Security Council rather than with the ICC. My argument thus implies replacing the Security Council mechanism – itself a highly political and a highly inegalitarian institution – with a more democratic procedure, one that represents a more diverse community than the small number of states represented in the Security Council. And, there are other ways to initiate a prosecution of non-member states: in the wake of the aggressive attack on Ukraine by Russia, non-ICC member Ukraine has accepted the ICC's jurisdiction under Article 12(3) of the Rome Statute, therefore making the prosecution of crimes committed on Ukrainian territory by Russian forces possible. In that sense, the ICC is at least coming closer to a less selective, and truly global jurisdiction.

[6] I adopt this term from Zürn (2016).

The second way in which my argument in this book might founder in the face of the real world is that its institutional aim is ineffective. Might not these institutions be wholly inadequate if they operate in conditions that are unfavourable to their capacity of exercising their function? The plausibility of my argument depends on whether ICJ institutions are effective in the sense that they do in fact help deter crimes; otherwise, the whole argument loses its point. While I hope to have presented convincing arguments for the argument that punishment beyond the state is morally permissible, I have been silent on the likely effectiveness of ICJ thus far. The reason for this is that these types of judgements of effectiveness lie in the realm of social scientists rather than philosophers. Fortunately, a number of high-quality and reliable studies about the deterrent effects of international criminal law have been published in the last few years, and I will survey their findings in what follows.

Before I do so, notice that I do not discuss empirical evidence for the effectiveness of deterrence in general, but concentrate specifically on the deterrent effect of international criminal law.[7] Although they presumably share some features, the deterrence of human rights crimes on the international level might depend on very different factors and mechanisms than the deterrence of petty crimes on the national level. One of the most important features of the deterrence argument is the hypothesis that would-be criminals make a cost–benefit calculation of whether the crime is 'worth' committing. The deterrence argument relies on the idea that the threat of punishment tips the scale on this calculation towards higher costs, so that it becomes too costly for the criminal to commit the crime. This cost–benefit calculation and the logic of action may or may not be very different in different contexts; this is why I will only review the evidence that explicitly refers to those crimes that are prohibited and covered by international criminal law. Any evidence that is more general will be of little use for our specific case.

Plenty of articles on the impact of international criminal courts have been published, but some of them are speculative or their arguments lack systematic empirical evidence.[8] Systematic empirical studies on the deterrent effects of international criminal courts are sparse for various reasons. The time frame needed to measure the deterrent impact of such

[7] For the deterrent effect of human rights prosecutions in transitional countries, see Kim and Sikkink (2010).

[8] See, for example, Goldsmith and Krasner (2003), Ku and Nzelibe (2006), and Cronin-Furman (2013).

courts is short because the only permanent court has been operative for about two decades. Given that international criminal trials are intensive in regard to both cost and time, the number of cases that can be used to measure impact is small. A theoretical problem lies in the design of the empirical research model: for determining deterrence or prevention, studies must measure non-events, which are more difficult to measure clearly. Besides these difficulties, we must also keep in mind that what follows are early findings that have yet to be confirmed by more extensive empirical research.

To begin, international relations scholars Geoff Dancy and Kathryn Sikkink correctly point out that one may safely assume that improvements in the status quo ante through international courts are likely, simply because the practice of impunity has hardly been better for peace (Dancy and Sikkink 2017, 50; Sikkink 2011). And indeed, recent systematic empirical research suggests that international criminalization of civilian killing and the institutionalization of punishment in the form of an international court have a deterrent impact. The idea that deterrence is one of the main functions of the ICC is neither mine nor is it new.[9] In the preamble of the Rome Statute, which is the legal treaty that established the ICC, the state parties to it affirm that 'the most serious crimes of concern to the international community as a whole must not go unpunished and that their effective prosecution must be ensured by taking measures at the national level and by enhancing international cooperation', and that they are 'determined to put an end to impunity for the perpetrators of these crimes and thus to contribute to the prevention of such crimes'.[10]

How exactly does the ICC prevent human rights crimes? In the literature on deterrence, a distinction is usually made between general deterrence and special deterrence. Special deterrence is the idea that inflicting a punishment on a person will deter that person from committing a crime again. General deterrence relies on the idea that if a potential offender knows that the consequences of their crime will involve infliction of harm on them, it will often be rational not to commit the crime.

[9] See Buitelaar (2016), Jo and Simmons (2016), and Akhavan (2001). To repeat, I do not suggest that deterrence is the only function of international criminal law, although I do think that it is the only function that can justify the authority of the institution. Other functions include the expression of moral condemnation, the expression of solidarity with the victims, etc. See May and Fyfe (2017) for a similar point.

[10] See the Preamble of Rome Statute of the International Criminal Court.

Seeking to avoid punishment when punishment means the infliction of harm, for example in the form of liberty deprivation, seems like a strong incentive to abide by the law. Moreover, punishment not merely involves hard treatment such as the deprivation of liberty, but also expresses moral condemnation (Feinberg 1965) and inflicts social stigma, so that those concerned about their social standing will have (additional) reason to abstain from committing crimes in order to avoid social exclusion. Obviously, the threat of punishment and the threat of social condemnation are not the only reasons why persons obey rules; they are probably not even the strongest reasons in most cases. In the case of international crimes in particular, a genuine moral motivation can explain compliance. The pull of complying with the law often does not merely come from a cost–benefit calculation, but from the firm belief that some deeds are genuine moral wrongs. Massive human rights violations often incite genuine indignation and moral outrage. Still, the massive human rights crimes committed in the last century alone make us painfully aware that moral reasons do not always suffice as a motivation for compliance.

Both aspects of punishment – the threat of hard treatment and the threat of social stigma – are important in light of who the perpetrators of international crimes typically are: government officials who govern or rebel groups whose aim is to govern. Both will want to avoid being punished and therefore deprived of liberty, and they will also want to avoid being dragged into a (time-intensive) criminal trial. Both groups also potentially seek political legitimacy domestically as well as internationally and will likely be deterred by the social stigmatization. Criminal groups that have no intention of governing are less concerned about their social standing; accordingly, they can be expected to be less deterred by the existence of an international criminal court.

This is precisely what a recent empirical study by Hyeran Jo and Beth Simmons suggests (Jo and Simmons 2016). Jo and Simmons statistically examine the deterrent effect of the ICC on the intentional killing of civilians. They distinguish between prosecutorial deterrence and social deterrence. Prosecutorial deterrence is 'a direct consequence of legal punishment: it holds when potential perpetrators reduce or avoid lawbreaking for fear of being tried and officially punished' (Jo and Simmons 2016, 444). Part of the prosecutorial deterrence is indirect: for example, states tend to introduce legal reform after being preliminarily investigated – thus creating incentives for states to strengthen their own legal systems, or heads of states who have fewer asylum options even when they are not indicted (Jo and Simmons 2016, 448). Therefore, it seems crucial that the ICC does not respect the immunity of high government officials. Social deterrence is defined a little wider, in that it describes when the potential perpetrators are deterred by the social informal consequences of lawbreaking (Jo and Simmons 2016, 448). Social deterrence can be observed when offenders are stigmatized, shunned, shamed, or excluded from profitable relationships (Jo and Simmons 2016, 450). This may, for example, also be true for relationships between states, when one state is receiving some form of financial assistance. Specifying and institutionalizing the prohibition of international crimes in the form of a court may strengthen the impression of a global moral community or a community of values. Additionally, it can raise and shape expectations of criminal justice for grave atrocities.

Jo and Simmons's paper is a fascinating read, and here is a summary of their findings:[11] the ICC contributes to prosecutorial deterrence; its member states, and especially those who have ratified the Rome Statute, are incentivized to improve their capacity to prosecute massive crimes domestically; implementing ICC-consistent statutes into domestic criminal law results in a reduction in civilian killings; the ICC mobilizes international and domestic agents to demand justice; deterrence is stronger with foreign-aid-dependent governments; and rebels are harder to deter than governments, but they still reduce intentional civilian killing when confronted with the possibility of prosecution (Jo and Simmons 2016, 469). In another article, Jo, Ratke, and Simmons argue that '[t]he evidence that the Rome Statute has contributed to strengthening of the laws and institutions to deter international crimes is strong and systematic' (Jo et al. 2018, 206). Similarly, Benjamin Appel finds that the ICC can in fact deter human rights violations and that members of the ICC (those who have ratified the Rome Statute) tend to commit fewer atrocities (Appel 2018). This finding is in accordance with an earlier argument made by Beth Simmons and Allison Danner, who argue that governments join the ICC in order to make their commitment to reducing violence against civilians credible (Simmons and Danner 2010).

For the case of Libya, Courtney Hillebrecht comes to a similar conclusion. Hillebrecht argues that the ICC's involvement in Libya seems to have deterred violence against civilians (Hillebrecht 2016). Claudio

[11] Jo and Simmons remind their readers that their method yields only probabilistic, not deterministic, results (Jo and Simmons 2016, 470). Also note the corrigendum they published, which dampens the confidence on some of their findings regarding the behaviour of rebel groups and prosecutorial deterrence (Jo and Simmons 2017).

Corradetti detects a deterrence correlation between the ICC and the violence that occurred after the elections in Kenya in 2007–2008 and 2013 (Corradetti 2015). In several articles, Geoff Dancy and Florencia Montal argue that overall the empirical studies show that the impact of ICJ is positive and that international prosecution of human rights crimes correlates with improvement in core human rights protection (Dancy 2017; Dancy and Montal 2017a, 2017b). Based on these empirical findings, and until more systematic studies become available, we can assume at least for now that a system of criminal law does prevent future human rights crimes and therefore helps protect human rights. This gives us reasonable hope that the ICC is capable of fulfilling its deterrent role.

Despite the contributory developments, the two problems I discussed show how the theory I defend in this book lies at some distance from the real world. Where does this leave the ICC? Should we stop supporting institutions that operate under non-ideal conditions? Not necessarily. Instead, we use the theory as a normative ideal to evaluate real-world institutions and define what they should aspire to, and how far they have come. Normative ideals can serve as a critical guide to understanding what the problems of real-world institutions are. From my arguments, it should be clear that one of the requirements for holding authority, in terms of a right to punish, is that prosecutions should be distributed more fairly than is the case now. An ICC that orients itself toward more democratic principles should, for example, do better in terms of selective prosecution. It is then a matter of practical judgement whether the current ICC is close enough to the ideal to warrant its legitimate survival, or whether the gap between the ideal and the real-world institution is so large that it ultimately renders it illegitimate. I tend to think that it is just close enough to the ideal and that it has potential to get closer, but reasonable people certainly disagree about this question.

In any case, and to reiterate this point again, a system of criminal prosecution and punishment is *but* one mechanism for making the world more just. We know that it is not enough to punish and that we also must work on the political conditions that enable powerful agents to commit international crimes. Carlos Nino, an Argentine law professor who was involved in the transition from military dictatorship to a democracy in his native country, observes in his brilliant book *Radical Evil on Trial* that

> those deeds that collectively can be described as radical evil can only be performed under favorable political conditions, most commonly a totalitarian or authoritarian regime which constrains criticism and prevents the diffusion of knowledge. It is not clear whether punishing radical evil will

> prevent similar evil acts from taking place when these favorable conditions are present, nor is it clear whether punishment forestalls the emergence of these conditions. (Nino 1996, x)

In part, Nino's concern is illustrated in the dispute between the British and the Japanese officers I described earlier in this chapter: the 'good' legal rules and laws, the ones that the British commander considers fundamental and that he believes are shared globally, just bounce off political conditions that function according to a completely different code, like the one the Japanese commander holds. But there is no reason to think that operating a system of ICJ and creating political conditions unfavourable to international crimes is an either-or-decision; one may reasonably hope that ICJ indeed *contributes* to forestalling the emergence of justice-adverse political codes and conditions. It can do so by conceptually transforming what, for the longest time, has been regarded as justified sacrifices and simply a part of politics, and turn it into ordinary crimes. This conceptual transformation is ultimately a consequence of understanding international crimes in separation from political ideologies such as nationalism or racism that often deem them necessary, even heroic. The criminal prosecution from Nuremberg to the ICC contributes to stripping the perceived inevitability and glory of those atrocities and showing what they really are: unspeakable *crimes*. It is in this role, too, that ICJ is a radical project.

WORKS CITED

Adams, N. P., Antoinette Scherz, and Cord Schmelzle. 2020. 'Legitimacy beyond the State: Institutional Purposes and Contextual Constraints'. *Critical Review of International Social and Political Philosophy* 23 (3): 281–91. https://doi.org/10.1080/13698230.2019.1565710.

Akhavan, Payam. 2001. 'Beyond Impunity: Can International Criminal Justice Prevent Future Atrocities?' *American Journal of International Law* 95 (1): 7–31. https://doi.org/10.2307/2642034.

Alexander, Michelle. 2012. *The New Jim Crow: Mass Incarceration in the Age of Colorblindness.* Rev. ed. New York: New Press.

Altman, Andrew. 2006. 'The Persistent Fiction of Harm to Humanity'. *Ethics and International Affairs* 20 (3): 367–72.

Altman, Andrew, and Christopher Heath Wellman. 2009. *A Liberal Theory of International Justice.* Oxford; New York: Oxford University Press.

Anderson, Elizabeth. 1999. 'What Is the Point of Equality?' *Ethics* 109 (2): 287–337. https://doi.org/10.1086/233897.

Anderson, Scott. 2010. 'The Enforcement Approach to Coercion'. *Journal of Ethics and Social Philosophy* 5 (1): 1–31.

2011. 'Coercion'. In *Stanford Encyclopedia of Philosophy* (Spring 2023 Edition), edited by Edward N. Zalta and Uri Nodelman. https://plato.stanford.edu/archives/spr2023/entries/coercion/.

Appel, Benjamin J. 2018. 'In the Shadow of the International Criminal Court: Does the ICC Deter Human Rights Violations?' *Journal of Conflict Resolution* 62 (1): 3–28. https://doi.org/10.1177/0022002716639101.

Applbaum, Arthur. 2010. 'Legitimacy without the Duty to Obey'. *Philosophy & Public Affairs* 38 (3): 215–39.

Austin, John. 1995. *Austin: The Province of Jurisprudence Determined.* Edited by Wilfrid E. Rumble. 1st ed. Cambridge: Cambridge University Press. https://doi.org/10.1017/CBO9780511521546.

Ba, Oumar. 2020. *States of Justice: The Politics of the International Criminal Court.* Cambridge: Cambridge University Press. https://doi.org/10.1017/9781108771818.

Bachrach, Michael. 2000. 'The Protection and Rights of Victims under International Criminal Law'. *The International Lawyer* 34 (1): 7–20.

Bassiouni, M. Cherif. 2014. *Introduction to International Criminal Law*. 2nd rev. ed. Leiden: Martinus Nijhoff Publishers.

Beitz, Charles R. 1979. *Political Theory and International Relations*. Princeton, NJ: Princeton University Press.

Bogdandy, Armin von, and Ingo Venzke. 2014. *In Whose Name? A Public Law Theory of International Adjudication*. 1st ed. International Courts and Tribunals Series. Oxford: Oxford University Press.

Boghossian, Paul. 2010. 'The Concept of Genocide'. *Journal of Genocide Research* 12 (1–2): 69–80. https://doi.org/10.1080/14623528.2010.515402.

Bosco, David. 2015. *Rough Justice: The International Criminal Court in a World of Power Politics*. New York: Oxford University Press.

Brighouse, Harry. 1996. 'Egalitarianism and Equal Availability of Political Influence'. *Journal of Political Philosophy* 4 (2): 118–41. https://doi.org/10.1111/j.1467-9760.1996.tb00045.x.

Buchanan, Allen. 2002. 'Political Legitimacy and Democracy'. *Ethics* 112 (4): 689–719.

2004. *Justice, Legitimacy, and Self-Determination: Moral Foundations for International Law*. New York: Oxford University Press. https://doi.org/10.1093/0198295359.001.0001.

2010. 'The Legitimacy of International Law'. In *The Philosophy of International Law*, edited by Samantha Besson and John Tasioulas, 79–96. Oxford: Oxford University Press.

2013. *The Heart of Human Rights*. Oxford: Oxford University Press.

Buchanan, Allen, and Robert O. Keohane. 2006. 'The Legitimacy of Global Governance Institutions'. *Ethics and International Affairs* 20 (4): 405–37.

Buitelaar, Tom. 2016. 'The ICC and the Prevention of Atrocities: Criminological Perspectives'. *Human Rights Review* 17 (3): 285–302. https://doi.org/10.1007/s12142-016-0414-6.

Butler, Melissa A. 1978. 'Early Liberal Roots of Feminism: John Locke and the Attack on Patriarchy'. *The American Political Science Review* 72 (1): 135–50. https://doi.org/10.2307/1953604.

Byrd, B. Sharon. 1989. 'Kant's Theory of Punishment: Deterrence in Its Threat, Retribution in Its Execution'. *Law and Philosophy* 8 (2): 151–200.

Christiano, Thomas. 2008. *The Constitution of Equality: Democratic Authority and Its Limits*. Oxford; New York: Oxford University Press.

2010. 'Democratic Legitimacy and International Institutions'. In *The Philosophy of International Law*, edited by Samantha Besson and John Tasioulas, 119–138. Oxford: Oxford University Press.

2011. 'Is Democratic Legitimacy Possible for International Institutions?' In *Global Democracy: Normative and Empirical Perspectives*, edited by Daniele Archibugi, Mathias Koenig-Archibugi, and Raffaele Marchetti, 69–95. Cambridge: Cambridge University Press. https://doi.org/10.1017/CBO9780511977992.004.

2012. 'The Legitimacy of International Institutions'. In *The Routledge Companion to Philosophy of Law*, edited by Marmor Andrei, 380–393. New York: Routledge.

2020. 'The Arbitrary Circumscription of the Jurisdiction of the International Criminal Court'. *Critical Review of International Social and Political Philosophy* 23 (3): 352–70. https://doi.org/10.1080/13698230.2019.1565715.

2021. 'The Problem of Selective Prosecution and the Legitimacy of the International Criminal Court'. *Journal of Social Philosophy*, 1–19. https://doi.org/10.1111/josp.12448.

Churchill, Winston. 2005. *Closing the Ring: The Second World War*. Vol. V. London: Penguin Classics.

Clarke, Phil. 2018. *Distant Justice: The Impact of the International Criminal Court on African Politics*. New York: Cambridge University Press.

Corradetti, Claudio. 2015. 'The Priority of Conflict Deterrence and the Role of the International Criminal Court in Kenya's Post-Electoral Violence 2007–2008 and 2013'. *Human Rights Review* 16 (3): 257–72. https://doi.org/10.1007/s12142-015-0373-3.

Cronin-Furman, Kate. 2013. 'Managing Expectations: International Criminal Trials and the Prospects for Deterrence of Mass Atrocity'. *International Journal of Transitional Justice* 7 (3): 434–54. https://doi.org/10.1093/ijtj/ijt016.

Dahl, Robert A. 1999. 'Can International Organizations Be Democratic? A Skeptic's View'. In *Democracy's Edges*, edited by Casiano Hacker-Cordón and Ian Shapiro, 19–36. Contemporary Political Theory. Cambridge: Cambridge University Press. https://doi.org/10.1017/CBO9780511586361.003.

Dancy, Geoff. 2017. 'Searching for Deterrence at the International Criminal Court'. *International Criminal Law Review* 17 (4): 625–55. https://doi.org/10.1163/15718123-01704007.

Dancy, Geoff, and Florencia Montal. 2017a. 'From Law versus Politics to Law in Politics: A Pragmatist Assessment of the ICC's Impact'. *American University International Law Review* 32 (3): 645–705.

2017b. 'Unintended Positive Complementarity: Why International Criminal Court Investigations May Increase Domestic Human Rights Prosecutions'. *American Journal of International Law* 111 (July): 689–723. https://doi.org/10.1017/ajil.2017.70.

Dancy, Geoff, and Kathryn Sikkink. 2017. 'Human Rights Data, Processes, and Outcomes: How Recent Research Points to a Better Future'. In *Human Rights Futures*, edited by Stephen Hopgood, Jack Snyder, and Leslie Vinjamuri, 1st ed., 24–59. Cambridge: Cambridge University Press. https://doi.org/10.1017/9781108147767.002.

Deitelhoff, Nicole. 2009. 'The Discursive Process of Legalization: Charting Islands of Persuasion in the ICC Case'. *International Organization* 63 (1): 33–65. https://doi.org/10.1017/S002081830909002X.

Devlin, Patrick. 1965. *The Enforcement of Morals*. Oxford: Oxford University Press.

Drumbl, Mark A. 2007. *Atrocity, Punishment, and International Law*. Cambridge: Cambridge University Press. https://doi.org/10.1017/CBO9780511611100.

Duff, Antony. 2010. 'Authority and Responsibility in International Criminal Law'. In *The Philosophy of International Law*, edited by John Tasioulas and Samantha Besson, 589–604. Oxford: Oxford University Press.

Dworkin, Ronald. 1966. 'Lord Devlin and the Enforcement of Morals'. *The Yale Law Journal* 75 (6): 986–1005. https://doi.org/10.2307/794893.

2013. 'A New Philosophy for International Law'. *Philosophy and Public Affairs* 41 (1): 2–30.

Edmundson, William A. 1995. 'Is Law Coercive?: William A. Edmundson'. *Legal Theory* 1 (1): 81–111.

Enoch, David. 2014. 'Authority and Reason-Giving 1'. *Philosophy and Phenomenological Research* 89 (2): 296–332.

Feinberg, Joel. 1965. 'The Expressive Function of Punishment'. *The Monist* 49 (3): 397–423.

1970. *Doing & Deserving: Essays in the Theory of Responsibility*. Princeton, NJ: Princeton University Press.

1987. *The Moral Limits of the Criminal Law Volume 1: Harm to Others*. New York: Oxford University Press. https://doi.org/10.1093/0195046641.001.0001.

Fichtelberg, Aaron. 2006. 'Democratic Legitimacy and the International Criminal Court: A Liberal Defence'. *Journal of International Criminal Justice* 4 (4): 765–85. https://doi.org/10.1093/jicj/mqk002.

Føllesdal, Andreas. 1998. 'Survey Article: Subsidiarity'. *Journal of Political Philosophy* 6 (2): 190–218. https://doi.org/10.1111/1467-9760.00052.

Fuller, Lon L. 1958. 'Positivism and Fidelity to Law: A Reply to Professor Hart'. *Harvard Law Review* 71 (4): 630–72. https://doi.org/10.2307/1338226.

Gallant, Kenneth S. 2013. 'Addressing the Democratic Deficit in International Criminal Law and Procedure: Defense Participation in Lawmaking'. In *The Sierra Leone Special Court and Its Legacy: The Impact for Africa and International Criminal Law*, edited by Charles Chernor Jalloh, 572–86. Cambridge: Cambridge University Press. https://doi.org/10.1017/CBO9781139248778.040.

Glasius, M. 2012. 'Do International Criminal Courts Require Democratic Legitimacy?' *European Journal of International Law* 23 (1): 43–66. https://doi.org/10.1093/ejil/chr104.

Goldsmith, Jack, and Stephen D. Krasner. 2003. 'The Limits of Idealism'. *Daedalus* 132 (1): 47–63.

Goodin, Robert E. 1988. 'What Is So Special about Our Fellow Countrymen?' *Ethics* 98 (4): 663–86.

Gosepath, Stefan. 2001. 'The Global Scope of Justice'. *Metaphilosophy* 32 (1–2): 135–59. https://doi.org/10.1111/1467-9973.00179.

2004. *Gleiche Gerechtigkeit: Grundlagen Eines Liberalen Egalitarismus.* 1. Aufl. Suhrkamp Taschenbuch Wissenschaft 1665. Frankfurt am Main: Suhrkamp.

2015. 'The Principles and the Presumption of Equality'. In *Social Equality: On What It Means to Be Equals*, edited by Carina Fourie, Fabian Schuppert, and Ivo Wallimann-Helmer, 167–85. Oxford: Oxford University Press.

Graf, Sinja. 2018. '"A Trespass against the Whole Species": Universal Crime and Sovereign Founding in John Locke's Second Treatise of Government'. *Political Theory* 46 (4): 560–85. https://doi.org/10.1177/0090591717752468.

Gur-Arye, Miriam, and Aron Harel. 2016. 'Taking Internationalism Seriously: Why International Criminal Law Matters'. In *Oxford Handbook of International Criminal Law*, edited by Kevin Jon Heller, Frédéric Mégret, Sarah M. H. Nouwen, Jens David Ohlin, and Darryl Robinson, 215–237. Oxford: Oxford University Press.

Hanna, Nathan. 2012. 'It's Only Natural: Legal Punishment and the Natural Right to Punish'. *Social Theory and Practice* 38 (4): 598–616.

Hart, H. L. A. 1967. 'Social Solidarity and the Enforcement of Morality'. *The University of Chicago Law Review* 35 (1): 1–13. https://doi.org/10.2307/1598946.

1968. *Punishment and Responsibility: Essays in the Philosophy of Law.* Oxford: Oxford University Press.

2012. *The Concept of Law.* Clarendon Law Series. Oxford: Oxford University Press.

Hillebrecht, Courtney. 2016. 'The Deterrent Effects of the International Criminal Court: Evidence from Libya'. *International Interactions* 42 (4): 616–43. https://doi.org/10.1080/03050629.2016.1185713.

Hobbes, Thomas. 11996. *Hobbes: Leviathan: Revised Student Edition.* Edited by Richard Tuck. Cambridge Texts in the History of Political Thought. Cambridge: Cambridge University Press. https://doi.org/10.1017/CBO9780511808166.

Jacob, Daniel. 2014. *Justice and Foreign Rule: On International Transitional Administration.* Houndmills, Basingstoke, Hampshire: Palgrave Macmillan.

Jo, Hyeran, and Beth A. Simmons. 2016. 'Can the International Criminal Court Deter Atrocity?' *International Organization* 70 (3): 443–75. https://doi.org/10.1017/S0020818316000114.

2017. 'Can the International Criminal Court Deter Atrocity? – Corrigendum'. *International Organization* 71 (2): 419–21. https://doi.org/10.1017/S0020818317000042.

Jo, Hyeran, Mitchell Radtke, and Beth A. Simmons. 2018. 'Assessing the International Criminal Court'. In *The Performance of International Courts and Tribunals*, edited by Andreas Follesdal, Geir Ulfstein, Oran R. Young, and Theresa Squatrito, 193–233. Studies on International Courts and Tribunals. Cambridge: Cambridge University Press. https://doi.org/10.1017/9781108348768.007.

Kant, Immanuel. 1977. *Die Metaphysik der Sitten*. Edited by W. Weischedel. Frankfurt am Main: Suhrkamp.

Kim, Hunjoon, and Kathryn Sikkink. 2010. 'Explaining the Deterrence Effect of Human Rights Prosecutions for Transitional Countries'. *International Studies Quarterly* 54 (4): 939–63.

Kolodny, Niko. 2014a. 'Rule Over None I: What Justifies Democracy?' *Philosophy & Public Affairs* 42 (3): 195–229. https://doi.org/10.1111/papa.12035.

2014b. 'Rule Over None II: Social Equality and the Justification of Democracy'. *Philosophy & Public Affairs* 42 (4): 287–336. https://doi.org/10.1111/papa.12037.

2016. 'Political Rule and Its Discontents'. *Oxford Studies in Political Philosophy* 2: 34–70.

Koskenniemi, Martti. 2006. 'Constitutionalism as Mindset: Reflections on Kantian Themes about International Law and Globalization'. *Theoretical Inquiries in Law* 8 (1), 9–36. https://doi.org/10.2202/1565-3404.1141.

Ku, Julian, and Jide Nzelibe. 2006. 'Do International Criminal Tribunals Deter or Exacerbate Humanitarian Atrocities?' *Washington University Law Review* 84 (September), 777–833.

Ladenson, Robert. 1980. 'In Defense of a Hobbesian Conception of Law'. *Philosophy and Public Affairs* 9 (2): 134–59.

Ladwig, Bernd. 2013. 'Global Justice, Cosmopolitanism and Moral Path Dependency'. *Philosophy & Social Criticism* 39 (1): 3–20. https://doi.org/10.1177/0191453712467750.

Lazar, Seth. 2020. 'War'. In *Stanford Encyclopedia of Philosophy* (Spring 2020 edition), edited by Edward N. Zalta, https://plato.stanford.edu/archives/spr2020/entries/war.

List, Christian, and Mathias Koenig-Archibugi. 2010. 'Can There Be a Global Demos? An Agency-Based Approach'. *Philosophy and Public Affairs* 38 (1): 76–110.

Locke, John. 1965. *Essays on the Law of Nature*. Edited by W. von Leyden. Oxford: Oxford University Press.

1975. *An Essay Concerning Human Understanding*. Edited by P. Nidditch. Oxford: Oxford University Press.

1988. *Two Treatises of Government*. Student Edition. Edited by Peter Laslett. Cambridge Texts in the History of Political Thought. Cambridge: Cambridge University Press.

Lorca, Rocio. 2016. 'The Presumption of Punishment: A Critical Review of Its Early Modern Origins'. *Canadian Journal of Law & Jurisprudence* 29 (2): 385–402. https://doi.org/10.1017/cjlj.2016.17.

Lu, Catherine. 2018. *Justice and Reconciliation in World Politics*. 1st paperback ed. Cambridge Studies in International Relations 145. Cambridge; New York: Cambridge University Press.

Luban, David. 2004. 'A Theory of Crimes against Humanity'. *Yale Journal of International Law* 29: 85–167.

2010. 'Fairness to Rightness: Jurisdiction, Legality, and the Legitimacy of International Criminal Law'. In *The Philosophy of International Law*, edited by John Tasioulas and Samantha Besson, 569–588. Oxford: Oxford University Press.

Lyons, David B. 1976. 'Rights against Humanity'. *The Philosophical Review* 85 (2): 208–15. https://doi.org/10.2307/2183731.

Maliks, Reidar. 2013. 'Kantian Courts: On the Legitimacy of International Human Rights Courts'. In *Kantian Theory and Human Rights*, edited by Andreas Follesdal and Reidar Maliks, 153–174. New York: Routledge.

May, Larry. 2005. *Crimes against Humanity: A Normative Account*. Cambridge Studies in Philosophy and Law. Cambridge: Cambridge University Press.

2008. *Aggression and Crimes against Peace*. Cambridge: Cambridge University Press.

2010. *Genocide: A Normative Account*. Cambridge: Cambridge University Press.

May, Larry, and Shannon Fyfe. 2017. *International Criminal Tribunals: A Normative Defense*. Cambridge: Cambridge University Press.

Mayerfeld, Jamie. 2004. 'The Democratic Legacy of the International Criminal Court'. *The Fletcher Forum of World Affairs* 28 (2): 147–56.

Meckled-Garcia, Saladin. 2015. 'Specifying Human Rights'. In *Philosophical Foundations of Human Rights*, edited by Rowan Cruft, S. Matthew Liao, and Massimo Renzo, 300–315. Oxford: Oxford University Press. https://doi.org/10.1093/acprof:oso/9780199688623.003.0017.

Morris, Madeline. 2002. 'The Democratic Dilemma of the International Criminal Court'. *Buffalo Criminal Law Review* 5 (2): 591–600. https://doi.org/10.1525/nclr.2002.5.2.591.

Müller, Luise. 2017. 'Rawls's Relational Conception of Human Rights'. In *Moral and Political Conceptions of Human Rights: Implications for Theory and Practice*, edited by Johan Karlsson Schaffer and Reidar Maliks, 58–76. Cambridge: Cambridge University Press. https://doi.org/10.1017/9781316650134.005.

2019a. 'Universal Jurisdiction, Pirates and Vigilantes'. *Critical Review of International Social and Political Philosophy* 22 (4): 390–411. https://doi.org/10.1080/13698230.2017.1390660.

2019b. 'International Crimes and the Right to Punish'. *Ratio Juris* 32 (3): 301–19. https://doi.org/10.1111/raju.12253.

2022. 'Which Practice? – Rescuing the Practical Conception of Human Rights'. *Critical Review of International Social and Political Philosophy* 25 (1): 128–42. https://doi.org/10.1080/13698230.2020.1859226.

Murphy, Jeffrie G. 1969. 'A Paradox in Locke's Theory of Natural Rights'. *Dialogue* 8 (2): 256–71.

Nagin, Daniel S. 1998. 'Criminal Deterrence Research at the Outset of the Twenty-First Century'. *Crime and Justice* 23: 1–42.

Nagin, Daniel S., and Raymond Paternoster. 1993. 'Enduring Individual Differences and Rational Choice Theories of Crime'. *Law & Society Review* 27 (3): 467–96. https://doi.org/10.2307/3054102.

Nickel, James. 2015. 'Personal Deserts and Human Rights'. In *Philosophical Foundations of Human Rights*, edited by Rowan Cruft, S. Matthew Liao, and Massimo Renzo, 153–65. Oxford: Oxford University Press.

Nino, Carlos Santiago. 1983. 'A Consensual Theory of Punishment'. *Philosophy & Public Affairs* 12 (4): 289–306.

1996. *Radical Evil on Trial*. New Haven, CT; London: Yale University Press.

Nozick, Robert. 1974. *Anarchy, State, and Utopia*. New York: Basic Books.

Otsuka, Michael. 2005. *Libertarianism without Inequality*. 1st publ. in paperback. Oxford: Clarendon Press.

Perry, Stephen R. 2013. 'Political Authority and Political Obligation'. In *Oxford Studies in Philosophy of Law: Volume 2*, edited by Leslie Green and Brian Leiter, 1–74. Oxford: Oxford University Press.

Peter, Fabienne. 2017. 'Political Legitimacy'. In *The Stanford Encyclopedia of Philosophy* (Winter 2023 edition), edited by Edward N. Zalta. https://plato.stanford.edu/archives/win2023/entries/legitimacy.

Pettit, Philip. 1988. 'The Consequentialist Can Recognise Rights'. *Philosophical Quarterly* 38 (150): 42–55.

2002. 'Is Criminal Justice Politically Feasible?' *Buffalo Criminal Law Review* 5 (2): 427–50.

2008. 'Three Conceptions of Democratic Control'. *Constellations* 15 (1): 46–55.

2010. 'Legitimate International Institutions: A Neo-Republican Perspective'. In *The Philosophy of International Law*, edited by Samantha Besson and John Tasioulas, 139–159. Oxford: Oxford University Press.

2014. 'Criminalization in Republican Theory'. In *Criminalization: The Political Morality of Criminal Law*, edited by R. A. Duff, Lindsay Farmer, S. E. Marshall, Massimo Renzo, and Victor Tadros, 132–50. Oxford: Oxford University Press.

Pitkin, Hanna. 1965. 'Obligation and Consent – I'. *American Political Science Review* 59 (4): 990–99. https://doi.org/10.2307/1953218.

1966. 'Obligation and Consent – II'. *American Political Science Review* 60 (1): 39–52. https://doi.org/10.2307/1953805.

Quong, Jonathan. 2015. 'Proportionality, Liability, and Defensive Harm'. *Philosophy & Public Affairs* 43 (2): 144–73. https://doi.org/10.1111/papa.12056.

Rawls, John. 1955. 'Two Concepts of Rules'. *The Philosophical Review* 64 (1): 3–32. https://doi.org/10.2307/2182230.

1999. *A Theory of Justice*. Rev. ed. Cambridge: Belknap Press of Harvard University Press.

2001. *Justice as Fairness: A Restatement*. Edited by Erin Kelly. Cambridge: Harvard University Press.

2003. *The Law of People with 'The Idea of Public Reason Revisited'*. Cambridge: Harvard University Press.

2005. *Political Liberalism*. Expanded ed. Columbia Classics in Philosophy. New York: Columbia University Press.

2007. *Lectures on the History of Political Philosophy*. Edited by Samuel Richard Freeman. Cambridge: Belknap Press of Harvard University Press.

Raz, Joseph. 1986. *The Morality of Freedom*, Vol. 37. Oxford: Oxford University Press.

2006. 'The Problem of Authority: Revisiting the Service Conception'. *Minnesota Law Review* 90: 1003–44.

2013. 'On Waldron's Critique of Raz on Human Rights'. *University of Oxford Legal Studies Research Paper 80/2013; Columbia Public Law Research Paper 13.359*. https://scholarship.law.columbia.edu/faculty_scholarship/1817?utm_source=scholarship.law.columbia.edu%2Ffaculty_scholarship%2F1817&utm_medium=PDF&utm_campaign=PDFCoverPages.

Renzo, Massimo. 2010. 'A Criticism of the International Harm Principle'. *Criminal Law and Philosophy* 4 (3): 267–82. https://doi.org/10.1007/s11572-010-9098-1.

2012. 'Crimes Against Humanity and the Limits of International Criminal Law'. *Law and Philosophy* 31 (4): 443–76.

Ripstein, Arthur. 2009. *Force and Freedom: Kant's Legal and Political Philosophy*. Cambridge: Harvard University Press.

Risse, Thomas. 2000. '"Let Us Argue!": Communicative Action in World Politics'. *International Organization* 54 (1): 1–39.

Risse, Thomas, Stephen C. Ropp, and Kathryn Sikkink, eds. 1999. *The Power of Human Rights: International Norms and Domestic Change*. Cambridge Studies in International Relations. Cambridge: Cambridge University Press. https://doi.org/10.1017/CBO9780511598777.

Rittberger, Volker, Bernhard Zangl, and Andreas Kruck. 2012. *International Organization*. 2nd ed. Basingstoke: Palgrave Macmillan.

Sadat, Leila. 2021. *The International Criminal Court and the Transformation of International Law: Justice for the New Millennium*. Leiden, The Netherlands: Brill | Nijhoff. https://doi.org/10.1163/9789004479739.

Scanlon, T.M. 1977. 'Rights, Goals, and Fairness'. *Erkenntnis* 11 (1): 81–95. https://doi.org/10.1007/BF00169845.

Schabas, William. 2012. *Unimaginable Atrocities: Justice, Politics, and Rights at the War Crimes Tribunals*. 1st ed. Oxford: Oxford University Press.

Schauer, Frederick. 1987. 'Precedent'. *Stanford Law Review* 39 (3): 571–605. https://doi.org/10.2307/1228760.

Scheffler, Samuel. 2003. 'What Is Egalitarianism?' *Philosophy and Public Affairs* 31 (1): 5–39.

2015. 'The Practice of Equality'. In *Social Equality*, edited by Carina Fourie, Fabian Schuppert, and Ivo Wallimann-Helmer, 20–44. Oxford: Oxford University Press. https://doi.org/10.1093/acprof:oso/9780199331109.003.0002.

Schemmel, Christian. 2021. *Justice and Egalitarian Relations*. Oxford Political Philosophy. New York: Oxford University Press.

Shelby, Tommie. 2022. *The Idea of Prison Abolition*. Princeton, NJ: Princeton University Press.

Sikkink, Kathryn. 2011. *The Justice Cascade: How Human Rights Prosecutions Are Changing World Politics*. 1st ed. New York: W. W. Norton & Co.

Simmons, A. John. 1979. *Moral Principles and Political Obligations*. Princeton, NJ: Princeton University Press. https://doi.org/10.2307/j.ctvzxx97q.

1989. 'Locke's State of Nature'. *Political Theory* 17 (3): 449–70.

1992. *The Lockean Theory of Rights*. Studies in Moral, Political, and Legal Philosophy. Princeton, NJ: Princeton University Press.

1993. *On the Edge of Anarchy*. Locke, Consent, and the Limits of Society. Princeton, NJ: Princeton University Press. https://doi.org/10.1515/9781400863549.

1994. 'Original-Acquisition Justifications of Private Property'. *Social Philosophy and Policy* 11 (2): 63–84.

1999. 'Justification and Legitimacy'. *Ethics* 109 (4): 739–71. https://doi.org/10.1086/233944.

2000. *Justification and Legitimacy: Essays on Rights and Obligations*. 1st ed. Cambridge: Cambridge University Press. https://doi.org/10.1017/CBO9780511625152.

2010. 'Ideal and Nonideal Theory'. *Philosophy & Public Affairs* 38 (1): 5–36. https://doi.org/10.1111/j.1088-4963.2009.01172.x.

2016. *Boundaries of Authority*. New York: Oxford University Press.

Simmons, Beth A., and Allison Danner. 2010. 'Credible Commitments and the International Criminal Court'. *International Organization* 64 (2): 225–56. https://doi.org/10.1017/S0020818310000044.

Song, Jiewuh. 2015. 'Pirates and Torturers: Universal Jurisdiction as Enforcement Gap-Filling: Pirates and Torturers'. *Journal of Political Philosophy* 23 (4): 471–90. https://doi.org/10.1111/jopp.12044.

Stemplowska, Zofia. 2015. 'Can Moral Desert Qualify or Justify Human Rights?' In *Philosophical Foundations of Human Rights*, edited by Rowan Cruft, S. Matthew Liao, and Massimo Renzo, 166–76. Oxford: Oxford University Press.

Stilz, Anna. 2011. 'Collective Responsibility and the State'. *Journal of Political Philosophy* 19 (2): 190–208. https://doi.org/10.1111/j.1467-9760.2010.00360.x.

2015. 'Decolonization and Self-Determination'. *Social Philosophy and Policy* 32 (1): 1–24. https://doi.org/10.1017/S0265052515000059.

Tusa, Ann, and John Tusa. 2010. *The Nuremberg Trial.* New York: Skyhorse Pub.

Vernon, Richard. 2002. 'What Is Crime against Humanity?' *Journal of Political Philosophy* 10 (3): 231–49.

2013. 'Crime against Humanity: A Defence of the "Subsidiarity" View'. *Canadian Journal of Law and Jurisprudence* 26 (1): 229–42.

Viehoff, Daniel. 2013. 'The Right against Interference: Human Rights and Legitimate Authority'. *Law and Ethics of Human Rights* 7 (1): 25–46.

2014. 'Democratic Equality and Political Authority'. *Philosophy & Public Affairs* 42 (4): 337–75. https://doi.org/10.1111/papa.12036.

2019. 'Power and Equality'. In *Oxford Studies in Political Philosophy Volume 5*, edited by David Sobel, Peter Vallentyne, and Steven Wall, 3–38. Oxford: Oxford University Press. https://doi.org/10.1093/oso/9780198841425.003.0001.

Waldron, Jeremy. 1999. *Law and Disagreement*. Oxford; New York: Clarendon Press; Oxford University Press.

2002. *God, Locke, and Equality: Christian Foundations in Locke's Political Thought*. Cambridge: Cambridge University Press. https://doi.org/10.1017/CBO9780511613920.

2017. *One Another's Equals: The Basis of Human Equality*. Cambridge: The Belknap Press of Harvard University Press.

Walen, Alec. 2021. 'Retributive Justice'. In *Stanford Encyclopedia of Philosophy* (Winter 2023 edition), edited by Edward N. Zalta and Uri Nodelman. https://plato.stanford.edu/archives/win2023/entries/justice-retributive.

Wellman, Christopher Heath. 1996. 'Liberalism, Samaritanism, and Political Legitimacy'. *Philosophy and Public Affairs* 25 (3): 211–37.

2001. 'Toward a Liberal Theory of Political Obligation'. *Ethics* 111 (4): 735–59.

2005. 'Samaritanism and the Duty to Obey the Law'. In *Is There a Duty to Obey the Law?*, edited by Christopher Wellman and A. John Simmons, 1–90. Cambridge: Cambridge University Press.

2009. 'Rights and State Punishment': *Journal of Philosophy* 106 (8): 419–39. https://doi.org/10.5840/jphil2009106839.

2012. 'The Rights Forfeiture Theory of Punishment'. *Ethics* 122 (2): 371–93. https://doi.org/10.1086/663791.

2013. 'Does the Existing Human Rights Regime Have Political Authority?' *San Diego Law Review* 50 (4): 931–54.

2017. *Rights Forfeiture and Punishment*. New York: Oxford University Press.

2023. 'The Space between Justice and Legitimacy*'. *Journal of Political Philosophy* 31 (1): 3–23. https://doi.org/10.1111/jopp.12272.

Wellman, Christopher Heath, and John Simmons. 2005. *Is There a Duty to Obey the Law?* Cambridge: Cambridge University Press.

Wenar, Leif. 2021. 'Rights'. In *Stanford Encyclopedia of Philosophy* (Spring 2023 edition), edited by Edward N. Zalta and David Nodelman. https://plato.stanford.edu/archives/spr2023/entries/rights.

Wolff, Jonathan. 1998. 'Fairness, Respect, and the Egalitarian Ethos'. *Philosophy and Public Affairs* 27 (2): 97–122.

Wright, V., and Sentencing Project (U.S.). 2010. *Deterrence in Criminal Justice: Evaluating Certainty verses Severity of Punishment.* Sentencing Project. https://books.google.de/books?id=w56XAQAACAAJ.

Young, Iris Marion. 2010. *Inclusion and Democracy.* Reprint. Oxford Political Theory. Oxford: Oxford University Press.

Ypi, Lea. 2013. 'What's Wrong with Colonialism'. *Philosophy & Public Affairs* 41 (2): 158–91.

Zürn, Michael. 2016. 'Survey Article: Four Models of a Global Order with Cosmopolitan Intent: An Empirical Assessment'. *Journal of Political Philosophy* 24 (1): 88–119. https://doi.org/10.1111/jopp.12070.

Zürn, Michael, Martin Binder, and Matthias Ecker-Ehrhardt. 2012. 'International Authority and Its Politicization'. *International Theory* 4: 69–106.

INDEX

For EU product safety concerns, contact us at Calle de José Abascal, 56–1°, 28003 Madrid, Spain or eugpsr@cambridge.org.

www.ingramcontent.com/pod-product-compliance
Lightning Source LLC
LaVergne TN
LVHW011815200926
848484LV00005B/1201

* 9 7 8 1 0 0 9 3 7 8 1 3 0 *